Essays on Performance Practice

Books by David Whitwell

Philosophic Foundations of Education
Foundations of Music Education
Music Education of the Future
The Sousa Oral History Project
The Art of Musical Conducting
The Longy Club: 1900–1917
A Concise History of the Wind Band
Wagner on Bands
Berlioz on Bands
Chopin: A Self-Portrait
Liszt: A Self-Portrait
Schumann: A Self-Portrait in His Own Words
Mendelssohn: A Self-Portrait in His Own Words
La Téléphonie and the Universal Musical Language
Extraordinary Women
Essays on the Modern Wind Band

Aesthetics of Music

Aesthetics of Music in Ancient Civilizations
Aesthetics of Music in the Middle Ages
Aesthetics of Music in the Early Renaissance
Aesthetics of Music in Sixteenth-Century Italy, France and Spain
Aesthetics of Music in Sixteenth-Century Germany, the Low Countries and England
Aesthetics of Baroque Music in Italy, Spain, the German-Speaking Countries and the Low Countries
Aesthetics of Baroque Music in France
Aesthetics of Baroque Music in England

The History and Literature of the Wind Band and Wind Ensemble Series

Volume 1 The Wind Band and Wind Ensemble Before 1500
Volume 2 The Renaissance Wind Band and Wind Ensemble
Volume 3 The Baroque Wind Band and Wind Ensemble
Volume 4 The Wind Band and Wind Ensemble of the Classical Period (1750–1800)
Volume 5 The Nineteenth-Century Wind Band and Wind Ensemble
Volume 6 A Catalog of Multi-Part Repertoire for Wind Instruments or for Undesignated Instrumentation before 1600
Volume 7 Baroque Wind Band and Wind Ensemble Repertoire
Volume 8 Classical Period Wind Band and Wind Ensemble Repertoire
Volume 9 Nineteenth-Century Wind Band and Wind Ensemble Repertoire
Volume 10 A Supplementary Catalog of Wind Band and Wind Ensemble Repertoire
Volume 11 A Catalog of Wind Repertoire before the Twentieth Century for One to Five Players
Volume 12 A Second Supplementary Catalog of Early Wind Band and Wind Ensemble Repertoire
Volume 13 Name Index, Volumes 1–12, The History and Literature of the Wind Band and Wind Ensemble

www.whitwellbooks.com

David Whitwell

Essays on Performance Practice

EDITED BY CRAIG DABELSTEIN

WHITWELL PUBLISHING • AUSTIN, TEXAS, USA

Whitwell Publishing, Austin 78701
www.whitwellbooks.com

© 2013 by David Whitwell
All rights reserved.

Printed in the United States of America

This book includes essays originally written between 2000 and 2010.

PAPERBACK
ISBN-13: 978-1-936512-70-6
ISBN-10: 193651270X

Composed in Bembo Book

Contents

	Acknowledgement	ix

Part I: Everything Begins with the Music

1	On the Definition of Aesthetics in Music	3
	On the Classification of the Musical Experience	25
	On the Nature of the Present Tense in Music	30
2	Applied Aesthetic Problems	35
	What Shall we do with Marches?	35
	Why do some Conductors feel they must TALK to the Audience?	40
	Whitwell on Seating-plan Acoustics	45
	On the Difficulty of Staying Awake	48

Part II: Essays on Making Band Masterpieces Musical

3	Gustav Holst, *Suite in E-flat*	55
4	Gustav Holst, *Suite in F*	61
5	Paul Hindemith, *Symphony for Band*	67
6	Darius Milhaud, *Suite Française*	73
7	Richard Wagner, *Trauermusik*	79
8	On the other Wagner Band Works	85
9	Ludwig van Beethoven, *Siegessinfonie*	97
10	Anton Reicha, *Commemoration Symphony for Band*	101
11	Hector Berlioz, *Symphony for Band*	111
12	Nineteenth-Century Italian Sinfonias	119
13	Special Memorial Compositions for Band	123
14	Special Variation Collections for Band	127
15	On the Five Whitwell Symphonies	129
	The Viennese Legacy (1987)	129
	Sinfonia da Requiem (1988)	131
	Meditations on Hamlet (1989)	136
	Symphony of Songs (1990)	137
	Sinfonia Italia (1991)	139

Part III: On Performance Practice

16 General Principles of Early Performance Practice — 153
- *bona fides* — 143
- Why is knowledge of performance practice important to the performer? — 144
- General Principles — 146
  - Incomplete notation — 146
  - Time and Placement — 148
  - Music and Movement — 149
  - The Music is Not on the Paper — 151
  - Modern Style: Chops, but no Soul — 153
  - Once more with Feeling! — 155

17 Classical Period Performance Idioms — 159
- Cadences — 159
  - Ritard Indications
    - Adagio — 159
    - *pp* meaning rit. — 159
  - Standard Stair-step cadence — 162
  - Standard Macro Meter Dance cadence — 163
  - Fermata as stop sign — 164
  - Improvisation signs
    - Cadenza — 165
    - Eingang — 166
- Inexact Notation — 167
  - Shortening notes — 167
  - Lengthening notes — 169
  - Inequality — 170
- Accentuation — 170
  - Agogic accents — 170
  - Ornaments — 173
    - Portamento — 173
  - Written Accents — 174
    - Staccato as accent — 175
- Tempo and Dynamics — 178
  - Tempo — 178
  - Dynamics — 186
- Improvisation — 187

PART IV: SCORE DISCUSSIONS

    18 Applied Performance Practices   193
          Mozart *Gran Partita*, K. 361   193
          Mozart *Partita*, K. 388   198

       About the Author   215
       About the Editor   217

Acknowledgments

I am indebted to my friend and colleague, Craig Dabelstein, for his help in preparing this book for publication.

David Whitwell
Austin, 2013

PART I

Everything Begins With The Music

Aesthetic Background in Selecting Repertoire

Although music is usually associated with the other arts, painting, sculpture, acting, etc., it is actually quite unique. In 2005 I wrote an essay which explains how music stands apart from, and must have a separate definition of aesthetics from, the other arts.

On the Definition of Aesthetics in Music

Unlike painting and acting, which are representations of something else, music is not a representation, nor a symbol, nor a metaphor of anything else. It is more accurately a language, a special non-rational language through which we communicate the experiential side of our nature. For the listener, it is this musical language which allows him to communicate directly with the composer's original inner idea and through contemplation learn more about himself.

The distinction, for example, between painting and music works like this:

$$\text{Object} \rightarrow \text{Painter} \rightarrow \text{Technique} \rightarrow \textit{Canvas}$$

The painter often has an object, say a vase of flowers, from which he develops an inner artistic vision, which through the technique of oils, brushes, etc., he turns into the work of art, a canvas.

$$\text{Composer} \rightarrow \text{Technique} \rightarrow \text{Notation} \rightarrow \textit{Performance}$$

The composer has no comparable object, but rather begins directly with an inner artistic vision, which he turns into a score, the notated form of music. But this notated form, the score, is not the art work. Written music, like written English, is only a symbolic language, symbolic of something else—which in the case of music is the composer's more complete inner idea.

Equally important is the process of the listener, who goes in the opposite direction. In the performance of music, the listener *experiences* the music immediately and has an *instantaneous* connection with the inner artistic idea of the composer. Here lies one of the great educational values of music, the direct exposure to great minds.

The observer of a canvas, on the other hand, first employs *exclusively* the eye. If he is going to be successful in going beyond this to see the inner artistic idea of the artist, he must make a *shift* from vision to mental contemplation. In other words, he must get past the experience of the eye before he can get to the experience of the artist.

But there are additional important distinctions. First, the art work of the painter is 'frozen' in time. In this way it is like a photograph. If you think of someone you know well, you can 'see' in your mind much of his features. But if you happen to have a photograph of that person, when you look at that a much more vivid picture of the person comes to mind. But the picture *never becomes the real person*. A recording, by the way, has this same analogy with real music.

In the case of the performance of music, the direct experience through which the listener communicates with the composer is always in the present tense, and seems so even when one listens to older music. For example you can listen to thirteenth-century dance music and with little effort your emotional and experiential empathy allows you to 'see' in your mind the palace room, the dancers, and, through meter and rhythm, often the actual dance steps, as if you were actually present. A significant part of this empathy comes from the fact that the genetic emotions have changed very little in the interval. But, on the other hand, *looking* at a thirteenth-century painting of a dance scene would give you none of this, indeed a thirteenth-century painting would appear to be little more than a cartoon.

A final important distinction lies in the nature of the existence of the art work. A finished canvas exists as a work of art even if it is hanging in a closed museum where no one can see it. A composition, on the other hand, exists as genuine music *only* in performance, which implies the presence of a listener—as there would be no purpose in a performance if there were no one to hear it. Therefore in a musical performance the listener is not a mere observer, but a *participant* in a live aesthetic experiential exchange.

On the Nature of the Aesthetic Experience in Music

Unlike a painting, which is, and may be judged as, a finished art object, music, in its genuine sense, exists only when it becomes a live, present tense experience. It follows, therefore, that the difficulty in formulating a meaningful and universal theory of aesthetics in music is that it must take into account not only the product of the composer, but the circumstances through which it is re-created in performance and heard. Because composer, performer and listener all play a role in determining the final aesthetic experience in music, we must begin by examining each of the constituent parts of the musical experience: The composer and his inner idea, which through his technique in writing music he expresses in the form of a notated score, which is re-created in the form of a live performance, which is perceived by a listener.

The Composer and his Inner Idea

Composer → Technique → Notation → Performance → Listener

If music were a static art, if there were no performances of music and instead one examined a score on display and *imagined* the music, as one examines a painting and imagines the artist's inner idea, then all of aesthetics in music would be centered here, in the study to imagine the composer's idea. While this is not the case, everything that we do mean by aesthetics in music *begins* here, with an original idea which will be communicated through performance to a listener. Let us begin, then, by considering the nature of this inner idea.

Does only the 'genius' have the ideas from which great music is constructed? When Mozart died, his wife immediately sold all his completed works, thinking she would get the best price while he was still remembered. But, interestingly enough, she *saved* his incomplete works and sketches for her two children, reasoning that if one of them wanted to be a composer he would be guaranteed success by having Mozart's melodies to use! It certainly would be a good place to begin, but unfortunately it is the working out of the material, not just the material itself, which results in great music. One only has to see the sketches of Beethoven to observe how a composer can begin with a rather mundane idea and gradually shape it into something special. So the answer to this question is, No!

Are great composers born and not made? This is probably true, but on the other hand the genes apparently play no role in the transmission of genius. This is demonstrated over and over again in cases where father and son are composers: genius does not transfer, nor is it inherited. And the same thing is true in the rational disciplines, as the example of Einstein and his parents will demonstrate.

It does seem that the Mozarts and the Einsteins are born with their genius and no amount, or absence, of education seems to contribute to the quality of their genius. But if we accept the idea that some men are simply born different, born with genius, how do they differ from us? They probably have much more in common with the rest of us than we might suppose. For, as Croce points out, it is only because we have so much in common that we are able to recognize their genius.

> Nor can we admit that the word *genius* or artistic genius, as distinct from the non-genius of the ordinary man, possesses more than a quantitative signification. Great artists are said to reveal us to ourselves. But how could this be possible, unless there were identity of nature between their imagination and ours, and unless the difference were only one of quantity? It were better to change *poets are born* into *men are born poets*, some men are born great poets, some small. The cult of the genius with all its attendant superstitions has arisen from this quantitative difference having been taken as a difference of quality. It has been forgotten that genius is not something that has fallen from heaven, but humanity itself. The man of genius who poses or is represented as remote from humanity finds his punishment in becoming or appearing somewhat ridiculous. Examples of this are the *genius* of the romantic period and the *superman* of our time.
>
> But it is well to note here, that those who claim unconsciousness as the chief quality of an artistic genius, hurl him from an eminence far above humanity to a position far below it. Intuitive or artistic genius, like every form of human activity, is always conscious; otherwise it would be blind mechanism. The only thing that can be lacking in artistic genius is the reflective consciousness, the superadded consciousness of the historian or critic, which is not essential to it.[1]

We recognize a part of ourselves in every composer and in every composition and this is because of the common emotional characteristics which are passed down to us genetically. We differ, both in ordinary life and in art, in the quality of the expression and individual meaning of these emotions.

---

[1] Benedetto Croce, *Aesthetic* (New York: Noonday), 14.

The idea that the greatest composers are 'born and not made' should not disturb us. With regard to the rational world, we accept without concern the fact that the wheel of fortune allots to each of us a different level of 'intelligence,' that which we measure as I.Q. It should be no surprise that with regard to the experiential side of ourselves we are also born with varying levels of sophistication. As one can, to some degree, improve I.Q., there is no reason to suppose we cannot also refine the properties of experience. Indeed, one of the strong justifications for performing only the best music is that of permitting ourselves the opportunity to communicate on this level with great minds.

In any case, the composer begins with an *inner* idea or thought of a purely experiential nature. Here language becomes a problem, because 'thought' normally is associated with reason. The word most often substituted is 'intuitive,' but this seems vague to us and we prefer just 'thought,' with the understanding that we mean non-rational thought.

In this regard, Croce takes the very rigid position that this inner thought is everything. He maintains that the formulation of this inner idea is synonymous with the finished art work, that if the idea is not perfectly defined it cannot be expressed in art.

> One often hears people say that they have many great thoughts in their minds, but that they are not able to express them. But if they really had them, they would have coined them into just so many beautiful, sounding words, and thus have expressed them. If these thoughts seem to vanish or to become few and meager in the act of expressing them, the reason is that they did not exist or really were few and meager. People think that all of us ordinary men imagine and intuit countries, figures and scenes like painters, and bodies like sculptors; save that painters and sculptors know how to paint and carve such images, while we bear them unexpressed in our souls. They believe that any one could have imagined a Madonna of Raphael; but that Raphael was Raphael owing to his technical ability in putting the Madonna on canvas. Nothing can be more false than this view.[2]

Durant was correct to question this idea when he asked, 'Have we never had thoughts and feelings more beautiful than our speech?'[3] Any lover who has ever tried to write a love letter can answer this question, for these feelings, which can be very profound and precise, are never satisfactorily communicated in words. Croce is certainly wrong in this viewpoint with respect to music, for music is experiential and musical notation is rational, a symbolic language just like English, can never satisfactorily communicate the composer's complete inner idea.

How can we then determine who is a good composer and what is good music? We must first assume that if some composers are persons of greater depth and universality and are also capable of communicating their inner ideas, even if imperfectly, that we are capable of recognizing this form of communication, even as we are capable of recognizing levels of importance in communication in rational matters. We begin by recognizing that it is the *ideas* among artists which separate them in degrees of importance. Croce expressed this same distinction and added that the first place to measure the success of varying artists in communicating universals of the spirit is in our own spiritual nature.

---

[2] Ibid., 9.

[3] Will Durant, *The Story of Philosophy* (New York: Simon & Schuster, 1961), 356.

The whole difference, then, is quantitative, and as such is indifferent to philosophy, *scientia qualitatum*. Certain men have a greater aptitude, a more frequent inclination fully to express certain complex states of the soul. These men are known in ordinary language as artists. Some very complicated and difficult expressions are not often achieved, and these are called works of art ...

We must hold firmly to our identification, because among the principal reasons which have prevented Aesthetic, the science of art, from revealing the true nature of art, its real roots in human nature, has been its separation from the general spiritual life, the having made of it a sort of special function or aristocratic club.[4]

Having said this, what do we look for in the composer and his composition? How do we find high quality in music?

We must begin, once again, by avoiding the pitfalls of language. Because in English all music is included under one word, 'Music,' some have made the mistaken conclusion that all music is therefore somehow equal. A wide variety of music is available to us which uses the same notational language, but to say this makes all music equal in significance is just as absurd as saying Shakespeare and comic books are equal in significance because they both use letters of the alphabet or words of the same language. The reason great literature and great musical literature are more significant than less significant works has to do not with the language (although, of course, Shakespeare and Mozart *did* use beautiful language), but with the importance of what it is that that language communicates.

One characteristic of the very best music is universality—music which speaks so clearly and compellingly that it creates its own audience. It is this kind of music that Rossini once spoke of, in answer to a question from Ferdinand Hiller regarding whether poetry and music could ever arouse an equal interest at the same time. Rossini replied,

If the magic of music has really seized the hearer, the word undoubtedly will always come off second best. But if the music doesn't seize the hearer, what is the good of it? It is useless then, if not superfluous or even detrimental.[5]

A nice summary of some additional qualities of good music is given by Percy Scholes:

First, good music has vitality and bad music often has not. It is easier to recognize this characteristic than to define it. A melody which wanders aimlessly is not vital. Compare with such a melody the opening phrase of anyone of Beethoven's sonatas, symphonies or string quartets—a phrase which in every instance arrests the attention ... We feel ourselves at once to be in the presence of *life*. And in a 'good' piece of music this feeling continues to the end of the composition ...

Originality. We may say that good music is 'individual' and 'personal.' Music lacking vitality is generally found to be a diluted extract of that of some other composer, or perhaps of so many other composers that no one composer can be named; or it may even be a thickened extract, for if there has been poured out upon the world much Mendelssohn and Water, there has equally been poured out much Mendelssohn and Glue ...

---

[4] Croce, *Aesthetic*, 13ff.

[5] Quoted by Wagner in 'A Fragment on Rossini (1869) in Richard Wagner, *Richard Wagner's Prose Works*, ed. William Ashton Ellis (New York: Broude), VIII, 377.

> There is no acid test for 'goodness' in music. The thoughtful consideration of a trained taste must be applied, directed by some such method of analysis as that indicated above. It may not be possible by such means to prove a composition to be a masterpiece, but at all events great masses of second-rate music can thus be put aside …
>
> Not all short-lived music is to be utterly condemned, for soundly-written journalism is a kind of literature. But it *must* be soundly written. There is, in fact, no excuse (beyond the commercial) for really 'bad' music in any place or for any purpose.[6]

The most important characteristic of good music is that it be *inspired* music, music written without purpose other than the composer's honest desire to communicate his feelings. This we contrast with what we might call *constructed* music, music being turned out in great abundance by educational publishers today. This music is designed for a certain portion of the educational market, designed for mass sales, and is carefully written to meet the technical needs of that market. But it is certainly not inspired music. It is exactly the kind of music Mendelssohn had in mind when he wrote,

> Music composed with a purpose will never reach the heart, because it does not come from the heart.[7]

This kind of music has been around for a long time and for centuries serious musicians made the same complaint. This example by Liszt can serve as the representative of numerous others.

> A work which offers only clever manipulation of its materials will always lay claim to the interest of the immediately concerned—of the artist, student, and connoisseur—but, despite this, it will be unable to cross the threshold of the artistic kingdom. Without carrying in itself the divine spark, without being a living poem, it will be ignored by society as though it did not exist at all, and no people will ever accept it as a leaf in the breviary of the cult of the beautiful.[8]

Wagner found this same lack of inspiration in much of the music of Meyerbeer, his much more popular rival in Paris.

> In Meyerbeer's music there is so appalling an emptiness, shallowness and artistic nothingness, that—especially when compared with by far the larger number of his musical contemporaries—we are tempted to set down his specific musical capacity at zero.

However, Wagner notes, there are moments here and there when, inspired by the libretto, Meyerbeer would rise to moments of great beauty and inspiration. In these passages, Wagner, in 'sincerest joy and frank enthusiasm,' acknowledges these moments as examples of,

---

[6] Percy A. Scholes, *The Oxford Companion to Music*, 7th edition (London: Oxford University Press, 1947), 770–773.
[7] Letter to his Family, September 2, 1831.
[8] Letter to August Kiel, September 8, 1855.

that genuine art-creation which must come to even the most corrupted music-maker, so soon as he treads the soil of a necessity stronger than his self-seeking caprice; of a necessity which suddenly guides his erring footsteps, to his own salvation, into the paths of sterling art.[9]

To discover good music the musician must first have cultivated good taste himself, as Croce implied above. He must then have the integrity to select the best music available to him and to reject everything else. Archibald T. Davison, the famous conductor of the Harvard University Glee Club, made this argument with regard to educational music in 1945.

The most serious demand is for teachers whose knowledge and experience of music is wide enough to guarantee a sound musical taste. Only when there is intelligent revolt against much educational material that now passes for music will there be hope for a productive music education in this country.[10]

Schumann was another who called upon musicians to fight this fight.

You ought not help to spread bad compositions, but, on the contrary, help to suppress them with all your force.[11]

Does this kind of integrity in the selection of music really matter? Wagner once addressed this very question.

Why make such a fuss about the falsification of artistic judgment or musical taste? Is it not a mere bagatelle, compared with all the other things we falsify: commercial goods, sciences, food, public opinions, State culture-tendencies, religious dogmas, clover seeds, and what not? Are we to grow virtuous all of a sudden in Music? ...
   The acceptance of the empty for the sound is stunting everything we possess in the way of schools, academies, and so on, by ruining the most natural feelings and misguiding the faculties of the rising generation ... But that we should pay for all this, and have nothing left when we come to our senses ... this, to be frank, is abominable![12]

In a parody of a familiar Protestant Credo, Wagner proposes a special kind of punishment for those who willingly propagate poor music.

I believe in God, Mozart and Beethoven, and likewise their disciples and apostles;
   I believe in the Holy Spirit and the truth of one, indivisible Art;
   I believe that this Art proceeds from God, and lives within the hearts of illumined men;
   I believe that he who once has bathed in the sublime delights of this high Art, is consecrated to Her forever, and never can deny Her; I believe that through this Art all men are saved; ...

---

[9] 'Opera and the Nature of Music' (1851), quoted in Wagner, *Prose Works*, II, 100ff.
[10] Quoted in Willi Apel, *Harvard Dictionary of Music* (Cambridge: Harvard University Press, 1947), 472.
[11] 'Maxims for Young Musicians,' 1848.
[12] Quoted in Wagner, *Prose Works*, VI, 146ff.

> I believe in a last judgment, which will condemn to fearful pains all those who in this world have dared to play the huckster with chaste Art, have violated and dishonored Her through evilness of heart and ribald lust of senses; I believe that these will be condemned through all eternity to hear their own vile music.[13]

The Composer and his Technique

Composer → *Technique* → Notation → Performance → Listener

The inspired composer's original inner idea is usually at heart one associated with *feeling*. It is not something he could express very well in words and at first something he might not express very well in music (Mozart excepted!). At some point the composer decides to communicate his ideas with others through musical composition. To do this, whether well or poorly, depends on the *technique* of composition, the next step in the aesthetic chain in music.

What do we mean by technique in terms of communicating ideas through music? Technique in composition in music exists on two primary levels, the first of which is purely *knowledge*, the grammar of music. This is a highly technical form of knowledge that deals not only with every aspect of how to write music, but also with a whole range of technical information regarding the acoustic and performance considerations upon which music depends. Some of this knowledge is very specialized and absorbed through what we might call the composer's *practical* experience. A case in point is the composer's understanding of how music carries the listener along in time. When is a sense of movement in time desired and when is a 'sense of arrival' appropriate? One composer who understood perfectly how to combine his aesthetic ideas with these kinds of practical considerations was Beethoven, as the distinguished composer, Jan Meyerowitz, observes.

> Even with very little training we can place any short quotation from a Beethoven movement in the exact spot where it belongs in the piece, where it fulfills a very definite function in the whole structure. You can recognize whether it is a first or a second theme, an episode, a transition or a retransition, a coda, a beginning, a climax, the end of a development, etc. Each passage, each motif is so clearly devised for its very special, exclusive function that we can place it in its correct spot *in a composition we do not even know!*[14]

Of course, technique has its limits, for, in the end, all the technique in the world does not produce beautiful music. And, of course, the reverse is true: one may have beautiful ideas, but lacking technique one's ideas can never be turned into music.

But, there is a more significant limitation to technique: technique is a form of *knowledge*, that is to say, it is *rational*, it can be taught and learned. Thus we immediately encounter an aesthetic paradox: music is the communication of feelings and feelings are non-rational. Therefore, there must be an entirely different definition of 'technique' in composition and this has to do with the composer's ability to communicate feelings through a symbolic language

---

[13] Ibid., VII, 66ff.

[14] Jan Meyerowitz, 'Do We Overestimate Beethoven?,' *High Fidelity Magazine* (January, 1970), 79.

which has no specific symbols for feeling. In order to achieve some understanding of what we mean by *this* kind of technique, we must consider briefly the development of symbolic languages themselves.

The earliest writing we know of early man are the pictures in the caves of France, dating from the last Ice Age. In a written language composed of pictures, as one also finds in the Egyptian tomb paintings, and in the ancient Asian languages, you have a language in which the written symbol is synonymous with one's experience (the symbol for 'cat' is a picture of a cat).

With regard to the development of rational language, a fundamental change occurred with the introduction of the much more efficient phonetic writing (now 'c–a–t' represents a cat, but does not look like a cat). This had the effect of putting a barrier between man's experience and his language, as explained by Marshall McLuhan.

> The phonetic alphabet did not change or extend man so drastically just because it enabled him to read. Tribal culture had already coexisted with other written languages for thousands of years. But the phonetic alphabet was radically different from the older and richer hieroglyphic or ideogrammic cultures. The writing of Egyptian, Babylonian, Mayan and Chinese cultures were an extension of the senses in that they gave pictorial expression to reality, and they demanded many signs to cover the wide range of data in their societies—unlike phonetic writing which uses semantically meaningless letters to correspond to semantically meaningless sounds and is able, with only a handful of letters, to encompass all meanings and all languages. This achievement demanded the separation of both sights and sounds from their semantic and dramatic meanings in order to render visible the actual sound of speech, thus placing a barrier between men and objects and creating a dualism between sight and sound. It divorced the visual function from the interplay with the other senses and thus led to the rejection from the consciousness of vital areas of our sensory experience and to the resultant atrophy of the unconscious. The balance of the sensorium—or *Gestalt* interplay of all the senses—and the psychic and social harmony it engendered was disrupted, and the visual function was overdeveloped. This was true of no other writing system.[15]

Once man adopted this new kind of writing, where the language-picture no longer corresponds with experience, things in our rational world become confusing.

> Verbal identifications and confused abstractions begin at a tender age ... Language is no more than crudely acquired before children begin to suffer from it, and to misinterpret the world by reason of it.[16]

Another very important point is that from that moment we needed an intermediary, a teacher, to connect *us* with our language. Someone has to answer our questions, 'Why isn't Gnat spelled with an *N*,?' or 'When do we use *to*, *too*, or *two*?'

---

[15] Marshall McLuhan, 'An Interview,' *Playboy*, March, 1969.
[16] Stuart Chase, *The Tyranny of Words* (New York: Harcourt, Brace, 1938), 56.

The development of our experiential language, music, followed much the same course. Although early man had no pictorial equivalent for his music, his music *was* a means of directly communicating his feelings. This was such an effective system of communication that no further 'improvements' were needed over a great period of time.

The 'improvement' which came was music's equivalent of a phonetic alphabet, and we call it our modern musical notation. But our notation was the invention of Church mathematicians and they carefully observed the Church's intolerance of emotion by inventing a notational system which has not a single symbol for feelings or emotions—even though, then as now, music is basically a language for the expression of emotion.

As with rational language, once notation arrived it also required an intermediary to connect the musician's experience with the notation, to show him how you really play what is on paper. It is no surprise, therefore, that this was also when the concept of the conductor appeared. But as Wagner points out, until the nineteenth century the composer was also present to tell the players how the music should *really* be played, a role now given over to the conductor.

> Even today, although we have accustomed ourselves to a most minute notation of the nuances of phrasing, the more talented conductor often finds himself obliged to teach his musicians very weighty, but delicate shadings of expression by *viva voce* explanation; and these communications, as a rule, are better understood and heeded, than the written signs.[17]

In another place,[18] Wagner discusses the development of the dominance of the rational, and the separation of man from his feelings, in terms remarkably similar to McLuhan. 'Understanding,' by which he means what we call today the rational left hemisphere,

> through the process of imagination acquired a language by which it would make itself intelligible *alone* and in a direct ratio: as the rational man became more intelligible the feeling man became less. In modern Prose we speak a language which we do not understand as being related to Feeling, since its connection with the objects, whose impression on our faculties first generated the roots of speech (pictures), has become lost to us.

It is very difficult to speak objectively of the technique by which a composer communicates *feelings* through musical notation because, unlike the more academic kind of technique, *this* technique is a very personal one. Indeed, Wagner once said that the composer has to actually invent this kind of technique for himself. A musical thought, he says, is not something physically real, but,

> is something which has made in *im*pression on our feeling and which, in order to communicate it to others, we must invent an *ex*pression.

---

[17] Wagner, *Prose Works*, IV, 192.
[18] Ibid., II, 230ff.

Wagner, in another place, defines more precisely how the composer does this. He points out that the poet, who deals in words, must go into more and more detail to define his meaning, while the composer does the reverse. The composer must concentrate his emotional ideas into the most condensed and refined form, which he refers to as the *Melos*.

> To address the Feeling to any degree, the Poet wandered into that vague diffuseness in which he became the delineator of a thousand details, intended to set a definite shape before the imagination as clearly as possible. But the imagination, bombarded by a host of motley details, only masters the proffered object by trying to grasp these perplexing details one by one, thereby losing itself in the function of pure Understanding ... The composer's purpose, on the other hand, is to condense an endless element of Feeling into a definite point in order that it might be understood.[19]

Presently we shall speak of how the performer and the listener find *personal* meaning in the Melos, but for the moment we should only like to point out that this form of feeling in music, that which we call the Melos, is the aspect of emotion in music which might be called 'Universal.' For example, nearly everyone, we believe, would find it emotionally 'wrong' to sing *Crucifixus* in place of *Hallelujah* in Handel's 'Hallelujah Chorus.' Why does it sound 'wrong?' It is not just because we are used to the word we know, it is because the *inherent* emotion of this music does not correspond to the word *Crucifixus*. Music, in other words, *does* have its own inherent emotional meaning. The composer must have the sensibility to create music which accurately reflects the emotional content of his inner aesthetic idea.

The Composer's Score

Composer → Technique → *Notation* → Performance → Listener

> It is usual to distinguish the internal from the external work of art: the terminology seems to us infelicitous, for the work of art (the aesthetic work) is always *internal*; and what is called *external* is no longer a work of art.[20]

What Croce reminds us here is very important. Although the score is a vital step, even an irreplaceable step in art music, the score is not to be considered *music*, it is only grammar, a technical representative of the music.[21] The score is a document in symbolic language which only *represents* the composer's original aesthetic inner idea. No matter to what degree of detail the composer notates his ideas on paper, no matter how much time and effort he expends, the score can never be considered as synonymous with his inner musical idea.

---

[19] Ibid., II, 277ff.

[20] Croce, *Aesthetic*, 50–51.

[21] In German this distinction is clear, for there is one word, *Die Noten*, for the notation and a separate word, *Die Musik*, for music.

Furthermore, in the case of music, even if another musician is capable of looking at the score and reading it while simultaneously 'hearing' in his mind every detail of what he sees, he still cannot take this written document as being synonymous with the composer's inner idea. Croce mentions this and reminds us that it is not the score which is beautiful, only that which it represents.

> Writings are not physical facts which arouse directly impressions answering to aesthetic expressions; they are simple *indications* of what must be done in order to produce such physical facts. A series of graphic signs serves to remind us of the movements which we must execute with our vocal apparatus in order to emit certain definite sounds. If, through practice, we become able to hear the words without opening our mouths and (what is much more difficult) to hear the sounds by running the eye along the stave, all this does not alter in any way the nature of the writings, which are altogether different from direct physical beauty. No one calls the book which contains the *Divine Comedy*, or the score with contains *Don Giovanni*, beautiful in the same sense in which the block of marble which contains Michael Angelo's *Moses*, or the piece of colored wood which contains the *Transfiguration*, is metaphorically called beautiful.[22]

Why can the score never be the same as the music? First, as we have said, the score is written in a rational symbolic language. It is being asked to represent the composer's non-rational musical idea, which is something it cannot by nature do. The problem is made even worse by the fact that the left hemisphere of the brain generally denies the very existence of the right hemisphere. The left hemisphere can read the musical symbols on paper, but it has no idea that they represent something else.

Second, musical notation is not capable of precision. We have, for example, only one way of writing a dotted eighth-note followed by a sixteenth-note, while in the actual practice of performance this figure is played with great variety, under the influences of tempo, articulation and style. And in this regard, we skip over symbols such as dynamic markings, which are not only incapable of precision, but were never intended to be precise.

Third, thanks to the medieval Church we have no symbols whatsoever which represent feeling.

Having said all this, we must not lose sight of the fact that the score is, nevertheless, the special step in the chain of the aesthetic experience in music, which makes *real* music possible. The score remains the only way a composer can transmit his ideas and it is the only place the performer can look to discover the composer's inner idea. But the problem remains: musical notation cannot completely notate all there is to music. It will be read by performers, all of whom have different experiential histories and all of whom, therefore, will tend to see behind this notational language differently.

---

[22] Croce, *Aesthetic*, 100–101.

Finally, we must, however, assume that the score represents the composer's idea as precisely as the notation is capable or as precisely as the composer intended. That is, we must assume that it *is* the physical representation of the composer's idea.[23] It is for this reason that if a performance fails to communicate the composer's inner idea, the blame will always be assigned to the performer and not to the score.

The Performance

Composer → Technique → Notation → Performance → Listener

If it is understood that music is something to be listened to, and if the end of music is the experience of the listener, then performance must lie at the heart of any theory of aesthetics in music, for only in performance does music actually exist in the present tense.

At the same time, if we presume, as a matter of artistic integrity, that the performer's goal is to re-create the composer's original aesthetic idea, then it follows that we must assume the performer is indeed capable of doing this. Croce bases his assumption that the performer can do this on the following reasoning. The faculty of the composer which we call *genius* has its corollary in what we might call the *taste* of the performer. He says these are 'substantially identical' characteristics of artistic discernment.[24]

We prefer to base the assumption that the performer should be able to re-create the composer's aesthetic idea on the genetically shared emotional characteristics of the species. In any case, we must assume this goal of the performer is possible, otherwise re-creation in performance would be inconceivable.

On the other hand, we must acknowledge that in saying the performer *should* be able to achieve this goal, we cannot say he always does. We know all too well that with respect to rational language one may speak or write well, but based on erroneous concepts. In the same way, a performer may perform well, yet distort the composer's intent. Certainly it is wrong to think of a 'beautiful performance' as the aesthetic goal. As Liszt once observed,

> A successful performance cannot as a rule be considered as a criterion of artistic worth.

It is rather the performance of the *composer's* beautiful idea which is the aesthetic goal.

Thus, by a 'poor performance' we mean not only that which is technically deficient, but also that which fails in its obligation to the composer. There are many ways this can result. In the performance of older music this often results in part from a lack of knowledge of performance practices. This knowledge is essential if the composer is to communicate with us.

---

[23] We omit here the sins of editors and publishers who change the notation without telling us.
[24] Croce, *Aesthetic*, 120.

Equally misinformed is the viewpoint that the performer should simply play the music as written, 'letting the music speak for itself.' The error in this viewpoint lies in the false notion that the work of art is the score, when in fact the work of art is that which the score *represents*. Koussevitzky, in particular, complained about those who failed to understand this.

> Nowadays we can often hear 'authorities' exclaim, in reviewing a performance: 'Let the music speak for itself!' The danger of this maxim lies in its paving the way for mediocrities who simply play a piece off accurately and then maintain that they 'let they music speak for itself.' Such a statement is not right, in any event, because a talented artist renders a work as he conceives it, according to his own temperament and insight, no matter how painstakingly he follows the score markings. And the deeper the interpreter's insight, the greater and more vital the performance.
>
> A perfect rendition of a work can have two different aspects which are equally faithful to the score. One part can be called mechanically perfect, the other organically perfect. The first gives the listener the beauty of mathematical balance, symmetry and clarity, the second the complete, vital, pulsing *elan vital* of the composition. The one wants to present a pretty facade, while in the other the musical creation—its basic idea—comes to life. The one may be compared to a completely symmetrical building, the other to a great Gothic cathedral, in parts asymmetrical and yet an organic unit. The one is always friendly and pleasant, but always retains something superficial, like a lively stage set. The other touches the listener, arouses him, fuses him with the reality of the basic idea, and allows him to experience the *elan vital* of the composition.[25]

Closely related to this is the error made by the performer who thinks of his responsibility as one of 'understanding' the score in a rational sense, or an academic sense. By this we mean looking at a score as an accumulation of forms, types of melody, harmonic practice, etc. In a word, he only studies the grammar of the score. In doing so, he 'fails to see the forest because of the trees.' The 'forest' in this metaphor is *feeling*, as Wagner reminds us.

> An artist addresses himself to Feeling, and not to Understanding. If his work is discussed in terms of Understanding, then it might as well be said he has been misunderstood.[26]

We do not ignore the grammar of music, but, as the great pianist, Alfred Brendel, suggests, in doing so we must not lose our focus on *feeling*.

> Although I find it necessary and refreshing to *think* about music, I am always conscious of the fact that *feeling* must remain the Alpha and Omega of a musician; therefore my remarks proceed from feeling and return to it.[27]

Wagner criticized the school of interpretation led by Mendelssohn on these very grounds.

---

[25] Quoted in Carl Bamberger, *The Conductor's Art* (New York: McGraw-Hill, 1965), 144.

[26] 'Eine Mitteilung an meine Freunde,' 1851.

[27] Quoted in *The New Yorker*, May 30, 1977.

Aesthetic Background in Selecting Repertoire   17

> At a time when I came into contact with a young musician who had been in Mendelssohn's company, I was perpetually told of the master's one piece of advice: In composing never think of making a sensation or effect, and avoid everything likely to lead to it. That sounded beautiful and right enough, and in fact not a single faithful pupil of the master's has ever chanced to produce a sensation or effect … I imagine all the teachings of the Leipzig Conservatory are founded on that negative maxim, for I have heard that the young folk there are plagued to death with its warning, whilst the most promising talents can gain themselves no favor with their teachers unless they forswear all taste for music not in strict accordance with the Psalms …
>
> Once I begged one of the most reputed older musicians and comrades of Mendelssohn to play me the Eighth Prelude and Fugue from the first part of the Well-tempered Klavier, as that piece had always had such a magical attraction for me; I must admit that seldom have I felt so great a shock as that experienced from his friendly compliance. At any rate there then was no question of gloomy German Gothic … under the hands of my friend the piece flowed over the keyboard with such a 'Grecian gaiety' … that involuntarily I saw myself seated in a neo-Hellenic synagogue, from whose musical rites every trace of the Old Testament accentuation had been decently purged away. That singular reading was still ringing in my ears, when one day I begged Liszt to cleanse my musical feelings from the painful impression. He played for me the Fourth Prelude and Fugue. Now, I knew what to expect from Liszt at the pianoforte … but I never expected what I learnt that day. For then I saw the difference between study and revelation; through his rendering of this single fugue Liszt revealed the whole of Bach to me, so that I now know of a surety where I am with him, can take his every bearing from this point, and conquer all perplexity and every doubt by power of strong faith.[28]

One type of performance which is most objectionable is that by the performer who simply substitutes his own interpretation without any consideration for the composer at all. This is usually a matter of excess. Certainly it is the performer's duty to seek the *Melos* of the composition and certainly no two performers will arrive at exactly the same understanding of this, but we speak of the performer who goes too far and simply creates the music after his own image. Wagner found the performers who were most guilty of this excess to be conductors.

> Lo there is the man who certainly thinks least about himself, and to whom the personal act of pleasing has surely no place, the man beating time for an orchestra. He surely fancies he has bored to the very inside of the composer, yes, he has drawn him on like a second skin! You won't tell me that *he* is plagued with the Upstart-devil, when he takes your tempo wrong, misunderstands your expression marks, and drives you to desperation at listening to your own composition.
>
> Yet *he* can be a virtuoso too, and tempt the public by all kinds of spicy nuances into thinking that it after all is he who makes the whole thing sound so nice. He finds it neat to let a loud passage be played quite soft, for a change, a fast one a wee bit slower. He will add for you, here and there, a trombone effect, or a dash of the cymbals and triangle. But his chief resource is a drastic cut, if he otherwise is not quite sure of his success. Him we must call a virtuoso of the Baton.[29]

We must then ask, Where is the line between a personal interpretation of the composer's intent and a performance in which the personality of the performer replaces the intent of the composer? How does the performer maintain integrity to the composer's original inner idea? What is the proper relationship between the performer and the score?

---

[28] Wagner, *Prose Works*, IV, 344.
[29] Ibid., VII, 114.

The highest aesthetic goal in performance is reached when the performer comes to understand that his duty is not to reproduce the score, but to reproduce what the score represents. The most important key to revealing what the score represents is to call upon his genetically shared emotions. It is this genetically shared language that allows him to understand what the notated symbols mean. The vital first step is that he recognize that the notated symbols of the score are not comparable to the notated symbols of rational language, including the entire range from newspapers to legal briefs. In other words, the highest aesthetic goal in performance *begins* when the performer comes to understand that not *all* the music is found on the score page. This is what is meant when some of the greatest musicians of all time understood:

Gustav Mahler
    The important things in music are not found in the notes.

Felix Weingartner
    There are musicians who only see the notes and those who see *behind* the notes.

Franz Liszt
    With notes alone nothing can be accomplished; one thirsts for soul, spirit, and actual life.

Bruno Walter
    The performer's duty is to recreate the spirit of the score, not the letter of the score.

The 'missing' music these artists are describing is that part of music for which we have no notational symbols. It is the central core of feeling, or emotional meaning, which Leopold Stokowski called, 'the inner spirit of the music and all the potentialities lying dormant on the printed page of the score,' Koussevitzky called the *elan vital*, and Weingartner, 'the spiritualizing internal factor that gives the music its very soul.'

It is when *this* is missing in performance that the re-creation of the music fails to achieve its highest aesthetic end. It is when the performer fails in this responsibility that the composer suffers, for he knows his most important and beautiful ideas have not been communicated. It is interesting, in this regard, to read Verdi's anguished cry regarding performances he heard of his opera, *Aida*.

> For my part, I vow that no one has ever, ever, ever, ever even succeeded in bringing out all the effects that I intended … No one!! Never, never … Neither singers nor conductors!![30]

In contrast, it is also interesting to read Weingartner's testimony that he found Wagner to be the model of what the contribution of the performer should be.

> He obviously aimed in his own performances not only at correctness, but at bringing out that to which the sounds and notes are only the *means* …

---

[30] Bamberger, *The Conductor's Art*, 312.

He sought the unifying thread, the psychological line, the revelation of which suddenly transforms, as if by magic, a more or less indefinite sound-picture into a beautifully shaped, heart-moving vision, making people ask themselves in astonishment how it is that this work, which they had long thought they knew, should have all at once become quite another thing ... Out of the garment of music there emerges the *spirit of the artwork*; its noble countenance, formerly only confusedly visible, is now unveiled, and enraptures those who are privileged to behold it. Wagner calls this form, this quintessence, this spirit of the artwork its *melos*.[31]

This is the performer's great contribution, to communicate *this* to the listener. But how does he find the 'music' that is not written in the score?

His goal must be to hear what the composer heard, not see what the composer wrote. To do this he must learn not to initially fix his concentration on the notation itself, but rather learn to see the notation somewhat passively, giving the notation (the composer) a chance to speak to him before he begins to apply his own personality to the notation. We are reminded of the old European rule of etiquette regarding conversation with a royal person: 'Don't speak until spoken to.' The great conductor, Eugen Jochum, describes this process perfectly.

> I take care first of all to have, so to speak, a passive attitude toward the work; that is, to establish a lack of bias, a receptiveness that will allow the work of art to best develop its own reality. First I abandon myself to the work, which I read through again and again ... without my thinking of particulars. What is this tempo? How does it relate to later tempi? What is the nature of the themes? How do they relate to one another? These questions are left for later.
>
> In this manner the tempo focuses 'by itself,' the piece becomes so self-evident that it begins to live its own life, still practically completely withdrawn from my conscious will and shaping impulses. The condition described as passivity now reveals itself as having many layers; only the intellectual layers of consciousness are actually passive. The possessive, forming will is only excluded by the thinking mind. On the other hand, the deeper layers of consciousness are vibrantly awake, straining toward the work, so that an emotional field of tension is formed in which the 'spark leaps over.' This is the decisive point. When it is reached, conscious work of the greatest precision can and must begin. It is only important that the impulse of the will and conscious control do not take over too soon, and that one's own personality is not brought in at the wrong moment. It is thus a question of humble acceptance of a law, of listening to an inner meaning.[32]

This is as it should be, for the symbols themselves are not the music. We might add that we believe memorization is the most immediate tool for discovering the music which is not on the page. Memorization allows the performer to mentally stand aside, so to speak, to hear the music in his mind, eliminating the intrusion of our most dominant sense, the eye, and its strong tendency to fix on the score, which, of course, consists of only symbolic symbols of the music. This wisdom is engagingly expressed in a famous Sufi parable.

> A student was walking through the village, whereupon he came to the house of his teacher. There he saw his teacher, on his hands and knees, apparently looking for something in the grass.
>
> 'Master, what are you looking for?'
>
> 'I am looking for my house key,' his teacher replied, 'Come and help me look for it!'

---

[31] Quoted in Ibid., 98ff.

[32] Quoted in Ibid., 260.

The student joined his teacher in the grass, but after a time he concluded that there was probably no key in the grass at all and that this was intended as some sort of lesson.

'OK, Master, where did you actually lose your house key?'

His teacher answered, 'Well, actually I lost it somewhere inside my house.'

'Why,' said the student, 'are we looking out here in the grass?'

'Because there is more light here,' reassured the teacher.

And so there is.

It is important to add that in the process by which the sincere interpreter seeks to understand what the composer felt beyond what he could place on paper with rational symbols, it is inevitable and appropriate that he will, to some degree, come to a personal interpretation. This is because he will always be influenced by his own experiential history. We say appropriate because this is the only possible way that the feelings of a dead composer can come to life in the present sense.

We think of this subsequent relationship between interpreter or performer and the score as being somewhat analogous to you and your banker both having a necessary key to open your safe deposit box. The score is certainly the most important 'key,' but the interpreter or performer has the other 'key,' a key made of his personal experiential knowledge of music.

The Listener

Composer → Technique → Notation → Performance → Listener

Both the composer's efforts to transmit his inner aesthetic ideas into a notated form and the efforts required to re-create these ideas through performance imply the expectation of a listener. Indeed, as two great composers observed, would music even make sense without a listener?

> Music remains meaningless noise unless it touches a receiving mind.[33]
> *Hindemith*

> Music is a means of communicating with people, not an aim in itself.
> *Moussorgsky*

The experience of the listener is the logical end of the aesthetic chain in music. This being the case, the question follows, What does the contemplative listener experience in music?

There are two broad areas of personal development affected when the contemplative listener experiences music. We might mention in passing that it is precisely these two areas where music education should be centered. First, as with the case of any other kind of intellectual exchange, we profit from the exposure to superior minds. For example, in a recent

---

[33] Paul Hindemith, *A Composer's World* (Garden City: Doubleday, 1961), 18.

study of Thomas Jefferson as a young man, the author observed, 'he was profiting immeasurably by contact with superior minds.'[34] By 'superior minds,' in the case of music, we mean the great composer, who differs with us not so much in kind as in degree. As Croce expresses this,

> What is generally called par excellence art, collects intuitions that are wider and more complex than those which we generally experience.[35]

By contemplative listening the listener is able to place himself in the perspective of the composer, to experience through his experience. By this process we are lifted to a higher level of insight, as Croce again explains.

> To judge Dante, we must raise ourselves to his level: let it be well understood that empirically we are not Dante, nor Dante we; but in that moment of contemplation and judgment, our spirit is one with that of the poet, and in that moment we and he are one thing. In this identity alone resides the possibility that our little souls can echo great souls, and grow great with them in the universality of the spirit.[36]

Because listeners vary greatly in their experiential histories, this opportunity for growth may be easy for some and more difficult for others. It was for this reason that Bruno Walter once observed that it is the special duty of musicians to remember those most in need of this kind of development.

> There are people for whom life begins anew every morning. It is they who are ever more deeply touched by every renewed encounter with Schubert's *Unfinished*, it is they whom the perusal of a familiar Goethe poem moves with the force of a first impression; people over whom habit has no power; people who, in spite of their increasing years and experience, have remained fresh, interested, and open to life. And there are others who, when they watch a most glorious sunset or listen to the Benedictus in Beethoven's *Missa Solemnis*, feel scarcely more than 'I know this already'; and who are upset by everything new and unusual—in other words, people whose element is habit and comfort. It is for the former that our poets have written, our artists created, and our musicians composed; and it is for them, above all, that we perform our dramas, our operas, oratorios, and symphonies. As regards the latter, we artists must try, time and time again, to burst open the elderly crust they have acquired, or with which many of them may have been born; our youthful vigor must call upon theirs or revive whatever is left of it.[37]

The second area of personal development for which the contemplative listener has access through music includes special and unique opportunities for self-discovery. It is here that the concept of the melos of the music achieves a personal meaning. As we have described above, it is the melos, the concentrated, pure form of emotion, which is communicated through performance. Each listener then takes in this form of the emotion, sifts it through his own experien-

---

[34] Claude G. Bowers, *The Struggle for Democracy in America* (Boston: Houghton Mifflin, 1966), 96.

[35] Croce, *Aesthetic*, 13.

[36] Ibid., 121.

[37] Bruno Walter, quoted in Bamberger, *The Conductor's Art*, 176ff.

tial understanding of that emotion, and in the process comes to understand in a more defined sense this aspect of himself. This is the same experience in music which Aristotle identified as *Catharsis* with respect to tragedy.

Wagner says this is the great value of music, to allow us to 'gaze into the inmost Essence of ourselves.' In addition to this very important observation, Wagner, in the following, also points out that music *is* the means by which the feeling part of us communicates, a part of us which cannot otherwise speak; that music, unlike painting, does this directly; and that the value of a composition is determined by the degree to which it does this.

> Music, who speaks to us solely through quickening into articulate life the most universal concept of the inherently speechless Feeling, in all imaginable gradations, can once and for all be judged by nothing but the category of the *sublime*; for, as soon as she engrosses us, she transports us to the highest ecstasy of consciousness of our infinitude. On the other hand what enters only *as a sequel* to our contemplation of a work of plastic art ... the required effect of *beauty* on the mind, is brought about by Music by her very *first entry*; inasmuch as she withdraws us at once from any concern with the relation of things outside us, and—as pure Form set free from Matter—shuts us off from the outer world, as it were, to let us gaze into the inmost Essence of ourselves and all things. Consequently our verdict on any piece of music should be based upon a knowledge of those laws whereby the effect of Beauty, the very first effect of Music's mere appearance, advances the most directly to a revelation of her truest character through the agency of the Sublime. It would be the stamp of an absolutely empty piece of music, on the contrary, that it never got beyond a mere prismatic toying with the effect of its first entry, and consequently kept us bound to the relations presented by Music's outermost side to the world of vision.[38]

The reason why this is so important is because music is our most effective language of our experiential self. We know the rational side of our self cannot do this. Language is one of our most important forms of communication, but anyone who has tried to write a love letter knows that language is quite inferior in the realm of the expression of emotions. Furthermore, when it comes to our most sensitive feelings we often don't want to talk about them at all! Here language fails us.

> Everybody knows that language is a very poor medium for expressing our emotional nature. It merely names certain vaguely and crudely conceived states, but fails miserably in any attempt to convey the ever-moving patterns, the ambivalences and intricacies of inner experience, the interplay of feelings with thoughts and impressions, memories and echoes of memories, transient fantasy, or its mere runic traces, all turned into nameless, emotional stuff. If we say that we understand someone else's feeling in a certain matter, we mean that we understand why he should be sad or happy, excited or indifferent, in a general way; that we can see due cause for his attitude. We do not mean that we have insight into the actual flow and balance of his feelings, into that 'character' which 'may be taken as an index of the mind's grasp of its object.' Language is quite inadequate to articulate such a conception. Probably we would not impart our actual inmost feelings even if they could be spoken. We rarely speak in detail of entirely personal things.[39]

---

[38] Wagner, *Prose Works*, V, 77.
[39] Susanne K. Langer, *Philosophy in a New Key* (New York: Mentor Books, 1948), 92.

In another place, Langer concludes,

> Language and music are similar in that both are means for expressing something. The difference is that language is principally a means for expressing ideas, and music is principally a means for expressing feelings.[40]

Two additional writers expressed this same truth as follows:

> Language is not subtle enough, tender enough to express all we feel, and when language fails, the highest and deepest longings are translated into music.
> *Robert Ingersoll*
>
> Where words fail, music speaks.
> *Hans Christian Anderson*

Most especially science will never come to our aid on the subject of emotions, because emotions are *individual* and science is only interested in the *general*. This represents a basic difference between the rational world of science and the experiential world of art. Even in the case of the study of human nature itself, science takes as significant only the general, the average (which represents no one in particular) and avoids the individual, which is in every case unique. The psychologist who studies aggressive behavior, for example, is interested only in those characteristics which create a syndrome of aggression, but can draw no useful conclusion from any one individual aggressive person. Art is just the reverse. We might say: The scientist dreads the presence of individuality as the death of science; the artist dreads the loss of individuality as the death of art.

> The reason why scientific description, so far from helping expression, actually damages it, is that description generalizes. To describe a thing is to call it a thing of such and such a kind; to bring it under a conception, to classify it. Expression on the contrary, individualizes ... Expressing an emotion has something to do with becoming conscious of it.[41]

Indeed, Liszt points out that it is one of the values of music that it relieves us briefly from our left hemisphere dominant world.

> Only in music does feeling, actually and radiantly present, lift the ban which oppresses our spirit with the sufferings of an evil earthly power and liberate us with the white-capped floods of its free and warmth-giving might from 'the demon Thought,' brushing away for brief moments his yoke from our furrowed brows.[42]

In summary, as the distinguished conductor Celibidache points out, it is this personal relationship with our feelings which gives music its universality.

---

40 Susanne K. Langer, 'The Cultural Importance of the Arts,' *The Journal of Aesthetic Education*, Spring 1966, 5–12.
41 R. Collingwood, *Principles of Art* (London: Oxford, 1938), 112.
42 Letter to August Kiel, September 8, 1855.

> Music is the shortest way to expressing how little music has to do with the notes. The notes are physical, coarse textured phenomena. But in its relationship to another note, a note can become something which finds an echo in the human emotions. The reasons for this can be experienced in phenomenology, and demonstrated wonderfully. If it weren't for this relationship between the physical phenomenon of sound and the emotional reaction, no one would want to make music, no one would have any interest in it. But it wakens something in us, and we sing and play to liberate ourselves again [through] this responsiveness.[43]

There are additional direct benefits which the contemplative listener gains through the experience of listening to important music, but for the present we conclude with the question, is there physical evidence of this relationship? In the matter in which it is so evident that 'we are what we eat,' can the same be inferred with respect to experiences? It is in this regard that our attention was drawn to a comment by Schumann.

> No children can be brought to healthy manhood on candy and pastry. Spiritual like bodily nourishment must be solid. The masters have provided it; cleave to them.

The fact is there is even extraordinary clinical evidence to suggest that something similar to 'You are what you eat' happens with respect to our brain's response to our experiences. Experiences actually change the brain physically! Thus the choice the listener makes, with respect to the quality of music he listens to, is a very serious responsibility, for it *literally* changes his brain.

> The brain's neurons change the communication pathways among themselves in response to experience, says Dartmouth's Bharucha. Working with a computer model of brain cells called a neural network, Bharucha found that as he exposed the model to music, the layer of brain cells responsible for processing individual notes sent signals to another layer whose cells gradually became specialized for recognizing specific groups of notes, or chords. These cells in turn signaled a third layer of cells that gradually became responsible for recognizing groups of chords as belonging to particular keys. This hierarchical grouping occurred even though Bharucha gave the brain model no explicit instructions as to how the cells should connect themselves. Instead, the network simply organized itself in a manner that reflected the intrinsic organization of music itself.[44]

We have seen that a definition of aesthetics in music must include the components of the participation of the composer and his expression through the score, the re-creation of the composer's ideas through performance, and the reception by a contemplative listener. The philosophical field of aesthetics was invented by Aristotle in his study of tragedy and he found that in the end aesthetics was of the province of the observer, not the play itself and not the

---

43 Sergiu Celibidache, quoted in *Los Angeles Philharmonic Notes*, April, 1989.

44 'The Musical Brain,' *U. S. News & World Report*, June 11, 1990. Diana Deutsch, of the University of California, San Diego, has found some evidence to suggest that we hear the octave as such a pure interval due to the channeling of nerve impulses to the same nerve cell in the brain. See, 'What Happens When Music Meets the Brain,' *Wall Street Journal*, August 30, 1985.

actors. It is the same with music, which like stage plays have both a written and a performance form. The contemplative listener is the only place in the equation where a meaningful discussion of aesthetics can be centered.

◈

GIVEN THE DEFINITIONS ABOVE, the next question is how does one establish the parameters which define art music versus everything else? An essay written in 2009 is focused on this important question.

ON THE CLASSIFICATION OF THE MUSICAL EXPERIENCE

Benedetto Croce, in his classic study of aesthetics, raises the issue of how the conditions in which the observer finds an art work can affect the aesthetics of that art work in so far as the individual observer is concerned.

> When speaking of the stimuli of reproduction we have added a caution, for we said that reproduction takes place, if all the other conditions remain equal. Do they remain equal? Does the hypothesis correspond with reality?
>
> It would appear not. In order to reproduce an impression several times by means of a suitable physical stimulus it is necessary that this stimulus be not changed, and that the organism remain in the same psychical conditions as those in which was experienced the impression that it is desired to reproduce. Now it is a fact that the physical stimulus is continually changing, and in like manner the psychological conditions.
>
> Oil paintings grow dark, frescoes fade, statues lose noses, hands and legs, architecture becomes totally or partially a ruin, the tradition of the execution of a piece of music is lost, the text of a poem is corrupted by bad copyists or bad printing. These are obvious instances of the changes which daily occur in objects or physical stimuli. As regards psychological conditions, we will not dwell upon the cases of deafness or blindness, that is to say, upon the loss of entire orders of psychical impressions; these cases are secondary and of less importance compared with the fundamental, daily, inevitable and perpetual changes of the society around us and of the internal conditions of our individual life. The phonetic manifestations or words and verses of Dante's *Commedia* must produce a very different impression on an Italian citizen engaged in the politics of the third Rome, from that experienced by a well-informed and intimate contemporary of the poet. The Madonna of Cimabue is still in the Church of Santa Maria Novella; but does she speak to the visitor today as to the Florentines of the thirteenth century? Even though she were not also darkened by time, must we not suppose that the impression which she now produces is altogether different from that of former times? And even in the case of the same individual poet, will a poem composed by him in youth make the same impression upon him when he re-reads it in his old age, with psychic conditions altogether changed?[45]

In the case of music, it is our contention that music only exists in performance. What is on paper we *call* music, but it is really not music. Aesthetics in music, we have argued, can only meaningfully be discussed in the relationship of live performance to the listener. But, as Croce

---

[45] Croce, *Aesthetic*, 123–124.

points out above, the conditions of the performance have a direct effect on the nature of the aesthetic experience. These conditions play a definite role in how we classify the aesthetic experience in music.

On the Classification of the Musical Experience

We believe the performance of music in actual practice falls naturally into four classes: Art Music, Educational Music, Functional Music and Entertainment Music. Music of high aesthetic quality is *possible* in each class, subject to the conditions of the performance.

We begin our discussion by defining Art Music, the highest aesthetic, the highest quality of experience. We believe Art Music is the most unequivocal in definition. The other three classes, in turn, seem to us more clearly defined in how their conditions and functions differ with Art Music.

I. Art Music

Art Music we believe is defined by four conditions, *all* of which *must always be present*, if the experience is to be classified as Art Music. These are:

1. *Art music is inspired.*

Art music is music in which it seems evident that the composer has made an honest attempt to communicate genuine feelings. Feelings must be presumed to be generally recognizable in music, as they are in any other art form, including painting, sculpture, dance, and architecture. Due to the common genetically understood nature of emotions, it must also be understood that in music emotions or feelings cannot be 'faked.' They will always be recognized as such by any contemplative listener. Croce adds the following observation.

> For by sincerity may be meant, in the first place, the moral duty not to deceive one's neighbor; and in that case it is foreign to the artist. For indeed he deceives no one, since he gives form to what is already in his soul.[46]

2. *Art Music has no purpose other than the communication of its own aesthetic content.*

Art Music is free of any purpose or function, save the spiritual communication of pure beauty. As Croce points out,

> Art is independent both of utility and of morality, as also of all practical value. Without this independence, it would not be possible to speak of an intrinsic value of art, nor indeed to conceive an aesthetic science, which demands the autonomy of the aesthetic fact as its necessary condition.[47]

---

[46] Croce, *Aesthetic*, 53.

[47] Ibid., 116.

3. *Art Music is that which enjoys a performance faithful to the intent of the composer.*

4. *Art Music must have a listener capable of contemplation.*

If any of these conditions are missing, the performance must result in a lesser aesthetic experience. For example, the *Ninth Symphony* of Beethoven played in a stadium, during the half-time of a professional football game, would fail for the lack of the presence of Condition Number Four. The same Symphony heard in a concert hall, but in a poor performance, not faithful to the intent of the composer, would fail for the lack of the presence of Condition Number Three.

II. Educational Music

Educational Music may or may not have the same conditions as Art Music and it may or may not occur within an educational institution. But Educational Music is generally burdened with Condition Number Two, it has a purpose. If it is music specifically composed for its educational purpose, it cannot be Art Music. However, Art Music *can* be performed by students for the purpose of education.

III. Functional Music

Functional Music is music put at the service of something else. We include here, for example, all kinds of religious music, music for weddings, music for the military, and occupational music. Functional Music may share the same conditions as Art Music, excepting Condition Number Two.

One may ask, How can a Mozart Mass be called Functional Music, and not Art Music? The answer is that if the observer were not contemplatively listening to the music, but were rather contemplating religious thoughts, then the Mozart Mass becomes merely a very high level of Functional Music. If, on the other hand, the observer is a contemplative listener of music, forgetting about religion, then the Mozart Mass is Art Music, but has failed in its purpose as church music.[48] Even Croce admits that aesthetic contemplation can hinder functional purpose.

> It cannot however be denied that aesthetic contemplation sometimes hinders practical usage. For instance, it is a quite common experience to find certain new objects ... so beautiful, that people occasionally feel scruples in maltreating them by passing from their contemplation to their use. It was for this reason that King Frederick William of Prussia showed such repugnance to sending his magnificent grenadiers, so well adapted to war, into the mud and fire of battle.[49]

---

[48] Such works as the Verdi *Requiem*, or the Mozart *Requiem*, are performed today as Art Music and are almost never used at anyone's funeral.

[49] Croce, *Aesthetic*, 102.

Military and wedding music are examples of music in which the contemplative listener is missing entirely. How about airport, supermarket and elevator music where there is no listener at all? According to the definitions we have given, recorded music without listeners is not to be considered music at all.

IV. Entertainment Music

Most Entertainment Music is music with no purpose other than to please, which is missing Condition Four, the contemplative listener. For this reason, Entertainment Music may be inspired music, but the composer is unlikely to be inspired by lofty and noble emotions, knowing there will be no contemplative listener.

It is for these reasons that Entertainment Music can never be Art Music. But, one might protest, when a tired businessman goes to the opera at the end of his work day, is this not for him Art Music which is also a very high level form of Entertainment Music? Franz Josef of Austria once posed this very question. When Mahler was music director of the State Opera in Vienna, he once became frustrated because of the disruption of those arriving late. Therefore he began a policy of having all late arrivals placed in a separate room until the first intermission. When informed of this, the emperor was puzzled and observed, 'But after all, the theater is meant to be a pleasure.'[50]

The answer is no, Entertainment Music and Art Music can never be the same thing because of Condition Number Two: Art Music has no purpose other than the communication of its own aesthetic content. It is inconsistent with the nature of great art to have any extrinsic purpose, including the purpose to entertain.

With the development of mass public audiences during the nineteenth century, this became an important question. Wagner was one of the first important critics to write about this aesthetic problem with respect to public music. It might be interesting to see how he viewed this question at that time. First, he states the principle mentioned above, as follows:

> The highest principle of aesthetics [is that] the 'objectless' alone is beautiful, because being an end in itself, in revealing its nature as lifted high above all vulgar ends it reveals at like time that to reach whose sight and knowledge alone makes ends of life worth following; whereas everything that serves an end is hideous, because neither its fashioner nor its onlooker can have aught before him save a disquieting conglomerate of fragmentary material, which is first to gain its meaning and elucidation from its employment for some vulgar need.[51]

It therefore follows, he adds, that even having the mere purpose of 'to please' must remove a composition of the category of the highest art.

---

[50] Quoted by Alma Mahler, *Gustav Mahler* (New York: Viking, 1969), 136ff.

[51] Quoted in Wagner, *Prose Works*, IV, 107.

Thus is born what alone we can term the *Good in art*. This is exactly like the *Morally good*; for this, as well, can spring from no intention, no concern. On the contrary, we might define the Bad as the sheer aim-to-please both summoning up the picture and governing its execution. As we have had to accord our public no developed sense of artistic form, and hardly anything beyond a highly varying receptivity, aroused by the very desire of entertainment, so we must recognize the work that merely aims at exploiting this desire as certainly bare of any value in itself, and closely approaching the category of the morally bad in so far as it makes for profit from the most questionable attributes of the crowd.[52]

Wagner was quite adamant about this, writing in another place,

> I assert that it is impossible for anything to be truly good if it is reckoned in advance for presentation to the public and this intended presentation governs the author in his sketch and composition of an artwork.[53]

And yet again,

> Popularity: the curse of every grand and noble thing.[54]

The great musicians have always understood a certain duty to their art to lead the public to higher aesthetic purpose by way of example. Liszt once wrote a beautiful thought in this regard, a plea to all musicians to think higher.

> Let us ... cast out all but the noblest ambitions, to concentrate our concerns on efforts that dig a deeper furrow than the fashion of the day! Let us renounce, too, for ourselves, in the dreary time in which we live, all that is unworthy of art, all that lacks permanence, all that fails to shelter some grain of eternal and immaterial beauty which art must lighten gloriously in order to glow itself, and let us remember the ancient prayer of the Dorians, whose simple formula was so reverently poetic when they petitioned the gods: 'to give them Good through Beauty!' Instead of laboring so to attract and please listeners at any price, let us rather strive ... to leave a celestial echo of what we have felt, loved, and endured! Let us learn ... to demand of ourselves whatever ennobles in the mystical city of art rather than to seek from the present, without regard to the future, those easy crowns which, scarce assumed, are at once dulled and forgotten![55]

It takes great courage and conviction to pursue the highest goals in music when the public is so easily satisfied by a diet of only entertainment. No one knew this better than Wagner.

---

[52] Ibid., VI, 67.
[53] Ibid., VI, 55.
[54] Ibid., VII, 74.
[55] Franz Liszt, *Chopin* (1852).

> To take a last look back upon the picture afforded us by the Public … we might compare it with a river, as to which we must decide whether we will swim against or with its stream. Who swims with it, may imagine he belongs to constant progress; because it is so easy to be borne along, and he never notices that he is being swallowed in the ocean of vulgarity. To swim against the stream must seem ridiculous to those not driven by an irresistible force to the immense exertions that it costs.[56]

⁂

I should like to post next an essay which expands on a thought mentioned above, the fact that in contrast to painting and sculpture music exists *only* in the present tense. This is an essential principle a conductor must have in mind in the selection of repertoire. There is a vast gap between music which looks good on paper, or contains clever manipulations of rational ideas, and that which communicates to the listener. And communication with a listener is the only point of music.

It might be worthy of thought here to wonder if this distinction in tense might not be one of the reasons why 'Program music' so often fails. One can imagine how a composer might be personally inspired in thinking of, say, the defeat of Napoleon. But it must surely be an additional burden in communication when he tries to take past tense events and transform them into present tense experiences for the listener.

On the Nature of the Present Tense in Music

A friend of many years wrote recently that he was preparing to move into a professional home for senior citizens. This friend has an extensive collection of early music, literary works and musical instruments and so I asked him how does one cope with the idea of giving everything away prior to making such a move? To illustrate his current frame of mind, he wrote as follows:

> I don't find it a matter of coping, but rather a matter of having no choice. I have too much stuff that I no longer need, though some of it has sentimental value. For example, I saved the programs of every concert I played, and I never even looked at them for 40 to 50 years. So what value do they hold for me? None.

It is a very interesting phenomenon that he points to. We all have similar collections of old programs, not to mention pictures and recordings. And like my friend, the curious thing is that we never feel an obligation to go back and look at these things. Suppose that today I said to myself, 'I wonder what music I performed in 1982?' If I were to dig out my programs for 1982 I would no doubt find it a very interesting exercise. There would be, for example, repertoire I had completely forgotten and names of guest artists and conductors would, by the mer-

---

[56] Wagner, *Prose Works*, VI, 94.

est exposure to the eye, bring back a flood of memories. The exercise would, no doubt, repay the investment in time with a very pleasant hour or two. But, again, the interesting question is, why do none of us do this?

I have a case on the wall of my office which contains some 200 cassette recordings of my concerts. They have a catalog number on the binding, and perhaps a date, but no information on the repertoire on the tape, which is to be found in a catalog which affords the necessary space for this information. So, sometimes when faced with a long drive across town I will grab a cassette at random and listen to it in the car as I drive.[57] Since for several decades I was one who joined the efforts at improving the image of the band by performing much very new music and dozens of premieres, there are on these tapes a great deal of music played one time and one time only. And so it often happens that I will hear, as I am driving, some composition which I do not recognize whatsoever. I cannot recall the music or the composer's name, I cannot recall ever having performed this music (which I am hearing on a recording of my own concert) and when I return home I have to consult my index to identify the composition. And yet I know that there was surely a time when I invested a great deal of time studying this score and, indeed, memorizing it for the concert.

How does one explain how such a performance, with all the personal investment it entails, can completely be deleted by the mind? I don't think the quality of my memory, in general, is to blame. I have a good memory. I have conducted all rehearsals for a performance of the *Rite of Spring* without a score and I retain extensive quantities of precise dialog from conversations held beginning with the 1940s.

All of our minds have a certain sense of discrimination when it comes to memory. For example, our minds seem to know, sometimes even in advance, whether to remember something for long periods (a phone number) or whether to let things enter and exit the mind without being retained at all (nearly all of today's newspaper).

But with music, there is another fundamental factor at play. Although the subject is never discussed in our educational formative years, the fact is that *real* music exists *only* in the present tense—it exists perfectly in step in time with us as we are hearing it. A musical score sitting on a shelf is not music. A recording of last night's performance is not music. What we pass out and is placed on the 'music' stands is not music.[58] This is why most of us do not enjoy listening to our own recordings. The recordings are not real music, they are only sounds frozen in the past tense. While we may retain in our mind the exhilaration of the concert itself, experiencing live music, now in the recording we find only a cold document of that concert. And in listening to this document we are listening outside of the actual experience and it is for this reason, as all artists know, that now as mere objective auditors we tend to notice small flaws which seemed almost beside the point in the live experience. And it is for the same reason, the

---

[57] Talk radio, of course, being an impossible waste of time, even if thought of as entertainment.

[58] Here other languages are more helpful. In Germany it is *die Noten* or *die Stimmen*, which is placed on the stands and would never be referred to a *die Musik*.

transformation of the experiential into past tense documentation, that musicians have little interest in looking back at programs and recordings of prior concerts. As my friend has suggested above, we collect and store them away for almost no purpose at all.

It is precisely because real music exists only in the present tense that we should not casually accept recordings as being 'music.' Music is present tense; recordings are past tense. They have only value as an aid in helping us to recall the real music, but they do not substitute for music. In this way they are analogous to photographs. A photograph can strengthen our recall of a loved one, but the photograph never becomes the loved one (for one thing, the loved one is not two inches tall).

Who Stole our Present Tense?

Nearly all of traditional education is geared to the future. Learn this or else! Practice or else! For young adults all experience seems deferred. They are focused on 'When I get,' not to mention everything about Wall Street.

Old people, of course, live in the past tense.[59] My wife, Giselle, has observed that only small children, before school age, live in the present tense, or as she says, 'in the moment!'

So who stole our present tense? How did we come to have a society in the Western world where we do not live in the present? If one wishes to pursue this question, there is perhaps no better place to begin than with the writers of the early Christian Church in Rome. Gibbon, in his famous study of Rome, gives five reasons for the remarkable rise of the early Church and one of these was 'the doctrine of a future life.'[60]

> When the promise of eternal happiness was proposed to mankind on condition of adopting the faith, and of observing the precepts, of the gospel, it is no wonder that so advantageous an offer should have been accepted by great numbers of every religion, of every rank, and of every province in the Roman empire. The ancient Christians were animated by a contempt for their present existence, and by a just confidence of immortality, of which the doubtful and imperfect faith of modern ages cannot give us any adequate notion.[61]

In other words, to the average person in fourth-century Rome the Church said, you may be poor, have inadequate clothes and shelter and be miserable, but do as we tell you and in the next life you will walk on streets of gold![62] And from that day to this both Catholic and Protestant churches emphasize the future tense more than the present tense.

We cannot help but add one more thought in this regard. As Gibbon points out in the book we have cited, before the Christian movement there was a long tradition in ancient literature dealing with various thoughts about a future life after death. It is very possible, therefore,

---

[59] I was speaking with the 85-year-old Fred Fennell once when a student reporter came up and asked him, 'Dr. Fennell, what are your plans for the future?'

[60] Edward Gibbon, *The History of the Decline and Fall of the Roman Empire* (Philadelphia,, 1845), I, 508ff.

[61] Ibid., 532.

[62] In the Middle Ages the aristocracy was quick to use the clergy and their promise to help control the population.

that these ideas were more commonly known two millennia ago and if so perhaps the Roman Church misunderstood one of the admonitions of Jesus. Maybe what Jesus meant was, 'if you don't take these teachings to heart *now* (in the present tense, 'in the moment' like a child), they won't be of any value in the *future,*' when he said,

> Truly, I say to you, whoever does not receive the kingdom of God like a child shall not enter it.[63]

On top of this, as we have pointed out, the schools also do not focus on the present tense. What is the affect on our civilization when we are reared in the wrong tense? It should be no surprise to us when we observe the wide-spread disorientation of youth and young adults.

Of course we are not going to be able to change religious philosophy, but one should hope that the educational world might devote more thought to the present tense of their students. Certainly only then will the educational world come to understand the potential of music, since it only exists in the present tense.

---

[63] Mark 10:15.

Applied Aesthetic Problems

THERE ARE, NO DOUBT, CONDUCTORS who have high standards of precision in performance by their organizations and who are of high integrity in their own score study and yet who are unaware that the very nature of their programming may have more to do with how an audience judges a concert than the performance itself. This has been a particular problem with band directors, who have a long heritage of entertaining the audience and a deep belief in the principle of variety.

There has been a very long agreement among philosophers that the result of a production upon an audience must either be Aesthetic, moving the emotions of the audience, or Entertainment. Drama critics, for example, held for a thousand years the belief that it had to be one or the other, that there can be no middle ground. Shakespeare was the first important playwright to break this rule, as for example with the comedic grave diggers scene in *Hamlet*. But Shakespeare was able to handle this problem sufficiently that the audience was, in the end, not confused in the nature of the play.

But in the case of a concert, where the listeners are far more intimately drawn into what they hear and indeed have their hearts in the hands of the conductor, it may well be true that there is no middle ground. For to mix the serious with the superficial would at least confuse the listener when he reflects on the evening and in the case of some listeners might create resentment.

In band concerts this aesthetic problem rather frequently presents itself in the example of ending a concert with a march. I have sometimes had the feeling that the conductor believed he must send the audience home happy which might suggest that all the previous concert was not important in some way. In 2010 I wrote a brief essay trying to explain the ramifications of such a choice.

WHAT SHALL WE DO WITH MARCHES?

I am old enough to remember a time when marches were the linchpins of band concerts. The epitome of that tradition came in the concerts of Sousa when he would routinely perform a march following each programmed composition. No one raised aesthetic objections to such disparate successions in style because it was all for the purpose of entertainment anyway. And for the same reason no one objected that the billboard at the Steel Pier in New Jersey listed a Sousa band concert followed by a diving horse act.

But today we can no longer do this. Even the most insensitive conductor knows he cannot follow the *Music for Prague, 1968* by a Sousa march, nor the other way around. In fact the old marches are almost never played at all any more. Perhaps in part historical distance plays a role, for they are being heard in fewer concerts.

In my mind there are two characteristics of marches which are deeply rooted in me due to my own experiences, their aesthetic heritage and form. The first of these characteristics only fully became part of my thinking after a Christmas party in 1968 in Salzburg. Carl Orff was present and after his participation, reading from one of his opera librettos, it was announced that now we would have folk-dancing. Our small group moved to a large classroom and records were produced. I, due to my well-known shyness, leaned against a wall and watched the others dance. But, when a recording of Sousa's *The Washington Post* began to play I, as a matter of education, had to join the dancers in the two-step. It is always nearly impossible to describe movement in words, so I will merely say that on this evening the two-step consisted of running in a circle at a very fast pace. It was exhilarating and far more fun than marching to a march.

This dance experience caused me to reflect for the first time on the folk roots of this dance form. All of us today know of the Hungarian roots of the march as a dance form, in particular the *Verbunkos* used for military recruitment. But the earlier Hungarian roots lay in folk choral music and it is this which still echoes in those wonderful sweeping melodies in the trios of Sousa marches.

In truth, in the nineteenth century social musical life of Europe, marches were found side by side in high society with waltzes, schottisches and polkas. They were all folk music, music of the people. Marches did not yet have the associations which came later of militarism and colonialism. And we still have marches in our repertoire which have nothing to do with war, such as those found in folk-song suites, those of the court *Hautboisten* and *Harmoniemusik* repertoire and even some marches composed for the church. And don't forget processional music is march music—Wagner's *Elsa's Procession to the Cathedral* is a march! I can't help thinking that if we could somehow remove the political associations and present marches as folk-music it might perhaps be easier to find a way to program them.

The other special characteristic of marches as part of our repertoire which I have long thought about came as the result of an invitation to make an LP recording of Sousa marches with the Luzern Wind Orchestra in Switzerland. The regular conductor, Albert Benz, asked me to select fourteen marches of which I would conduct half and he the other half. Working this into their already busy schedule resulted in a three-day period of rehearsal and recording in Zürich. Having to quickly absorb seven Sousa marches, and deciding on performance practice in so far as time allowed, resulted in the thought occurring to me that these marches were very much like so many divertimenti. The problem would be the same if I were preparing seven Mozart divertimenti, on some level they would all sound the same but they would also be distinctly individual. And for the first time I began to think of the march form as the divertimento of the band repertoire. I still think of them as exactly that, but, unlike divertimenti, one aesthetic problem is that they are too brief.

Aside from the social and aesthetic problems discussed above, there are definite performance problems which have limited the appearance of marches on my own programs. First, it has been my experience that to play a march well requires a great deal of rehearsal, at least three hours with good players. This amount of rehearsal is necessary in order to recreate the historical traditions of earlier dance music. And after all this rehearsal and concentration is spent, one is left with only three minutes of music. It is very uneconomical. Certainly in a normal university concert which contains major difficult contemporary repertoire one simply cannot afford the time.

This particular performance problem became central to my life one weekend during which I fulfilled an engagement with the Pasadena All-City Honor Band in California, a Saturday afternoon rehearsal, a Sunday afternoon rehearsal and evening concert. Since the school music programs had undergone a tremendous decline in quality I was careful to select for these brief hours of rehearsal one march and a couple of very easy additional works. It was necessary for the school administration to bus students in for these two days and some administrator concluded that it made more sense to bus in half of the students for Saturday and the other half for Sunday, rather than busing in all the students for both rehearsals—clearly redundant! Not being an official of the school system I knew nothing of this until I arrived on Saturday and saw half of the chairs empty. The second day found the other half of the band present and the students from Saturday were missing. Only the timpani player, an eager kid who owned his own timpani, appeared for both rehearsals. I made a point of thanking him and he replied, 'Well, it was the least I could do, in view of the fact …' Well, everyone knows how that sentence ended.

I explained to the supervisor of music that, in spite of my best efforts, I could only perform the one march, the other pieces being impossible in view of the rehearsal circumstances. She understood utterly without disappointment. The concert was held in the Ambassador Auditorium, one of the two great formal concert sites in LA at that time. This marble palace was filled with parents and friends as the concert began with the supervisor of music introducing me at length, to help consume time. It was the only time in my career that my entire resume has been read in public. Then, following thunderous applause, I appeared and conducted the three minute long march. Following more thunderous applause I commented at length on how hard the students had worked to create such a wonderful performance and if you don't mind we will play it again! Following this I gave a long speech on the importance of music education, and played the march again. And so it continued through several more speeches and several more performances of the march. As I returned home it seemed, in retrospect, like encores to a missing concert.

Apart from the problem of programming a three-minute composition, the greater programming problem is an aesthetic one. One march at the end of a concert will inevitably turn the entire concert into an entertainment event. A concluding march works like an electronic eraser, erasing the memory of all earlier compositions no matter how substantial or how serious. A simple law of nature you can depend on. Placing the march first on the program is nearly as bad, for it creates a certain atmosphere which may cause the second composition to be in an impossible aesthetic position.

I have tried to manage this aesthetic problem by playing a group of marches, such as three of them in contrasting styles or periods. But they must be contrasting for listening to three Sousa marches in a row is a bit like eating three strawberry sundaes in a row.[1] Programming three contrasting marches helps the aesthetic problem somewhat but it only really works if the entire program is of a similar contrasting nature.

But the programming problem remains if it is an aesthetic program. Recently I attended a concert by the Austin Symphony during which a fine pianist joined the orchestra in a wonderful performance of a Mozart concerto. Then, most regrettably, for an encore the pianist played a stupid arrangement of a trivial popular song by some current composer. It ruined the entire experience and sent some of us home very disappointed and confused. When one thinks of the vast number of short piano works, any one of which the audience would have loved to hear live, one is at a complete loss to explain this man's bad taste. A devastating blunder!

Why is this so important? It is important because our sensitive experiential identities are in a concert laid bare in the hands of the artist. This responsibility of the artist, or conductor, is very great and has been acknowledged and discussed since the time of Plato. As of yet there are no laws associated with offending the sensibilities of listeners, but Berlioz thought there should be. In 1852 there came to his attention a civic notice in Cologne forbidding wandering musicians with untuned instruments. 'Fine!,' cried Berlioz in an article in the *Journal des Débats* of 7 January 1852, reasoning that if we are going to control air pollution we should also control ear pollution. Such a law, he argued, should include,

> Imbecilic singers without a voice, incapable performers and conductors who tear apart a masterpiece, break its four members; extinguish its flame, make it physiognomy ignoble and grotesque, are beings incomparably more destructive than if they were spreading infectious odors in the room where they worked.

The question is not whether marches will adversely affect the sensibilities of the audience, but rather if their placement in a specific program would. The issue is one of creating a unified aesthetic character for the concert. This is not only a matter of something you present the audience member, but in the case of a concert the listener becomes part of the event, as a contemplative listener. He cannot be ignored because his involvement is mandatory. Aristotle, who invented the field of aesthetics in his discussion of the components of the tragedy, went to some length to stress the unity of the theme and the principle that if you change any component part you will change the whole.[2] This principle of the unity of the theme or the action was considered so important it was maintained for centuries by later playwrights and dramatic theorists. And to return to the idea of ending a serious concert with a march, Aristotle specifically points out that sometimes a playwright will 'accommodate themselves to the wish of

---

[1] Curiously, Sousa himself once used food as an analogy when speaking of his marches. When asked why his marches, unlike the long European tradition, did not have a da capo at the end of the trio (thus causing his marches to end in a different key than they began), he observed, 'After the ice cream, who wants to go back to the roast beef?'

[2] Aristotle, *The Poetic*, viii.

the spectators' by, for example, having a happy ending to a tragedy. But, points out Aristotle, this changes the whole from tragedy to comedy.[3] And that is exactly what happened with the concert by the pianist and the Austin Symphony mentioned above.

The associated problem is one of confusing the audience sensibilities, in which case they are likely not to return. Given no warnings to the contrary an audience comes to a concert expecting a concert to be a concert. If they find they were merely amused, they will be unlikely to return because they can remain at home, turn on the TV and find five hundred channels of amusement and save all that money spent on tickets, parking and transportation.

Finally, if the concert is one of contemporary music, the performance of a march suddenly raises the question of Tense, discussed in Chapter One. You cannot hear the *Milano March* by Ponchielli or the Fucik *Florentiner March* without being transported back into the Past Tense more than a century. When I hear that Fucik Trio I am back in the Empire living on Kärtnerstrasse and I see Mahler going by on the street car and most of the men wearing uniforms. But that is not today's world.

※

STRONGLY RELATED TO ARISTOTLE'S DEMAND that one must preserve a unified aesthetic experience from the beginning to the end of a concert, is another frequently seen example of a practice which causes havoc with the unity of the musical experience and that is the case of the conductor who feels he must talk with the audience before each composition. Why does he do this, a practice that one never saw before the 1980s? Is the conductor's desire to prove he is a nice guy? Does he feel an obligation to entertain the audience, or to balance the serious performances with his entertaining introductions? If the conductor really thought there was information about the music they should hear, he could schedule someone to do that before the concert, as orchestras frequently do.

If his desire is to help the audience understand the following program, he is quite mistaken. Talk is left hemisphere of the brain and the audience's genetic preparation to understand the music is in the experiential right hemisphere. To say it in another way, the audience's genetic right hemisphere's universal ability to 'understand' music will not and cannot understand the language of the left hemisphere. But a much more serious aesthetic problem is that a kind of mental confusion is created. Since the two hemispheres do not work together, the listener's brain must first determine that the left side should listen, then that the right side should listen, then the left, then the right, etc. A concert accompanied by brain ping-pong. The brain takes this kind of induced confusion seriously. Would we interrupt a formal orator by stopping him at a number of intervals and performing some music?

I once discussed other aspects of this practice in an essay.

---

3   Ibid., xiii.

Why do some Conductors feel they must TALK to the Audience?

I recently heard a performance of the Schönberg *Theme and Variations* for band which was preceded by the conductor describing briefly for the audience the fact that this was a set of variations, after which he proceeded to perform the unaccompanied theme at the beginning of the composition. Then, with no further comments, he began conducting the actual performance.

But why did the conductor feel obligated to do this? The audience came to hear music, the experience of music. But now this audience had been made to feel they must instead listen to a compositional technique and worse they are set up to feel they are failures in the event they cannot hear this theme at all times. But the question, Why?, remains unanswered.

Did this conductor really prefer that the audience focus on picking out the theme in the Third Variation, instead of being moved by the profound expression of pain and sorrow, deriving from the composer's experiences with World War II? No, surely no musician would elect to rob the listeners of such a priceless moment in favor of concentrating on dry academicism. Or did this conductor believe that 'uneducated' listeners could not 'understand' this music without his introduction? No, all conductors know that it is the genetic characteristics of music which make music understandable to all mankind and that this is why we say 'music is the international language.' Indeed it is the reverse which is true: it is the things which music can 'say' that language cannot that make music so important to humanity.

But clearly, this conductor on some basis arrived at the point that he believed he was helping the performance to follow. More likely, he accomplished the reverse, and certainly so in the case of anyone who paid attention to him and sat in their chairs employing the rational part of their brain instead of that part of themselves to which the music itself was addressed. For those listeners, he ruined the performance. I recall a similar case of a live performance by a major conductor and major orchestra which began with the conductor telling the audience how fortunate they were that they were going to be part of a very special evening and pleading with them to be especially quiet as the following performance was being recorded 'live' for an important subsequent commercial recording. In the first bar the solo trumpet performed a cataclysmic missed note, a forte smashed attack which echoed throughout the hall. There was an immediate and enormous sense of let-down among the audience for everyone had the immediate feeling that this concert was all for nothing, as clearly this performance could not be used as intended.

In both of these examples the audience was very unfairly treated psychologically and musically. We say unfairly because in fact the audience is completely equipped genetically to understand music. By talking to them about any aspect of the theory of music we embarrass them because the implication is given that this is something they should know or need to know in order to understand music. This is why one so often hears an adult begin a sentence by saying, 'Of course I don't know anything about music, but …' It is a completely unnecessary embarrassment because it is not true. Even those of us who are highly trained musicians do not listen to the theory, or the grammar, of the music. When listening to the performance of a Beethoven symphony not one of us sits there and thinks to himself, 'Hmm! A first inversion sub-dominant chord with a seventh!'

But why does any conductor feel he must talk to the audience? I do not recall Bruno Walter speaking to the audience, nor Fritz Reiner, nor Eugene Ormandy, nor von Karajan nor Solti. But I have heard a university orchestra conductor speak for nearly as many minutes as the duration of the composition itself, playing fragments of themes and alerting the audience that in measure 164 they will hear this theme upside down, etc. Why would a conductor feel he must do this?

We suspect that in many cases the conductor feels obligated to resort to language because he has a certain lack of faith in the ability of music to speak for itself. This mirrors a frequently observed clinical curiosity having to do with our bicameral brain. Because the right hemisphere of the brain (where the experience of music is found) lacks its own complete facility with language, the left hemisphere must speak for it. But since the left hemisphere really has little or no knowledge of what goes on in the right hemisphere it tends to go so far as to deny that the right hemisphere even exists. A familiar example of this is when we make a decision on an emotional basis, and not on a rational basis, and are asked why we made the decision we did. Since only the rational left hemisphere, where the language to answer the question lies, can answer for this right hemisphere choice, it denies that the decision had any actual basis at all by having you answer, 'I did it on a hunch.'

What the conductor must come to grips with, and believe, is the fact that forty years of clinical study has clearly established the fact that the right hemisphere exists as a separate form of understanding, equal to but apart from the traditional language of the left hemisphere. To the extent that the question is, Who is the real us?, the right hemisphere is clearly more reflective of the individual than the left hemisphere. It is also very important to understand that the right hemisphere does not lie; lies are found only in the left hemisphere.

With respect to music, we stress once again that it is the right hemisphere, the experiential side of the listener which understands music, not the rational side. If that were not the case we would not have concerts at all, we would have people going to the store to buy scores to take home to read. And it is for this reason, because music is going to communicate to the listener all by itself, that programming becomes so important. If a conductor has put together a program of music unworthy of public performance, it is no wonder he feels some compulsion to talk his way out of it.

Now let us consider some other familiar circumstances in which conductors seem obligated to talk to the audience.

To Make the Audience like You and the Ensemble knowing in advance it is going to be a weak Performance.

Sorry! Too Bad! It won't work. A concert does not have a score like a ball game. We can't please an audience by a score of 60 to 40. It is a cruel and inevitable fact that an audience will find a concert either good or bad.[4] There is no middle ground at all and no audience member ever said, 'It was almost a good concert.' The reason for this is again all wrapped up in genetics. The audience knows whether a concert is good or not and they cannot be fooled. Neither can their judgment be tempered by giving them a lot of excuses—we lost some rehearsal time, some students had to miss rehearsals, this music is very difficult, etc., et. al. Max Krone, the founder of the Idyllwild Music Camp in California many years ago, had painted on the wall of the concert stage, 'The Audience does not ask How Hard it is, only How Good it is!'

You might succeed in making yourself likable and we often hear an adult say, 'Oh he is such a nice man and he talks to the audience.' Well, take pleasure where you can but don't expect this feeling to have any influence on their judgment of your concert whatsoever.

Welcoming Speeches

I personally never walked out on stage and thanked the audience for coming or welcomed them. I think, in part, it is because I assume they are there for their own purpose, like people who anticipate and then go to church. It seems equally curious to me to hear a priest thank the congregation for coming to Mass. A more serious problem is again a Right-Left brain problem. Beginning a concert with talking changes the atmosphere and context of concentration from the perspective of the audience. After the speech they must immediately 'change gears' in terms of the receptivity of their minds. I believe it is difficult to do. And again, no one ever heard Solti thank the audience for coming.

But I can accept that others may feel obliged to welcome the audience before the concert begins. But if one does this, then one must take this into account in program planning. One should not begin by appearing so happy, and being so happy that the audience came, and the students are so happy to see them, happy and happy and then immediately plunge the listeners into the almost unbearable weight of a 1,000 years of pain and suffering by the Russian people by beginning the concert with *Marche Slav* by Tchaikowsky. This reminds me of the first performance in Meinningen of the Beethoven *Ninth Symphony* by Hans von Bulow. At the enthusiastic applause at the end, Bulow turned to the audience and said, 'I am so happy to see that you like this masterpiece that I am going to play it again. And don't bother to try to leave because I have ordered the doors locked!' To imagine having to sit another ninety minutes is one thing, but it is almost unimaginable to think of going from that incredibly joyous ending back one more time to the dark and foreboding first movement!

On rare occasions the reverse problem comes into play. An ensemble has programmed a lively and happy composition to begin the program but during the course of the day some widely known figure has died. Because a concert is *ipso facto* a celebration of the spirit, a 'celebration' may seem inappropriate on such a moment, to both musicians and audience. This is

---

4   In the case of a school concert, of course, the parents can be expected to lie to make their children feel good.

why often in such cases a special number is added and played first, something such as Bach's *Come Sweet Death*, in honor of the person who died. This allows the audience to have some sense of personal emotional connection with the event of the day and in the process a kind of catharsis which in turn helps clear their concentration for the concert.

I know a conductor who has a habit of always inviting a composer who is in attendance to come up before his work is performed and say a few words to the audience. This no doubt is well intentioned, but I do not recommend it. The music of a composer is an extremely personal thing which comes from the deepest reaches of his experiential self. There are no words to describe his music, any more than there are words to describe love. And so inevitably the composer appears rather at a loss for words, ill at ease if not embarrassed, and will never say anything deeply personal about his music. He is much more likely to try to say something funny, which may have an adverse affect on the psychological receptivity of the listener.

It is much better to bring the composer up on stage after the performance of his composition, for this will increase and prolong the applause—convincing him, human nature being what it is, that the audience really liked his composition. He will be more comfortable, will be proud rather than embarrassed and will feel even more indebted to you and the ensemble.

Oral Program Notes

In general it is the purpose of the printed program to introduce guest conductors, guest composers and guest soloists. When the lights dim, signaling the beginning of the concert, it is time for listening to music, not talk. Or, to say that differently, do not confuse the left hemisphere's moment (talking and the printed program) with the right hemisphere's moment (hearing and experiencing music).

There may be rare occasions when the conductor may want to share with the audience something relevant to the next composition to be heard which is information which should perhaps not be set in print—where it will survive forever. As an illustration, I recall first hearing the *Angel's Camp* by Charles Cushing and being deeply moved. After the concert I immediately sought him out to ask if I could obtain the parts for a performance of my own. I found a composer greatly offended by the performance we had just heard and he declared that as long as he lived he would never again let anyone perform his music! And, in fact, I had to wait ten years until after his death in order to obtain the materials from the family in order to perform the work and to begin to spread the word of this sublime masterpiece. I decided to tell this to my audience in order that they could share in how important this performance was to me, but it is not a story suitable for publication in the program notes.

The Conductor feels a need to Educate the Audience

One often hears or reads concern that all performers have an urgent need to 'educate' the audience. Certainly, with current estimates suggesting that perhaps only two percent of the American public listens to Classical music, this concern is self-evident. But, in this regard we cannot escape our bicameral nature. It must be music and its performance, which speaks for the importance of music—not rational words. And, it follows, once again the issue of programming is of such vital significance. Only important aesthetic music can speak for the importance of aesthetic music. The listener judges on the basis of his own individual experiential history as a listener. The talker, the conductor, will always be outside and apart from the individual listener's experiential history as a listener. His rational arguments will therefore have no affect on 'educating' the listener. He would be much better advised to select the finest music he can find, music which communicates with power to the listener, and let music speak for itself.

One fact needs to be engraved in bronze: Music which comes from the heart will always be diminished by talk.

⁂

ANOTHER EXAMPLE of some conductors' confusion of the senses has to do with the seating plan of the ensemble. Wanting to create some visual interest, I suppose, he places the percussion instruments in a broad arc behind the ensemble. He has temporarily forgotten that music is of for the ear, not the eye. The problem here is that while the audience will be fascinated by the percussion no matter where they are placed, the conductor has taken up the most valuable space on the stage, for wind bands need depth and not width to create a homogeneous sound.

The eye, by the way is a real problem in this musical world created for the ear. Because the eye is so dominant among our senses it tends, from evolution, to take over. So the conductor who has to read a score while he conducts must use his eyes, but the senses do not work together and so the conductor's ear is nearly shut down. I have attended many concerts where, for example, the inner-voices are muddled and not clear, or where the balance from bottom to top is incorrect. In such cases I find myself asking, 'why doesn't he hear that?'

For the most part, the clarity of the inner-voices and the quality of the bass tones are the product of the seating plan. I have found very few conductors who have really given much thought to their seating plan. Usually they tell me it is someone's plan they saw diagramed in a magazine.

Many years ago I was rehearsing the Ernst Toch, *Spiel* for forty-four winds with some very fine players. There was no problem playing the composition, but for some reason it did not sound good. One day, on the spur of the moment, I changed the seating plan and suddenly—to my very great surprise—the performance sounded great, with no further rehearsal. This was the moment I fully realized that there are acoustic principles at work which greatly affect performance. I then spent some years in experimentation and in addition was on a scientific committee hosted by a major instrument maker, during which we studied the individual characteristics of wind instruments' tone as the tone travels from stage to audience, etc.

What follows are some principles I arrived at, and which I believe in completely. I offer them for contemplation and suggest one might want to experiment with these principles. One can pass out a drawing of a new seating plan to the band and they can easily find their new positions. Play something familiar in your normal seating position. Then have the players quickly move to the new position and play the same thing again so you can listen [from the front] to the difference. You may not like the change, of course. But what you will hear with my plan is a more organ-like sound, a clear focused bottom of the sound and clearer, cleaner internal voices. During the 1980s I wrote an essay giving my recommendations for seating.

Whitwell on Seating Plan Acoustics

First Basic Principle

Wind instruments in ensemble sound better if there is more space between players than you would find in an orchestra. This is because string instruments, all being wood boxes, cross-resonate. Strings sound good even if they sit closely together. Winds do not. Wind instruments require a certain 'envelope of space' for the individual tone to develop on stage before it travels out to the audience. If they are sitting close together, the clothes of the nearby players absorb critical overtones before they have a chance to travel off stage to the audience.

Try using your present seating plan but have the players move more closely together. Perform some hymn-like music. Have them quickly move, keeping the same plan but moving apart until there is nearly one chair distance between players. Play the same passage again. You will be astonished.

Second Basic Principle

I am sure every conductor has heard of the pyramid principle. This has been discussed by conductors for centuries, as for example by Michael Praetorius in book III of his *Syntagma Musicum* of 1619. The problem is that the ear tends to hear upper partials more than lower partials. Today we know the reason. The human brain actually 'turns up the volume' for sounds in the octave above third space C, treble clef. The brain has learned to do this over thousands of years in order to help with hearing the consonants of language (probably beginning with hearing the tiger outside the cave). As a result, the listener in a concert actually hears something the ensemble did not perform. In order to counteract this, the conductor must artificially balance the ensemble = more bottom, less top. The conductor's goal is to create an illusion under which the listener thinks he heard what the composer wrote. This is critical with a wind band, for if the conductor does not do this, two things happen: [1] the band sound is top heavy and strident, not organ like (organ-like meaning like the overtone series) and [2] the audience does not enjoy being bombarded by high partials for two hours. It is unpleasant.

I employ this principle in other ways. When you have a melody which is doubled in octaves, no matter how many players on either line, my rule is to make the bottom octave ⅔ of the sound and the top octave ⅓ of the sound. If you do this, the listener hears them as 50–50%. If they actually play 50–50%, the listener thinks he hears ⅔ top and ⅓ bottom.

I also use this principle for the endings of long tones, as in a composition that ends in a whole-note. Instead of giving a gesture that makes everyone stop immediately together, I give a long gesture with the arm and tell the players to stop according to the instruments place in the overall tessitura. That is, the flutes and first clarinet stop as soon as the arm begins to move, horns and sax half way along, and the last person to stop is the tuba (with a little dimenuendo 'tail' to the sound). What the listener hears is a beautiful, resonant cut-off and the listener hears the full chord. If everyone stops together, what the listener hears is a chord with no bottom (the ear tries to hang on to the upper partials). You will hear this especially in the short note at the end of a march. Michael Praetorius goes so far as to recommend that it sounds great if the bass continues for four beats after everyone else stops! But, of course, he was thinking of the sound in a great cathedral. There, it *would* be a great effect.

Another problem: Because the brain hangs on to the upper partials the listener will also hear a little acoustic 'tag' that appears to go up (say 'mamma' with the last syllable being a higher pitch). This is something created by the brain and is not actually there. That is, you will hear it but you will not see it on an oscilloscope. But it is an important principle. My rule with a wind band on any kind of last note the band plays together: Let us never end together. Ironic!

Third Basic Principle

Wind bands sound better if the seating plan is deeper, and not wider. Many bands use only four rows. I use six rows, even with an ensemble of fifty players. This only means the percussion must go on one or both sides and not in back. They look good in back, but placing them there prevents the band from having a seating plan that sounds good. Also very important is that by having a seating plan that has depth, rather than width, it makes possible more space between the individual players.

Fourth Basic Principle

If the tubas (and euphonium) are centered in the last row, with the trombones centered in front of them, then a combination-tone effect takes place which makes the bass notes of chords centered, more beautiful and more clear and focused. This never happens if the tubas are on the same row as trombones. Then one only hears the individual instruments, never a unity of the sound.

The same principal applies to the tenor and baritone range instruments: bassoons, tenor and baritone sax, bass clarinets. They can go anywhere, but they must be in a block together if they serve to clarify the tenor-baritone sound of the chordal structure.

Fifth Basic Principle

Rows of flutes and clarinets must not face each other. Angle the rows so that the rows point slightly toward the audience, as if aiming just behind the conductor, and not at each other. If they face each other, their upper partials clash above the band, before traveling to the audience, giving a brittle sound to the entire band.

My personal seating plan recognizes the above principles and at the same time is a personification of the overtone series). The central core is in straight rows. These are, counting from the back row, moving toward the conductor:

tubas and euphoniums
trombones
horns
saxes
bassoons, low clarinets, etc
oboes
conductor

I put clarinets on my left, flutes on my right. Each in straight rows branching away from the central core, above. These rows are angled not towards each other, but as if they were pointing at a point behind the conductor, as mentioned above.

I put trumpets on my right, behind the flutes. This is so they can blow across the ensemble. The trumpets are the most directional of all wind instruments and the only instrument of the band whose tone quality (overtone structure) does not change from stage to the last row of the hall. By filtering their sounds through the players' bodies (rather than pointing at the audience) it allows them to fill the instruments and play with a full sound.

Because of this plan, based on depth instead of width, there is plenty of room for the percussion on the left and right sides (behind clarinets and trumpets). In fact, this brings them closer to the ensemble (for hearing purposes) and closer to the audience (for eye purposes).

☙❧

ONE FINAL PROBLEM in applied aesthetics is known to all listeners: sometimes listening to soft and gentle classical music makes one sleepy. And it happens to conductors, as you will often see a conductor look at his watch while conducting. At that moment he is not listening to the music at all, he is on another side of the brain. He has been listening to the music with his right hemisphere and he does not know the time so he has to shift gears, so to speak, to enter the left hemisphere where the numbers on the face of the clock will make sense.

But I also have a personal theory that dreams occur mostly in the right hemisphere, which is one reason we rarely remember them—there is too little language in the right hemisphere to relate the dream to someone else. If I am correct, then the right hemisphere dream center cannot be too far from the location where we hear and experience music. It might follow that what we call day-dreaming while music is playing may be a kind of disorientation in the brain itself. In any case it may be near an explanation for the otherwise unbelievable circumstances of a musician actually falling asleep while performing. In 2008 I wrote an essay which mentions such cases.

On the Difficulty of Staying Awake

We have all seen audience members sleeping during musical performances. Classical music, in particular, can be very soothing after a hard day's work, a large dinner and a little wine. One can sympathize (as long as it is not one of our concerts!). But have you seen performers fall asleep *while* performing?

On two occasions I have been in the audience when a conductor actually fell asleep while conducting! In both cases the conductor's head suddenly dropped, he began toppling off the podium and awoke before he completely fell down. On both occasions the ensemble continued to play[5] while the conductor made his way back up on the podium and resumed swinging his arms. One of these performances was during a Western Division Conference of the MENC in Salt Lake City and the other in a similar Western Division MENC concert in San Diego. The latter instance I found particularly odd because the composition was the Hindemith *Symphony for Band* and the conductor fell asleep in the fifth bar of the beginning movement, a moment very full, strong and forte.

Once when I was a student at Michigan a contrabassoonist fell asleep in a concert while he was playing. He had one of those old style contrabassoons with the long straight bell, looking like the smoke stack of a Mississippi steam ship. Suddenly, like a great tree falling, his instrument came falling forward, wiping out several students, music stands and almost hitting Dr. Revelli. Dr. Revelli, kind and understanding gentleman though he was, did not appreciate a musician falling asleep while he was conducting. On another occasion when I was a student at Michigan a fellow student fell asleep while playing piano during our beginning piano class. This class was scheduled just after lunch, in a hot old building with no ventilation, and the poor fellow simply fell asleep and crashed into the ancient upright piano. The teacher of the class, a doctoral student in piano, was duly shocked, on behalf of the history of the instrument, that anyone could fall asleep while playing a piano.

When I was in the Air Force Band in Washington there was a clarinet player who used to sleep through entire concerts and no one noticed. This occurred during the afternoon concerts of tours. This elderly gentleman would keep himself upright by putting the bell of his clarinet on the edge of his chair, with the mouthpiece in his mouth supporting his head. He then had a means of attaching the sleeve buttons of his uniform to the keys of the clarinet, which supported his arms and gave somewhat the appearance of playing the instrument. There he slept in the middle of the clarinet section during these hour-long concerts, the repertoire of which never varied day after day. In the fashion of 'Pavlov's dog' he would always wake up during

---

5   In both cases I had noticed the players did not look at the conductor anyway, so it probably had no effect on most of the band members.

the final work, Sousa's *Stars and Stripes Forever*. The band was never asked to stand and bow until this time so he was never caught by surprise during his nap. Our conductor, who was always oblivious to everything anyway, never noticed.[6]

There was one occasion during one of these long tours when the band was angry at the officers for some reason, in particular with Col. Howard who always conducted the final *Stars and Stripes*, and by pre-arrangement we played only the first four bars of this familiar march followed immediately by the last four bars. The conductor was apparently day-dreaming for he gave no indication that anything had happened; he heard the beginning and the end and probably assumed we had performed the entire march. I always wondered what the audience thought as they applauded automatically at the end.

This story will not be surprising to anyone who has experienced a long tour of, let us say, nine weeks. During such a tour the daily routine never varies: take a long bus ride in the morning, lunch and nap, afternoon concert, dinner and evening concert. The repertoire always is the same, so after two weeks or so all sense of time is lost. It is hard to explain how hypnotic this becomes and how, when one first boards a bus in September and returns home in November, one has no recollection whatsoever of the month of October. Neither does one have any idea what town one is in on a particular day. Frequently an audience member will ask, 'How do you like our town?' And one is embarrassed and can make no answer without revealing that he had no idea what town he was in.

I am sure most members of the band had the same experience I did, an almost zombie state caused by the constant repetition of the daily schedule. Often one would sit down to begin the evening concert and then be aware of leaving to catch the bus back to the hotel, with no real memory of the concert itself. Sometimes in the late afternoon one would find oneself asking a roommate whether we had played the afternoon concert or not. I fought this mind paralyzing routine by giving myself various intellectual challenges for the evening concert. One tour I decided to count the number of notes that I played during the two hours. The rules of my little game were strict. I could only count a note at the very moment I was playing it. If I lost count, as for example during a passage of sixteenth-notes, I had to wait until the concert the following day to resume, and always starting again at the very beginning of the concert. I had to mentally pronounce the number while playing (not an easy accomplishment) and, of course, had to remember the count. No pencil and paper. As best I can recall this occupied me on one tour for five or six weeks and I was quite disappointed, when the time came that I could count through an entire concert, to find it was not that many notes. I was playing only several hundred notes, while I had thought previously that it must be thousands.

On another long tour I occupied my mind by the challenge of memorizing my music. Again I could only do this as I played during the concert, no study of the music before or after allowed! And I begin by memorizing the final work, for then I could close the folder and tie

---

[6] During the year I was studying with Ormandy there was an old gentleman who was in the final year of membership necessary for qualification for a pension. The old man's hands shook, creating a problem for these proud string players. At the same time they wanted to see this long-term member make it to retirement. So they soaped his bow in order that he could bow away with the rest of the section yet never make a sound. Ormandy never knew of this.

it up and be ready to leave for town sooner. Then, I memorized the next to last composition, and so could tie up the folder even sooner. And thus I proceeded, composition by composition in reverse order, until it began to cause questions why my folder was not open.

Of course, if you have your part memorized it allows one to look around the auditorium and day-dream. This is possible as a typical illustration of the 'many-minds' phenomenon familiar to the reader, an ability of the mind to do something on a kind of automatic basis while at the same time another part of the mind, the real you, or id, is engaged in something completely different. When, for example, you are driving your car and engaged in conversation with a passenger the real you is engaged in conversation, but who is driving the car? Conductors experience this frequently in rehearsal as one part of our mind continues the right arm beat pattern while the real us part of the mind is thinking, 'should I stop and go back and rehearse that last passage?'

A very familiar experience for many is that of driving on a highway late at night and suddenly having the feeling of waking up and finding oneself further down the road than your conscious mind remembers. This experience is very frightening, as one contemplates what could have happened in that past half-mile or so, and it has the effect of really waking you up. I had such an experience during basic training, which in my time was thirteen weeks (today it is much condensed). The officers never had enough classes or training to fill thirteen weeks and so there remained long periods when, for lack of being able to think of anything else, they would have us out in the hot Texas summer sun, endlessly marching up and down the streets. On one of these afternoons, just like the driving experience, I suddenly had the feeling of waking and finding myself a block further down the street. Somehow the 'me' part of my mind slept while another part of the mind kept the body movement of marching going. Again, upon 'waking' I was frightened, only in this case it was fear for what the sergeant would do to me if he caught me sleeping while marching! The sergeant was always saying, while pointing at his heavy boots, things like, 'If you make this mistake again there will be no future generations in your family!'

A much more complex experience of this kind happened to me in 1966 when I was giving solo recitals throughout South America supported by the State Department. One of these recitals was in La Paz, Bolivia, and was given in the home of the American Ambassador. This was in a large old home in which several rooms in line had sliding doors which could be opened to form a large hall-like space. In this case we had been warned in advance by the wife of the ambassador that the piano was out of tune and that the only piano tuner in town was on an 'anti-American' strike. Of course I said, 'don't worry, we will use it as is.'

When I arrived at the designated time for the evening I found that a dinner came first, with the concert following. The dinner guests, and audience members, were the international diplomatic corps. Since I was, of course, the guest of honor, there followed dozens of toasts by various ambassadors. I was a good horn player, but not a natural one, and it had long been my experience that I could never successfully drink and play. But I had to respond to the endless toasts, at first taking just a tiny sip of wine, and then just pretending to sip. But even the smell had some effect after a time and by the time it was time to perform I was, shall we say, rather loose. The piano turned out to be more than a semi-tone flat, a greater distance than I could compensate for on the instrument's tuning slide. What to do? One, after this elaborate banquet, could not just turn around and say, 'Sorry!'

The repertoire of this recital was difficult for the accompanist, the Hindemith *Sonata*, Strauss and Mozart concerti arranged for piano, etc, too difficult to transpose on the spot. The only alternative left was for me to transpose the entire recital. If I had been told a day in advance I doubt that I could have done it, but coming in so an immediate circumstance, aided by the wine, I just did it. I retain the clearest memory of my state of mind during this recital, a feeling that I was a listener and that someone else was playing the recital. For me it was an extraordinary illustration of the 'many-minds' phenomenon. One part of my mind was transposing and performing the recital while another part of my mind, the real me, or id, was quite consciously only a listener. That is, I was quite clearly aware of listening to the concert as a listener would.

PART II
Making Band Masterpieces Musical

Gustav Holst, Suite in E-flat

MORE THAN THIRTY YEARS AGO, when only the original edition of this masterpiece was known, serious questions I had regarding this score forced me to visit the British Library to examine the autograph score. Immediately upon entering the music division it was clear that the institution was decades behind in cataloging manuscripts. Until such time as they could catch up they had prepared large scrapbooks in which they added a sequential number as works were donated to the Library. As there was no index whatsoever to these scrapbooks, I felt it obligatory to go through these books. In the process I found two band compositions by Holst which none of us knew. One was a complete original march, *Marching Song*, which the composer's daughter refused to believe existed until I gave her the 'Add.' number so she could go see for herself. The other manuscript, consisting of seven movements, one of which was an aleatoric movement (!!), composed for an early coronation ceremony, in which only two of the movements had been used. Restrictions established by the family prevented the staff from making copies for me so I copied both scores out by hand in order to perform these works in Los Angeles.

In examining the autograph score for the famous *First Suite*, the first thing which startles the reader is the unquestionable fact that the composer intended these three movements to be played without a pause. Not only is there a paragraph on the first page which requests this, but Holst also wrote 'segue' at the end of the first movement. But from the perspective of live performers, it is quite another matter as all conductors know. The magnificent, powerful climax of the first movement leaves the performers and conductor so exhausted, physically and emotionally, that to continue without a break into the soft second movement is nearly impossible.

What does one do? Holst, anticipating that the performance would continue without a pause not only scored the final chord of the first movement with very little third of the chord, to prevent a feeling of finality, but also wrote the resolving 'stinger' or 'bump-note,' as one would expect as the final note of most marches, in the first measure of the second movement in the form of a staccato eighth-note in the brass instruments. True it makes a deceptive resolution, but rhythmically and dynamically it functions like the concluding 'down-beat' of that previous great chord nevertheless. But that is true only if there is no pause between the movements.

Fred Fennell told me that he sometimes made a break between the first and second movement, but moved this brass chord back as if it were part of the first movement, making it follow the great final E♭ chord. Then when he began the second movement he left this staccato eighth-note out completely. His rationale, I think, was correct. The staccato eighth-note, regardless of where it is written, does belong to the previous movement. He also felt that, in any case, one had to rescore the great final chord of the first movement by adding more people playing the third of the chord, because it is simply too harsh as it stands—especially noticeable if one pauses between the movements.

After experimenting several times in performance, trying to judge how I felt, how the players felt and how the audience must have felt, I have elected to rescore the final chord of the first movement, with more third, making it the end of the first movement—then a pause to recover—then in beginning the second movement I simply do not play that staccato eighth-note, as in my judgment it is not part of the second movement. In other words, I differ with Fennell in that I simply never play this out-of-context staccato 'bump-note.'

First Movement

I have talked with conductors who are almost afraid to begin this movement out of their concern for accurately hitting the tempo they have in mind and, at the same time, getting a full-length first quarter-note. Fred Fennell told me he always beat out the 'missing' first two beats, not because he felt it was necessary for the players, but because he, himself, felt these two rests were part of the music. I have never had these concerns and have always begun this work as I would any other composition, by creating a preparatory gesture equal to one full quarter-note, no more and no less. Nevertheless, for those worried about hitting the 'right' tempo, Fred did have a nice trick. He thought of a great wheel turning at one rotation per bar. The conductor, in his mind only as he stands on the podium, gets that imaginary wheel going in his mind, going at the speed he has in mind for the movement. Then, at some point, he imagines that he grabs hold of the wheel at the ictus of beat two. The momentum of the wheel carries his hand and arm up at precisely the correct speed to produce the intended length and speed of the first notated quarter-note. It does work, particularly so when the meter is in three but the conductor is conducting in one, as for example a Viennese Waltz.

A much greater concern at the beginning, it seems to me, is the intonation between the euphonium and tuba parts, which are in octaves. What comes to our rescue here is the 'pyramid principle,' something Holst was clearly aware of, although not by that name, from his experience in working with choirs. While most American conductors now are familiar with the pyramid principle with respect to balance of sections of instruments, few understand that this principle is vital in linear practice. At Rehearsal Letter E in this movement one finds the melody in the cornet, doubled at the octave by the bass cornet, the euphonium. There is no question, in my mind, that what the composer heard in his head was a true combination sound, as if the listener was hearing each line as being 50% of the total volume. However if one performs it 50%–50%, the listener actually will hear 75%–25%, due to the pyramid principle. To make the listener think he hears 50%–50%, one must perform this with the euphonium being 75% of the sound and the cornet 25%. When one does this not only does a beautiful, balanced unified sound result but a crucial by-product occurs—instant good intonation. This is because it is very easy for the cornet to hear the correct pitches as overtones of the euphonium, whom he can now hear. All players, even the very young due to genetic characteristics, can easily do this, but tuning to a pitch above, or even one at the same pitch, is very difficult even for the finest professionals, again for genetic reasons.

The trick at the beginning of this Holst movement, then, is to make sure the euphonium is 25% of the sound and the tuba 75%. If you can achieve this, you will find that, magically, intonation problems are gone!

The pyramid principle governs nearly all the music which follows, as for example in the first variation (bar [9]) where it determines whether the listener hears the melody, which is in the bass, or only the noisy counterpoint played by the narcissistic cornets.[1]

At Letter B, the 'Brilliante,' the linear application of the pyramid principle is again vital in making the woodwinds appear to run at a constant dynamic. Otherwise the tendency will be for the listener to hear a squealing sound as the instruments go over the top of the tessitura and then hear them disappear completely in the lower register. For me there is another important problem here as I believe the melody in the isolated eighth-notes is not heard as a melody by the listener unless these eighth-notes have some length to them. I express this to the players with the word, 'woof.' If played as written ('ta'), the listener will hear these notes as only another percussion strike, but he will not hear the pitch. There is a passage just like this in *Til Eulenspiegel* by Strauss and when you hear this performed you will almost never hear that melody in the bass.

The most common error in the interpretation of this movement is the failure of most conductors to understand that there is a tempo change eight bars before Rehearsal Letter D. Perhaps I should first explain that there is a very long tradition that composers did not bother to mark what they considered to be obvious things on paper. In a word, they put some trust in the performer that he would understand what was needed by what they see on paper. This happens all the time in earlier music where a composer at the beginning writes 'Allegro' and assumes the music itself will tell the musicians what the appropriate speed is, whereas the word itself is quite ambiguous. A clear example can be found in the second movement of the great C Major Symphony of Schubert, where there is a ritard. that is not indicated at all on paper, other than an *a tempo* after it is finished. In the more complicated music of the later twentieth-century composers seemed to think that unless they wrote everything on paper the musicians would not understand, hence sometimes there is more information between the staves than on the staves. The conductor must remember that he has every right to change the tempo if the music 'tells' him to. This is a right legislated by a 300-year-old tradition. Further, we must remember that those Italian words at the beginning of the score, in the present case Allegro moderato, are, like metronomic markings, references only to how the music *begins*. Indeed, Bruno Walter said exactly this, 'The metronome marking is good only for the first few bars.'[2] Changing tempi in the middle of a movement, which used to be called 'elastic,'

---

[1] Same problem at Letter C.

[2] *On Music and Music-Making* (New York: Norton, 1957), 43.

was, as Brahms once pointed out,[3] not a new idea at all. Thus when Monteverdi warned a singer that the beat must be of the heart, and not of the hand, he meant to let the music itself tell you the tempo. And that is precisely the issue here.

In the present case, Holst takes the pitch E♭, in the ninth bar before D, and pivoting on this pitch turns the melody upside down and the tonality becomes C minor. The ear should tell the conductor that this music is slower, mysterious, spooky and with, at Letter D, the ponderous foot-steps of the frightening specter! These footsteps tell you the correct tempo—do not speed! The very purpose of the oboe part ten bars before D is to provide material in which the ritard. can be clearly heard by all players who are holding long pitches. I also make a slight fermata on the first two beats of the ninth bar before D to give a sense of cadence and rest before the mysterious music begins.

To return to this mysterious section of music by Holst, the most difficult aspect is that it must remain very soft throughout, all the way until the ninth bar after E. When the volume resumes, nine bars before Letter F, where Holst writes *crescendo poco a poco*, I find it helps if one staggers this crescendo a bit, having the running eighth-notes do most of the crescendo for four bars before the melody begins to change, and certainly no crescendo in the percussion until the last two bars before F.

The ending of this movement is very special. First, Holst calls it *Maestoso*, which is a *style,* not a tempo. What comes next is the critical thing, *rit. al Fine*, meaning a gradual slowing down to the very end of the movement—like a great train slowing down. The only change I find necessary here is that in the cadence in the horns, the seventh and eighth bars after F, the diatonic horn line needs to continue going up in all voices, with no dropping of the octave.

Second Movement

With the second movement of this composition we have one of the rarest of all things in music—a fast movement which is soft. Indeed, the entire movement is soft, with the exception of the four bars before Rehearsal Letter B, and it is very difficult to achieve this.

Except where slurs are given, everything should be rather on the staccato side, or at least an attempt must be made to achieve lightness. The key to the melody at the beginning of this movement is first in playing the second note of the syncopation figure earlier than it looks on paper. This figure is always printed incorrectly in order to make the music easier to read, but the quarter-note is never played in the middle of the bar the way it looks. Second, the sixteenth-note in the dotted rhythm must be played quite late. These two things together provide the necessary sparkle. If the music is performed as it appears on paper, the result will be very pedestrian, like a common folk tune. With regard to sparkle, the movement always reminds me of the Scherzo in Mendelssohn's *Midsummer Night's Dream* music, which is difficult to perform for the same reasons.

---

[3] Ibid., 129.

In the middle lyric section I think the melodic shaping takes care of itself, but I go to much effort in shaping the accompaniment figures. Where do they move the music forward? Where do they hold the music back?

Third Movement

Two things about the first two bars: First, remind the woodwinds to trill very fast—a slow trill sounds like a phone ringing and you will have your audience looking for their cellphones. Second, the three notes in the brass must be played: something, something louder and something louder still or the audience will hear a diminuendo. It is a linear form of the pyramid problem.

At Letter A [missing in the old edition] Fred Fennell had the wonderful idea of using the largest, darkest suspended cymbal he could find and letting it ring for four bars, with the entrance of the 'milk and honey' theme coming in below whatever the dynamic then is in the ringing cymbal. It is a glorious musical effect.

The main thing usually missing in performances of this section is the fact that there are three melodies going on, not just the one 'milk and honey' one. Another is the melodic line in the euphoniums which soars above while the 'milk and honey' theme relaxes in its cadences. The third melodic line is in the tuba, where Holst probably miscalculated by thinking of the resonant tutti string basses of the orchestra. So here I turn every quarter-note of the tubas into a half-note and encourage the players to add long slurs as they see fit and to add cresc. and dim. as they see fit. Trust me, they will do something beautiful. [Secret: I do this with the bass lines of all marches, where otherwise the tubas sound like nothing so much as more bass drums—all thump and no pitch.]

At Rehearsal Letter D, where we get two separate themes, the key for the audience in being able to identify them is in contrasting styles: broad for the 'milk and honey' in the brass and staccato for the woodwinds. It might be pointed out in this passage that Holst reverts to an older English system of percussion notation in the bass drum part. If he writes a half-note it means something louder than if he writes a quarter-note for the bass drum. It is a minute but important key to what he was feeling.

For me, I believe Holst felt it would be understood that a ritard. should begin in the bars before the *meno mosso* near the end, rather than attempting a sudden slower tempo.

The final suggestion I should like to offer is with respect to the final note of the third movement. The same phenomenon in the brain that necessitates the adoption of the pyramid principle in balancing high and low sounds also comes into play here, namely the fact that the brain tends to 'hang on' to the higher pitches. The result, from the listener's perspective, is that the piece ends with a squeak and we do not hear the actual chord. To prevent this one tells the upper woodwinds to play the shortest possible note and the lower brass to play a full quarter-note and everyone else something relative to where they are in the total sound. What the listener then hears is the strong accented chord which the eye sees on paper and you hear the full chord, not just a squeak on top. Do this for the final 'bump-notes' or 'stingers' of all marches, otherwise the strong masculine march ends with the high pitched squeak of a lady when her toes are stepped on by the drum-major.

Gustav Holst, Suite in F

First Movement

Because of the phenomenon by which the brain creates the illusion of a crescendo on things going up diatonically, the bass figure in bar ☐1 and woodwinds in ☐2 will sound to the audience like a crescendo and will have the effect of appearing to the listener (who does not have a score) as if the eighth-notes are pick ups and the quarter-note the down beat. Mozart sometimes did the reverse as a trick on the listener. In the beginning of his *Quintet* for horn and strings what the listener hears sounds like first beat, second beat, first beat, second beat, etc. But the music is actually notated second beat, first beat, second beat, first beat, etc., before it eventually straightens out. Consequently I go to great care in the first bar to get a strong accent on the first note. That usually takes care of the problem. If it doesn't, I have the players also make a diminuendo in the eighth-notes. It goes without saying that the quarter-note is played like a fifth eighth-note.

In bar ☐6 we find a version of a notational problem found frequently in the band music of both Holst and Vaughn Williams. On the second beat of this bar a wind player, in attempting to perform what his eye sees, will choke off the sound in the throat producing a sound which I can only describe as a 'yuk,' a very bad sound which, in so far as the listener is concerned, has no pitch. So in spite of the notation the conductor must demand enough length to actually hear the pitch. Our art is about the ear, not the eye.

The first lyrical section, at Rehearsal Letter E, is called 'Swansea Town.' For lack of a better term we can call this a folk-song, but it is certainly not the gentle folk-song of the shepherds of Cumbria. Swansea is the second largest town in Wales, a tough town, unprotected from the fierce storms of the North Atlantic. When I conducted the Swansea town band once, I was told of their difficulty in recruiting young men because the local brass bands threatened the boys with violence if they joined a 'military band,' meaning one with woodwinds. Talk about recruitment problems!

So maybe we should think of this folk-song with a title more like 'Marching Song of the Copper Miners of Swansea.' Certainly we can hear their heavy boots underneath the lyrical melody. However, I do not suggest for a minute making these boots heavier than they are as that would become unmusical. On the other hand I have always felt something was missing here. In my performances, therefore, I have always asked a single snare drum player to improvise a simple, subtle rudimental cadence at the *piano* level. It seems to me that this adds just enough masculinity to the music without trying to achieve this by making the accompaniment heavier. I must add, however, that while this was no problem thirty years ago, today I sometimes get a curious look of confusion on the face of the snare drummer when they hear the word, 'rudimental.' Is it possible that the paradiddle is now an endangered species?

Holst offers a contrast with this masculinity by creating in the following section, 'Claudy Banks,' music which is all grace, a folk-song which sings of a summer evening, a flowery garden, and a fair maid. To be faithful to this sense of grace I slur the eighth-note pick-up to each quarter-note after the bar-line. This is an aesthetic practice I learned from Ormandy, who never changed bows across a bar line if the note on the down-beat was a higher pitch.

Above I spoke of the 'pitch-yuk' problem in the notation of Holst and Vaughn Williams and one will see that this problem presents itself in every bar underneath the Claudy Banks folk-song until Rehearsal Letter J. The goal is to have enough length on each second note to hear the pitch and not a choked 'yuk.'

Second Movement

In the vamp consisting of the first two bars I employ a practice I always use in similar introductions. I make the first bar *mf* and only the second bar *pp*. This achieves the same soft mood before the movement begins but at the same time gives the players the confidence to begin with a clean initial attack with good tone.

The 'Song without Words,' used by Holst also in a choral arrangement, is based on a Cornish folk-song which does have words. If we are to assume that the words of this song may reflect what Holst was feeling as he wrote the music, then the beginning seems to appropriately reflect the emotional mood of the words in the beginning of this song.

> Abroad as I was walking, one evening in the spring,
> I heard a maid in Bedlam so sweetly for to sing;

But at Rehearsal Letter A there is obviously a considerable change in emotions. The music is suddenly restless and flowing and conveys a strong emotion of some kind. In the folk-song we discover the emotions are anger and pain.

> O cruel were his parents who sent my love to sea,
> And cruel was the ship that bore my love from me;

I do not believe it is possible to convey these strong emotions to the listener without moving the music at a somewhat faster tempo.

The ending of this movement is quite lovely if skillfully controlled. I believe nearly every good musician would feel that the final five bars should be played as an allargando. I perform it in such a way that it becomes quite slow by the final two bars. Most important, I recommend making the final tuba note, and accompanying brass above it, last at least until the point of the third beat of the final bar. In other words, the goal is a very long final eighth-note, softly drifting away in time and space.

There is a long tradition for this aesthetic practice. For example, in the third volume of his *Syntagma Musicum*, of 1619, where Praetorius discusses performance practice, this working conductor says he will sometimes have the bass voice extend as much as 4 beats [!] after the other voices have stopped.

> As a piece is brought to a close, all the remaining voices should stop simultaneously at the sign of the conductor or choir master. The tenors should not prolong their tone, a fifth above the bass or lowest voice … after the bass has stopped. But if the bass continues to sound a little longer, for another two or four *tactus*, it lends charm and beauty to the music [*Cantilenae*], which no one can deny.[1]

Certainly, in our Holst movement, any sort of 'cut-off' gesture by the conductor, any artificial abruptness caused by the conductor, will ruin this beautiful cadence. Here is advice to die for: Abruptness is bad in cadences and in kissing!

Third Movement

The interpretation of this music seems very obvious, I think. I would like to point out here that the figure consisting of two sixteenth-notes connected to an eighth-note is one which players nearly always spread out until it is almost indistinguishable from a triplet, in so far as the listener is concerned. Consequently I always have players add an accent to the first sixteenth-note and this seems to propel the next two notes sooner. This figure is, in fact, a relic of the Baroque mordant which was always accented and in which the second note was a lower neighbor.[2]

This movement ends with the blacksmith giving three final swings of his hammer and then he does what every blacksmith does when finishing work for the day, he thrusts the red-hot piece of iron he is shaping over the fire into a bucket of water to cool it down and prevent accidental fire. And that is what Holst is representing with the roll on the suspended cymbal on the final beat. This is all for nothing if the audience misses the point, so the conductor must take care that the cymbal is sufficiently loud not to be covered by the ensemble. In addition, when I conduct, I make a spear-like thrust with whichever arm is on the side of the ensemble that the cymbal player is on, to imitate the arm of the blacksmith in this action.

---

[1] This treatise is written in German, but in two places, of which this discussion of the pyramid principle is one, Praetorius switches into Latin, a language which would be been read only by conductors who were 'educated,' that is, who had attended the university. It is as if he considers this a secret for use only by intelligent conductors.

[2] In the Classical Period and nineteenth century it is an upper neighbor.

Fourth Movement

I have quite a different view of this music and I beg the reader for an open mind as I try to describe what I feel. This movement is based on a very old English melody. In *The Dancing Master*, the first edition of which was printed in 1651, it appears as a dance, a line-dance for a large group of dancers, 'for as many as will be standing thus' [a line of men on one side and a line of women on the other side].

But earlier, in 1606, it was a song, a ballad sung by the children of the court and was then already described as 'an old piece.' An early song version has a young lady who stops to admire a tree,

> It was a maid of my country
> As she came by a hawthorn tree,
> As full of flow'rs as might be seen
> She marvel'd to see the tree so green.
>
> At last she asked of this tree,
> How came this freshness unto thee,
> And ev'ry branch so fair and clean?
> I marvel that you grow so green.

It is my guess that what Holst originally had in mind, perhaps even before he wrote the notes on paper, was a scene inspired by both the song and the dance. After all we come here to one of the most basic and ancient characteristics of music itself. I once heard an interpretation clinic by the great Russian cellist, Piatigorsky, who told his listeners that all music 'is either a song or a dance.'

But I arrive at my thoughts from the music itself. It does not begin like a dance by a group of people, it begins more like a song by a single singer (a single wind player). And I think it is like this young lady in the ancient form of the song, she is stopped in place and she is contemplating as she looks at a tree. Therefore I begin this movement slow and in the character of a ballad singer, standing in place, singing freely, not concerned with meter or exact rhythms and perhaps in a contemplative or even nostalgic frame of mind. After eight bars someone else takes up the song, in the same slow tempo and in the same character, but now joined by a bagpipe, an instrument long associated with the dance. This, in turn, makes our singer think, 'yes, I could dance to this' and the downbeat at Rehearsal Letter A in the tuba, euphonium and bass clarinet are the singer's left foot firmly placed on the ground to begin his improvisation of a dance while he sings. From this moment on it is a dance and as more people join in the dancing as the music accelerates faster and faster until the ultimate tempo is reached at Letter B. The fact that it is only here that Holst writes *forte* for the first time suggests, I think, that here all the spectators begin dancing. It is tutti dance as well as tutti ensemble.

At Rehearsal Letter F I return to a slower tempo, although not as slow as in the beginning, in order to allow the dramatic chromatic line in the bass drive the accelerando and crescendo forward to the *ff* eight bars before G. By the way, seven bars before G we have once again the 'pitch-yuk' problem and once again the listener must hear the change of chord which takes place in the eighth-notes.

A final thought about the ending. It seems incontestable to me, given the sparse and soft music preceding it, and the fact that the final note is on a weak beat, that the final note was intended by Holst as a surprise for the listener. To make this possible, it follows, that the conductor must not conduct this final note with some great wind-up gesture, for this would only cause the listeners to anticipate the loud final note. I conduct it with only the sudden expansion of the fingers in one hand. Also, the piccolo player must be reminded to make one constant (fast) trill with no pulse of any kind on the first beat of the final bar, as this too would take away from the element of surprise. The purpose of the piccolo is to create a kind of suspended animation to heighten the element of surprise.

Paul Hindemith, Symphony for Band

When I was a student at the University of Michigan during the 1950s I was well aware of this famous German composer due to his sonatas and chamber works. It was unknown to me and my fellow students that Hindemith had composed an original symphony for band for no band was playing this work, which was then more than five years old. Why? For one thing, it did not 'fit' into the programs of university bands, who almost never performed original band music of any kind among their diets of marches, trumpet trios, comedy works, Broadway show music and transcriptions of excerpts of minor and unimportant orchestral works. Nevertheless, I am sure every university band director knew this composition existed and I am sure it was never absent from their conscience that one of the world's most famous living composers had composed an original band symphony and they were not performing it.

Second, it was an era when full scores were not usually yet published for band music. Conductors from that era were used to condensed scores of no more than six or eight staves, with everything transposed into 'concert pitch.' From the perspective of the experience of wind conductors today, who regularly work from the most complex and large scores, it is almost impossible to imagine the impression made on earlier conductors when they saw the Hindemith score for the first time. It may have been the first time many of them had ever seen a full score, not to mention one so large and complex—and all those transpositions! I was a member of the Michigan Band the first time the parts for the Hindemith *Symphony* were passed out. I am sure Revelli had studied this score and I am willing to accept that he understood it. But it was clearly a new experience for him having to actually conduct while reading such a score. It was very clear to all of us that he was having considerable difficulty following the score and before we had read even the first movement through, he closed his score and grumbled, 'Pass it in!' The students were very disappointed.

Then, during the 1970s and 1980s most university bands finally performed this composition. Today we have come full circle and it is almost never heard on a university campus. But it remains there on the library shelf nevertheless, an authentic, serious symphony by a famous composer who does not make the slightest gesture toward making it a 'fun' piece to play or 'entertaining' for the listener.

First Movement

First, a notational warning: the older Europeans used the traditional accent sign (>) to mean 'a full sound,' not the pointed, hard accent we play in America when we see this sign. Therefore, the first five eighth-notes (the quarter-note in such cases is always played as an eighth-note[1]) in the low brass in the first bar should be thought of as more or less five 'poms,' instead

---

[1] An eighteenth-century performance practice wherein the final note in a bar, if followed by rests, is played one-half its value.

of five 'ta's.' For anyone old enough to remember the period of Nelhybel's music, this was a particular problem. He used accent marks everywhere, thinking as a European, trying to get a full, dark sound in contrast to what he heard as an American sound, bright, edgy and pointed. Unfortunately a whole generation of American conductors misunderstood and took his accent signs to make the performances more pointed and brittle and, indeed, only resulted in making all his music sound the same. The man was basically a sixteenth-century contrapuntalist and we turned him into a nineteenth-century military band composer.

So, this is true in the melody at the beginning in the second and third bars. The accented quarter-notes were intended to be performed legato, but with a full tone. Otherwise, the style of the melody is very strong, but in a linear sense. That is, one must think of an organ where the tone is linear and the notes connected. This again is difficult for American band conductors who, following the nature of our repertoire (and their arms), think of everything as vertical—band conducting is all about the beat. The goal, then, is to have the cornets play with a big, warm sound with no spaces and no accents and which carries the listener forward through time. There are generations of Germanic contrapuntal genes behind this melody.

And what are we to think of the woodwinds at the beginning? To the eye it appears as if Hindemith were writing out some aleatoric-like improvisation and to the ear, in many performances, it becomes a blur of indistinguishable activity. Once again I hear the organ here, but a German baroque organ and not the nineteenth-century French organ with its undulating vibrato. I hear the high articulations of the old lead pipes and you will notice the composer makes this clear by writing lots of staccato dots for a few bars. But to sort out the lines I find it helpful also to tell players to just add a small accent on the first note of each ligatured group.

I should like to return one more time to a notational problem which involves the accent sign, namely let us focus on bar [20]. Hindemith once observed that for a composer there are only three ways to make one note more important than its neighbors in so far as the listener is concerned. If it is either higher, longer or louder the listener will understand it to be more important. Therefore when I look at the piccolo, oboe and clarinet figure in bar [20] I am very confident that Hindemith was very concerned that the first note would stick out too much, simply because it was the highest note. So when he added an accent mark he was trying to soften the effect through a certain fullness of the sound, as if one were saying 'low–lu–lu–lu.' But, of course, for most Americans he only compounded the problem, for if one adds an American style accent the result is quite objectionable to the ear.

In the middle of this movement we have a true German fugue. In a Baroque fugue the melody is called a 'subject' and the entire purpose of the composer is to write the fugue in such as way that the listener always hears each appearance of the subject. The second section of a fugue is called the 'episode,' a section by definition in which the subject is not heard at any time in any voice. The general idea at the time of Bach was to write the music of the episode so that it had a kind of 'marking-time' quality, music that just sits there, with nothing very interesting going on.[2] This, in turn, has the effect of creating in the listener of a nervous expectation that he will soon hear the subject return—where is it?—where is it?

Regarding the performance of this particular fugue, therefore, it is very important that the interpretation of the first episode section, 89 – 91 , be utterly undistinguished, like a calm pond without the slightest ripples. It is this which sets the stage for the second exposition section, 92 , and contributes, through contrast, to its power. The conductor will notice that the first subject section, the first exposition section, is *forte* and so is the next one at 92 , but the episode section is marked only ***mp***. In most performances I have heard the conductor has allowed the episodes to become something much louder than ***mp*** and thus the essential contrast between the exposition sections and the episodes is greatly diminished.

There is one more very important comment to be made about this fugue subject, namely the dotted rhythms. At some point Hindemith spent some time with the Philadelphia Orchestra, perhaps when Ormandy was preparing one of the several recordings the orchestra made of this composer's music. During the year I spent in Philadelphia (1967–1968) I heard references made by the players to the period when Hindemith was in town, because most of them were also private teachers and were eager to absorb as much as they could of his style for they were all using his sonatas in the studio. The one thing I heard over and over was of Hindemith's insistence for mathematically accurate dotted notes. This is a discipline very few players observe, or orchestras either for that matter. Consider that compound dotted figure in the first movement of the *Seventh Symphony* by Beethoven. You will be likely to never hear this played accurately, it is always 'bent' so that the figure is no longer compound but simple and you hear the music as if it were in $\frac{4}{8}$ and not $\frac{6}{8}$. You never hear this played accurately because it is so difficult, but if you do, the movement takes on a magically lilting dance quality which is surely what Beethoven had in mind. He generally was not interested whether something was difficult. And so with the Hindemith fugue in most performances you will hear the subject played as if the music were written in $\frac{12}{8}$, that is we take these figures and swing them. However, while the placement of the sixteenth-note is important, it is not important to try to sustain the dotted eighth-note, in fact they should be played nearly as short as a sixteenth note.

Take this to the bank: in the music of Hindemith play those sixteenth-notes late!

Second Movement

There are just a few stylistic points important to interpretation which should be mentioned in this movement. First, regarding the woodwinds in the initial bars, it is important to recognize this figure as a mordant and as such played on the beat with a little accent. The effect is like foot steps in shoes covered with thick lamb's wool. These are not grace-notes played before the beat.

---

[2] Bach was an exception. His great improvisation skills led him to making the episode section become so interesting, sometimes, that it almost distracts the listener. The great G-Minor *Prelude and Fugue* has an episode section which begins with an innocent little turn but eventually develops into extremely powerful music.

With the melody, presented in imitation, we have another urgent need for the linear application of the pyramid principle. To take the cornet solo, for example, the player must play a significant decrescendo within the first half-note in order to make an elegant approach to a high note which is made distinctly softer than the first note. If one does this, then the listener hears both notes at the same dynamic level contained in an elegant slur, which, of course, was the intent of the composer. If one does not do this, then the listener will hear the second note as significantly louder than the first note. As an intellectual idea this does not seem so bad, but in practice it sounds like the bray of a donkey, or a hiccup. Take your pick.

The following $^{12}_{\,8}$ section is called 'Fast,' but it is actually the same tempo. It only sounds faster to the listener as there are now three eighth-notes to the beat instead of two. Perhaps we might regard this as an old trick the Germans learned from Napoleon. While the Allies were marching along at quarter-note = 60 (the speed at which one could drag the small cannon) Napoleon had his composers write marches in $^6_8$. They were performed at the same tempo but it sounded faster, again because of the extra eighth-note in each bar, and it frightened the Western armies because they imagined the French were *running* towards them.

I generally have always found it a good rule when in a compound meter to add a bit of accent to every beat. It helps keep the players together as it prevents the beats from spreading out internally. This is particularly helpful in the final section where both first sections of music are played simultaneously.

I have always made the eighth-notes in the final two bars staccato, even a little on the marcato side. Without this, to my ear the music does not end; it otherwise seems to the listener as if something is going to happen on the following third beat.

Third Movement

In my mind it is clear that in this fugue subject the quarter-notes should be played like eighth-notes with eighth-note rests. First of all, in this tempo I cannot think of any example in earlier music where this figure is not slurred and yet has a long quarter-note. It would seem very awkward. The fact that the composer adds a staccato dot on the quarter-note when *piano*, at Letter C, does not suggest to me that the earlier quarter-notes were long, only that here they are shorter still to provide sparkle. Second, the shorter quarter-note helps clarity when the figure is interspersed with the very graceful answer at Letter A. Third, and very important, the shorter quarter-note in the subject makes it much more possible for the listener to hear the rapid imitation in the stretto sections, which are several.

Most important, this shorter quarter-note adds to the almost nieteenth-century German military quality of this subject, a rigid, clock-work, unyielding military precision which throws in much greater relief the following broad and lyrical lines which Hindemith calls 'espressivo.'

But this is not just any old 'espressivo.' This is music at the very opposite extreme of the militaristic facet of the Germanic personality. This is the down and dirty music of the Berlin cabarets of the 1920s and this melody needs to be played down and dirty. I always used to ask my students to go see Marlene Dietrich's old film, *The Blue Angel* (1930), the story of a cabaret singer, to get a feel for this period of Berlin life. They always came back to the next rehearsal and did a great job. We must always hope that this old film can still be viewed somewhere for the forces of the Politically Correct will never allow us to explain such things from the podium!

Hindemith had this 'against the stream' part of his character which we hear so clearly here. Once I was invited by Lukas Foss to join him and members of the Los Angeles Philharmonic in a performance requiring two conductors, a cantata written in 1929 by Hindemith called *Der Lindberghflüg*, with a libretto by Berthold Brecht and Kurt Weill. At this time the entire world was going crazy celebrating Lindbergh's famous solo flight across the Atlantic because it seemed to be the dawn of a new era of international travel and communication. Hindemith and his colleagues were apparently part of a small minority of intellectuals who were thinking, 'Wait … how do we know airplanes are going to be such a good thing for society.' So the cantata takes this anti-flight perspective in a very interesting and witty way.

Later in the third movement Hindemith begins to use these two themes at the same time, the rigid militaristic and the down and dirty cabaret music, it reminds me of that wonderful passage toward the beginning of the *Also Sprach Zarathustra* by Strauss where we hear the alternation of the leit-motivs for Nature and the Church—the Church says 'No!'—Nature says 'Yes!'—the Church says 'No!'—Nature says 'Yes!' It is an argument the Church always loses, hence the following section is called, 'Of Joys and Passions.'

In the remainder of the Third Movement of this Symphony, Hindemith more or less presents both ideas concurrently, the rigid militaristic and the music of the cabaret. What is a conductor to emphasize? Maybe that is why Hindemith brings back that strong Germanic theme from the first movement, to suggest that the good German character supersedes both the militaristic and cabaret urges.

Darius Milhaud, Suite Française

BAND CONDUCTORS love to conduct suites of folk-songs. In our repertoire we have folk-songs of England, Scotland, Ireland, Wales, Korea, Austria, Russia and on and on. Conductors love to program these works because they are technically straight-forward and pleasing to audiences. But one collection is quite different. Darius Milhaud says his folk-song suite, *Suite Française*, is all about 'destruction, cruelty, torture and murder' as the legacy of war.

The last time you heard this music as a member of the audience, did the performance communicate such profound emotions to you? If not, it may be that some conductors have negligently allowed the characteristics of the genre sweep this score up in its wake.

Milhaud composed this during one of his many residences teaching composition at a small college near San Francisco. One of my spies informed me that the composer had checked out volumes of French folk songs from the music department of the University of California at Berkeley and that the original call-slips were still obtainable. Thus I began a very long process of acquiring these volumes through interlibrary loan and playing through them at the piano looking for the ones he selected for his suite and hoping to find clues why. I believe I read through eight or nine hundred of them and eventually found, as I recall, perhaps eight which he used in the suite. But these eight were in no way more remarkable than the other nine hundred and clearly he had at his disposal the basic materials to toss off any number of traditional folk-song suites. The *Suite Française* is important music precisely because he did *not* do this. Rather, this composer took common materials and through introspection and seriousness of purpose reached for more profound emotions. Certainly you will not find 'destruction, cruelty, torture and murder' in any of the original tunes he chose from those early collections. But he was certainly filled with emotion when he thought of the geographical provinces which give their names to the various movements and in his notes for the young Americans he points out that these were the very areas where their fathers and grandfathers fought and died.

What Milhaud was doing in composing his *Suite Française* was much closer to what Mahler so frequently did. For that matter, sit back in your chair and think for a moment about the range and depth of emotions you hear in that French folk song, 'Fere Jacques,' in the third movement of Mahler's *First Symphony*. I am afraid some conductors assume the *Suite Française* is another superficial collection of folk songs and it is not. The purpose of this essay is to look at a few places in this score where the conductor can begin to think in a new direction.

2. Bretagne

This is Brittany, a peninsula which juts out into the North Atlantic Ocean. The first four bars are nostalgic but very painful, clearly reflecting the sense of loss of someone close during the war. How does the conductor convey this? First I want to recommend making the first note almost a fermata, because it is a cry, not a quarter-note. When I find a passage like this I always begin by just telling the players to do whatever they feel necessary to communicate, in this case, nostalgia and pain. Almost always the players will do something very beautiful and sincere (and without a lot of rehearsal time!). How is this possible? It happens because the basic emotions are universal and genetic. You don't have to worry when you say 'nostalgia and pain' that the students will play 'sweet and happy.' What makes it really musical, and contributes to developing a musical ensemble if you do this sort of thing on a regular basis, is that not only will they understand 'nostalgia and pain,' but they will express it in a genuinely *personal* way.

But with bar ⑤ the nostalgia is gone and we have now a real cry of pain which must be expressed with a significant crescendo in ⑤ and a significant ritard. in ⑥ ; the final two eighth-notes in the horn in ⑥ we treat once more as a little fermata to prepare the listener for the return of the original emotion. This great cry of anguish and pain in ⑤ and ⑥ , which Milhaud repeats over and over, is one of the most emotional and passionate moments in band literature. In most performances you will hear none of this, only a connecting bass line of no significance. How can a conductor look at these two bars and not feel this cry of pain? Because American conductors are trained to look at the score as data to be analyzed, not as a record of universal emotions. By the way, the two 'grace-notes' in ⑥ are not grace-notes. They should be played as a mordant on the fourth beat and with the first 'grace-note' accented exactly as a syllable in a name is accented. Remember the tempo is very slow here because of the ritard. and so this mordant represents language within the overall cry, perhaps someone's name uttered in anguish. Beginning with the second eighth-note of ⑥ we might think of something like, 'for my Renaldo's dead.' In the last appearance of this great cry, in the final four bars of the movement, Milhaud employs augmentation so that the strength of the emotion is not lost due to the diminuendo.

A few more comments about the second movement: first, the dotted quarter-note in ⑬ and following represents the lighthouse search light on the coast. Tell your students to think of how a search light at an airport looks—an initial sharp surprise, even though you know it is going to come around again—followed by a long decay in the brightness of the light. Then you tell them, 'play it so it sounds like that.' And they will! I don't have any idea how else to rehearse this.

The music at ㉕ is quite different. It is nostalgic, but without the strong pain in the melody. I believe that for Milhaud the pain is in the accompanying isolated eighth-notes, but I don't know how to put this into words. For me it is something like a jolt in the heart. Certainly it is in emotional conflict with the melody, which for me has always had the emotion of love attached to the nostalgia. In rehearsal I find it is more to the point if I sing the melody, as for example I feel a long first eighth-note in ㉗ . When they hear the singing voice the players understand immediately and they will not forget. Otherwise what would you do? Try to explain mathematically the relative lengths of these notes? And if you did, and the players were able to produce it, the result would only be notes with no feeling.

3. Ile de France

The 'Ile de France' is, of course, Paris and all audience members of any musical sophistication will recognize the dancing girls quotation from Offenbach in ⑫. Perhaps not so obvious is the recognition of the French Caribbean connection at the beginning, with its prominent maracas in the horns and trombones.[1]

For me the lovely, graceful and innocent melody at ㉕ is Milhaud's counter-weight to the naughty girls of Paris. I always see in my mind here the little girls all dressed up in their finest pink dresses walking with their parents in the parks on a Sunday afternoon in Paris. Their little brothers are off sailing little boats in one of the fountains, but the little girls are turning, in flowing motions creating their own little dance steps. I don't think I can otherwise communicate how to conduct this, so program it on a May concert and then tell your administrator in March that you must be provided a roundtrip ticket to Paris as an obligatory part of your score study!

Surely the ritard. in ㊸ must be understood to be a two-bar ritard., in ㊷ and ㊸. It is easy to conduct and play if one thinks of an accent on each half-note beat with the point of the baton bouncing higher on each subsequent beat. The bouncing baton, like a ball bouncing higher each time, is an invaluable trick for controlling a ritard. Nothing else works so effectively.

4. Alsace-Lorraine

Here is a wonderful region to visit. In Moselle they make something to drink, but I can't remember what it is. Strasbourg is a large city with one of Europe's great cathedrals, but also has one of the most beautiful areas of 'old Europe,' the *Petite France* neighborhood of Strasbourg.

Behind these beautiful scenes, however, are painful memories among the people for this region went violently back and forth between France and Germany for centuries. My own maternal family came from this region, my great grandfather moving from here to Kansas. I can remember talking to my grandmother and hearing her bemoan the extended family's sense of loss of identity in belonging first to one country, then the other, then back to the first, etc. From her I gathered this pain must be in the genes of everyone from this region.

This pain is exactly what Milhaud portrays in this movement, basically in contrasting a gentle rural scene and its violent and anguished disruptions caused by war. The music at the beginning is truly rural and we have a sun-filled morning with a simple carefree peasant walking and surveying his fields. But in the fourth bar an unexpected chill is felt in his spine. He doesn't know where this came from, or what it means, but it is frightening. To achieve this effect the grace notes must be played rather close to the quarter-note and while it may be ***mp***, it must have a certain sharp, or pointed quality to it. This becomes more frightening by its very repetition in ⑦ and it is because of this that the thirty-second-notes leading to ⑨ represent if not a little cry, at least an emotional sound in the throat.

---

[1] To which you need to add the characteristic accent on the first note of each group of four.

This tranquility is interrupted dramatically in ⟦17⟧ with the most anguished and painful emotional outburst. It is pure Mahler and must be played *subito forte*, as marked, but also *subito adagio*, so slow that the written out vocal slides are heard as exactly that and not as instrumental passing tones. These melodic slides have for centuries represented intense emotions in both vocal and string instrument music and they will be recognized by the listener for what they are as long as they are played like slides, just the way the individual player feels it with no attempt in rehearsal to create 'precision.'

This music might be thought of as a longer form of that chill in the spine, it now being a frightening, dark thought of some kind which eventually passes for in ⟦25⟧ we are back to the original tempo with the peasant again walking in his fields. Suddenly, in ⟦33⟧, a new painful interjection comes as the peasant is walking. The figure first heard here in the cornets becomes a basic emotional leit-motiv of this composition and must always, especially the first time, be performed like a painful cry, communicated by a distinct crescendo and descrescendo in the first bar. It must be performed in this pronounced manner every time it occurs in every instrument, for it is this figure alone which drives and increases the pain and anguish of the music as it moves toward the great climax in ⟦97⟧.

Measure ⟦97⟧ is the return of the profound Mahler-like cries of pain and this time it does not pass. Indeed it leads to the very Mahler-like bell tones in the trombones and baritone in bars [103] and [105]. These great bell sounds must be more prominent than anything else, with the exception of the pain leit-motiv above, now heard in augmentation (and still with its crescendo-decrescendo definition).

A final warning is needed at the end for the last chord will be heard by the listener as one beat too short due to the preparatory chord of three-beats before it. It is vital therefore that the final chord be taken off on the first beat of a missing next measure and nothing shorter than that. The music is simply too powerful and too emotional to be abruptly halted on what we used to call, and are no longer allowed to call, a 'feminine beat.'

5. Provence

Provence, lying on the Mediterranean, adjacent to Italy and possessing the most colorful history of any part of France is a diverse and extraordinary area. It is tempting, therefore, to take the opening music of this movement as merely a reflection of this dynamic region, as for example perhaps the busy streets of Marseille. But I think we must not forget the composer's reflection on the war years and because of this I feel confident that what we really have here is a celebration of the end of the war. The very first bar is full of joy, enthusiasm and a feeling of racing off to the future. But I have always heard the second measure as something in parenthesis, a timid soul with his hand over his mouth whispering, 'Is it really over?' And then in the third measure the crowd is rushing off again. So I always perform the second measure *subito p*, one quiet voice on the side line who must have represented many Frenchmen in 1945.

In ⑮ Milhaud presents another form of enthusiasm as he reaches back into the history of the area and finds a Renaissance dance. But this is not an aristocratic dance, such as you might find in Paris with a dance by Gervaise. This is a public dance with echoes of nearby Italy. And such dances were performed by the brittle sounding shawms or perhaps fifes, so this modern music does not really sound good unless the modern flutes play very marcato with a strong accent on each group.

Measure ㊱ is another form of celebration at the end of the war, a deep breath, relaxing the shoulder muscles as one looks out over the calm blue waters of the sea from one of the most beautiful coastal areas in the world. It is a feeling of acceptance that 'now we can enjoy life again.' It must be conducted alle-breve or it will not sound calm.

I should like to make a suggestion about the bar before, the molto ritard. in ㉟. It has been my experience that if one begins a molto ritard. at the beginning of this measure the players do not feel the ritard. at the sixteenth-note and eighth-note level and things fall apart. This problem seems resolved if one just waits until the second eighth-note of the second beat to begin the ritard. I believe there is a clue that Milhaud was actually feeling this himself and it is found in the final five bars of the movement. Measure ㉟ is like the first two beats of ㉟, although in augmentation. But the next measure is a further augmentation, in effect a written out ritard. By the way, the quarter-note in the snare drum during these measures is not tied but struck. And for me the movement does not have a sense of conclusion unless I can hear the final strike on the snare drum.

Richard Wagner, Trauermusik

I WONDER HOW MANY university wind ensemble conductors think of this composition as a major work? I wonder how many conductors are aware that the performance duration of this work is equal to that of all four movements of the Persichetti *Symphony*? The composition is almost entirely a setting for band of music by von Weber, but it is a work Wagner took very seriously and it is beautiful. No apologies are necessary.

The celebrated German composer, Carl Maria von Weber died in London in 1826 while on tour. Although he was buried with due pomp (in a casket shaped like a violin case) in Moorfields Chapel, his final resting place was soon forgotten. Fifteen years later, in 1841, an anonymous letter in the *Gazette Musicale* (Paris) recalled an admirer's difficulty in finding the coffin in the crypt and reported on its apparent state of neglect. This letter precipitated a movement in Dresden[1] to have the remains of the composer returned home to Germany and Wagner was the moving force in making this happen.

One of the sons of Weber went to London to bring his father's remains back to Dresden. An incorrect account in some English source supposed that the casket returned by train to Dresden, resulting in misleading many later interested persons. Fred Fennell, for example, told me that he once went to Dresden and walked with his stop watch from the train station to the Catholic Cemetery in order to gain insights regarding the repetitions[2] and tempo of the *Trauermusik*.

Actually, the remains returned by water on the Elbe River, landing at a dock about 1,300 yards from the final resting place in the Catholic Cemetery in Friedrichstadt. Wagner organized a procession to cover this distance consisting of a magnificent catafalque and a large gathering of artists and musicians.[3] Church bells tolled, the street was illuminated by innumerable candles placed in the windows along the route and Wagner himself made a lengthy oration at the cemetery. Wagner's own account of the performance of his *Trauermusik* by eighty wind players contains some surprising details, together with an account of his rehearsal.

> This transference was to take place in the evening, by torchlight and in solemn train; I had undertaken to provide the mourning music then to be performed. I compiled it from two motives of 'Euryanthe' that portion of the overture which represents the spirit vision I made connect with the cavatina of Euryanthe, '*hier dicht*

---

[1] In Dresden at this time Weber was most remembered for his work with the Dresden Opera, from 1817 until his death in 1826. Wagner, while not an immediate successor, was associated with the Dresden Opera from 1842–1848. In 1813–1816 Weber had been in charge of the Opera in Prague and his successor there was a man familiar to those interested in *Harmoniemusik*, Josef Triebensee.

[2] Fred, under the misinformation about the remains arriving at the train station, made the incorrect assumption that the purpose of the repeat sign in this composition was for the purpose of allowing the conductor to keep repeating the first part of the music until the procession reached the cemetery.

[3] There are similar works, the *Marche Funebre* by Filippa, composed for the return of the remains of Rossini and a work by Halévy for the return to Paris of the remains of Napoleon. The music for these works is available at www.whitwellbooks.com.

am Quell,'—also quite unchanged, though transposed to B♭,—and ended with the transfiguration of that first motive, as it recurs at the close of the opera. This quite appropriate symphonic piece I expressly orchestrated for 80 picked wind instruments, taking particular care only to use their smoothest registers, however great the volume; in the section taken from the overture I replaced the tremolo of the violas by twenty stopped trumpets in the gentlest *piano*; and even at the rehearsal in the theater the whole thing struck so deep a chord in our memory of Weber that not only was Frau *Schroder-Devrient*—who was present at the time, and at any rate was a personal friend of Weber's—most profoundly touched, but I could not help admitting to myself that I never had wrought out anything so completely answering to its aim. No less successful was the music's execution in the open street when the cortege took its way: as the extremely slow tempo, accentuated by no plain rhythmic landmarks, was bound to offer peculiar difficulties, I had had the stage completely cleared at the rehearsal, to gain the necessary room to let the bandsmen march around me in a circle while they played the piece, already duly practiced. I was assured by witnesses who watched the cortege passing, from their windows, that the impression of solemnity had been unspeakably sublime.[4]

The discussion of the interpretation of this masterpiece must begin with the question of the repeat sign. The fact that this repeat sign was present already in the very first piano score[5] confirms that Wagner had this in mind in his original conception and that he intended this repeat to be honored. But in American performances it is rarely honored, perhaps because the conductors think they are merely playing the composition twice, followed by a 'coda,' a designation which inexplicably continues to appear in each new publication even though Wagner himself never used that word. The reason why Wagner would never have thought of the final music as a true coda and the reason why he considered the long repeat not arbitrary is because the form itself is the ancient German Bar Form: AAB.

But, strictly speaking, in the case of any long passage of music, one should not just 'play the music twice,' for such a decision ignores the experience of the listener. For example the first time this theme is heard, at [17], it is full of outgoing optimism. However, when the time comes for this same music to be repeated, a great deal of contemplative music has been heard by the listener in addition to a long, ever slowing, ever softer sensitive cadence ending with a ***pp*** unison pitch. Emotionally, one simply cannot go from this back to the outgoing, almost macho, repeat of [17]. I find it necessary for musical reasons to begin the return of the music at [17] at the same level of ***pp*** and slower and more contemplative. Beginning with [19] I make a gradual return to the tempi and dynamics heard the first time in this music.

---

4   Richard Wagner, *Wagner's Prose Works*, ed. William Ashton Ellis (New York: Broude), VII, 228ff and Richard Wagner, *My Life* (New York: Tudor, 1911), 357ff, contain a very lengthy account by Wagner of the political problems in making this ceremony happen together with the complete text of his oration. This material is given in David Whitwell, *Wagner on Bands*, 2nd edn., ed. Craig Dabelstein (Austin: Whitwell Publishing, 2011), http://www.whitwellbooks.com.

5   I believe I may have been the first person to identify the original piano score, which had been labeled merely as 'a sketch' in a small bibliothek which existed at one time in Wagner's home, Wanfried, in Bayreuth. At that time all of Wagner's furniture and his extraordinary silk wall coverings were still in place giving one the strongest possible feeling of the presence of the composer. In a recent visit I was horrified to find that the government had taken over the administration of the home, had removed all the furniture and everything which had belonged to Wagner, repainted the walls to give the appearance of some modern museum of handcrafts. The graves of Wagner and his wife had been covered with a huge expanse of ugly concrete (worry about vandals?) and the grave of his loyal dog had been moved off out of the sight of the tourists. May God forgive the government agency who did all this.

It is very important for the conductor to mark a change in 23, a bar in which the dynamics are incorrect in all published scores. The down beat of 23 is not *pp*, *subito pianississimo*, but rather *forte,* or whatever follows logically the crescendo in 22. Weber wrote an accent in all the moving parts at this point, with the *pp* coming later. In 25 Weber has written *dolce*, a term which Weber always seems to associate with a moment of great calm, like a chorus of angels. Since most musicians find such passages in Weber require a slower tempo, then in retrospect we realize that the *pp* in 23 is not a reference to dynamics but rather means a calming down, a little rallentando.

The reason for this error in the various band versions is because it is found in Wagner's first sketches for piano. But we know Wagner was not working from the autograph score of Weber, because after the premiere of *Euryanthe* in 1823 in Vienna the autograph score went back into the possession of Weber's family and was not available to Wagner when he made his band transcription in 1844. It was common practice in European opera houses to have a copyist make a 'conductor's score' from the autograph opera scores. This was because the heavy volume containing an act of an opera was too heavy for the delicate frame of the keyboard instrument where the conductor sat. Furthermore, with the full score the conductor would be turning pages every few bars, making it difficult to also tend to his duties supporting the singers. I once saw just such a score in Mozart's handwriting, with his 'conductor's score' (*dirigenten partitur*) written at the top by Mozart, for *The Marriage of Figaro*. At the time Mozart conducted this opera he was not only the composer, but owned the autograph scores. But he took the time and effort to make a two-stave reduction of the entire opera which he could use for conducting purposes! So it was such a copy by some unknown copyist employed by the Dresden Opera which Wagner used when making his version for band. Whatever he saw was lost to us in the fire-bombing of Dresden at the end of World War II.

Returning to the *dolce* at 25, this passage must be very slow and if it is, what appears as merely a progression of half-note chords becomes hauntingly beautiful. The opera is, sad to say, a rather melodramatic story, which is one reason it is not produced more often. At this moment, Euryanthe has made a mistake causing her lover to leave, so she decides to kill herself. In 25 she is contemplating her burial place in a beautiful, quiet meadow which she sees in the distance. The trumpet solo in 26 is Euryanthe singing 'and over there,' followed by 'where pastures lie.' Then comes the very beautiful chromatic line where she sings 'and there—I beg—on death—for me.' If the tempo for this passage is not slow the musical magic is lost. If it is, for example, the same tempo as 17, then these deeply expressive eighth-notes are heard as mere grace notes. By the way the following bars, 32 and 33, is a 'great snake' which figures in the story, so the conductor must make a great, scary crescendo and diminuendo to represent the snake waking up. Surely it was this 'great snake' which becomes the dragon in *Siegfried*.

From an educational perspective, during rehearsal this composition represents a wonderful opportunity to discuss harmony with the students and in particular how harmony affects interpretation. To begin with it is difficult to even think of Wagner's music without thinking of harmony. But it is also an essential characteristic of German music. When the Netherlands School and the Italian School were so interested in counterpoint, the Germans were far behind, still enjoying the vertical joys of music. Even with Bach, though he was an extraordinary master of counterpoint, we are not surprised, that on that famous occasion when he was taken to meet the king at Potsdam for the first time and the court harpsichordist transfixed like others to see the famous Bach enter the room, stopped playing with his hands in mid air, leaving a chord unresolved, that Bach first crossed the room and resolved the chord on the keyboard before turning and allowing himself to be introduced to the king. And that is the power of harmony.

What invests harmony with such power? Certainly there must be a genetic role at work, considering that the overtone series with its powerful organization of harmonic relationships was in place as a natural law of physics and being heard already by all creatures before us who had ears to hear. And for conductors, it is extremely important to remember that you have the feelings of the listeners in your hands and much of the power you hold over their feelings lies in your decisions regarding the role of harmony, both in its linear and vertical employment. And in a composition like this one the decisions by which you convey this harmonic power invests you with profound responsibilities.

Let us consider some examples of the power of harmony employed in linear movement. First, in an example typical of sixteenth-century counterpoint in 73 [second bar of the 'coda'] the soprano E♭ is completely at rest until the third beat when the movement in the horn to F *forces* the E♭ to move to D. Similarly, in 46 we hear the melody at rest until the F♯ in the horns forces the melody to resume. In my performances I stretch this measure and the length of the F♯ to allow the listeners to feel the pressure of the upward movement.

In several of the cadences of this composition there are some wonderful (musical) examples of the use of 'Placement,' a term often used today by performers of early music. Placement means that the arrival of something is determined not by chronology (the literal time expressed in the notation) but by psychology, or allowing yourself to judge when it *feels* like the right time to play.

The most important of these examples is the final cadence. First, there are two vital errors which seem to creep into all editions. The lowest bass note should be a B♭ in the staff in the next to last bar and only drop to below the staff for the final note. The second vital correction which is necessary is that all the woodwind parts in the last two bars which consist of two whole-notes are supposed to be *tied*, they represent a *longa*, a symbol equal to two whole-notes. The overall effect which Wagner had in mind during this cadence is a suspension of time while the listener hears the two separated sounds in the next to last bar, as if they were a great bell or a great choral 'A-men.' But this beautiful effect is lost on the listener unless there is a considerable space between, and after, these two half-notes. In my performances I make each one like a separate bar of dotted half-note and quarter-rest. This is Placement: you conduct the second half-note when it feels right to do so and the final bar as well. Once the third entrance of the brass 'bell' is heard, which coincides with the beginning of the last bar, then I recommend the upper woodwinds immediately fold their volume into the brass, so that the extended last chord is not top-heavy. Wagner did not write a fermata over the final bar but he would have been the first to agree that the length is again a matter of feeling.

Another perfect example of an appropriate moment for Placement is in ⑪. Here the conductor shows the release on beat 3 of some voices but treats the whole-note as a fermata, allowing him to give the downbeat only later, when it feels right to do so. Any concept of straight time in ⑪ and ⑫ will greatly minimize the beauty of the arrival of the next **pp** music.

In the role of Placement in ⑮ and ⑯ we have an interesting case where the conductor's conception of how Wagner heard the principal melody in ⑰ determines the Placement application to ⑮ and ⑯. If the conductor had concluded that ⑰ should be strong in character then he would prepare the listeners by creating a crescendo in ⑯ to give direction to the added 7th. However it would probably be bad to create a space between ⑯ and ⑰ as that would produce the effect of an accent on the first note of ⑰ from the perspective of the listener. On the other hand, if the conductor's conception was that Wagner imagined in ⑰ something mysterious, soft and even angelic, then perhaps no crescendo in ⑯ would be appropriate for the added 7th alone would suffice. In this case I would probably make a cut off at the end of ⑯ and then give the downbeat very small and high in the air.

An obvious need for Placement is present with regard to the length of ㉑, that is, the conductor only by ear must feel when the music should proceed. Certainly if it is the second time (repeat) when the music moves forward to the B section ['coda'] then of course one does not make any space where the barline is between ㉑ and ㉒. The sustained F of ㉑ must connect with the B♭ of ㉒ without pause.

Another occasion where Placement has a great influence on how harmony affects the listener is in ㊸ and ㊹. Wagner did notate the crescendo in ㊸ but I suspect he imagined it only for the purpose of making the 7th of the chord move forward in time to its resolution in ㊹. In any case Placement becomes an important factor, with regard to the listener, in ㊹ because the more the crescendo in ㊸ then the longer the first half of ㊹ must be. In other words the listener needs enough time to not only perceive the resolution but also time for the music to calm down and to anticipate the *dolce* music at ㊺.

By the way, Weber did write '*dolce*' here, although over ㊺ and not in ㊹ as some editions have it. Again, I believe it suggests a slower tempo, which allows the musical conductor to make this passage very *rubato*, exactly as a singer might.

On the Other Wagner Band Works

DUE TO WAGNER's pressing work on his operas and his time spent in trying to produce them, his composition in other fields represent a small catalog, and many of these were occasional works written as needed. Among these compositions is one major work for band, the *Huldigungsmarch*, a fine and heroic composition which Wagner conducted himself in public.

Its performances in the United States have failed to interest other conductors primarily because earlier conductors did not have the necessary background in older European traditions. In particular, the beginning section was intended to be slow and passionate music and only later become the *alla-breve* and *Maestoso* march style. When conductors conduct the work from the beginning as a fast march work the composition is fundamentally and terminally trivialized.

Huldigungsmarsch

Composed
August 1864, for large concert band

Sources
Munich-Wittelsbacher Ausgleichsfonds: full score

Publication
Richard Wagner Werke (Leipzig, 1912–1929), xvii
Samtliche Werke (Mainz, 1970), 18/iii (full score)

First Performance
Munich, 5 October 1864

As is well-known, after a long period of frustration professionally, financially and personally, Wagner was 'rescued' by the appearance of Herr Pfistermeister, the secretary to the newly crowned King of Bavaria, Ludwig II, who announced the intent of the new king to guarantee the financial support of Wagner and his music. Wagner first met the king on 4 May 1864 and in gratitude began the composition of the *Huldigungsmarch* in honor of the king. The first performance, by three combined infantry bands stationed near Munich, was given on the king's nineteenth birthday, 25 August 1864.

Wagner conducted this work himself on several occasions, including one the following year reported by Hans von Bülow.

> Finally last night came the banquet: a big private concert in the Residenztheater with the house brilliantly illuminated, and no audience except His Majesty and between thirty and forty special Wagnerites. Wagner conducted.

First, the Pilgrims' March from *Tannhäuser*, with a surprise: on the final E♭ of the cellos, eighty military band players struck up the *Huldigungs Marsch* behind the scenes. The effect was magnificent, the point of it all being the special relationship between the composer and the King.[1]

In 1870, Cosima organized a performance of this work as a surprise for Wagner's birthday.

She had devised all kinds of surprises and retained the regimental band, forty-five men strong ... At eight o'clock the children, adorned with garlands of roses, burst into Wagner's room, the band struck up the *Huldigungsmarsch,* and Richard sobbed with delight at the surprise.[2]

By far the most important performance of this work was for the cornerstone ceremony of the theater in Bayreuth on 22 May 1872, which, of course, was also the composer's birthday. In recognition of all this, the King sent a telegram of 'Felicity and blessings.'

For the ceremony itself flags had been set out to mark the outline of the proposed theater. In spite of a rain storm, a crowd gathered to watch the cornerstone being lowered into place as a regimental band played the *Huldigungsmarsch*. Inside the stone was a poem by Wagner,

O may the secret buried here
Rest undisturbed for many a year;
For while it lies beneath this stone,
The world shall hear its clarion tone.

Wagner then took up the hammer and said, 'Bless you, my stone, long may you stand and firm may you hold!'[3]

Some have pointed out the deep significance, which all present understood, of the performance of the *Huldigungsmarsch*, for without the king's encouragement the world would have never seen this theater, not to mention the completion of the *Ring* itself.

Some anti-Wagner newspapers gave a somewhat nasty aftertaste to this ceremony. A paper in Leipzig, for example, wrote, 'We consider it a farce ... Many of the scenes that occurred there are simply nauseating.'[4]

I used to own two original first editions of piano arrangements of this work, one by Hans von Bülow and one by Wagner himself which he arranged the year following its composition. The Wagner arrangement is especially interesting as it reflects how the composer himself might have played the composition on the piano. It has some effective improvements compared to the original band version and I have incorporated these into my modern edition for band. In the first fast tempo, the triplet figure is doubled up, so that it occurs on both the second *and* fourth beat which gives considerably more drive to the movement. Also the very long tone (four bars of tied whole-notes) near the end is given new movement.

The reader can see sample score pages and hear a performance at www.whitwellbooks.com.

---

[1] Letter of Hans von Bülow to Karl Klindworth, July 13, 1865.
[2] Richard Count du Moulin-Eckart, *Cosima Wagner,* trans. Catherine Alison Phillips (New York: Knopf, 1931), I, 396ff.
[3] Curt von Westernhagen, *Wagner,* trans. Mary Whittall (Cambridge: Cambridge University Press, II 446.
[4] Henry T. Finck, *Wagner and his Works* (New York: Greenwood Press), II, 274.

'Elsa's Procession to the Cathedral,' *Lohengrin*, Act II, Scene 4

This music in the opera is virtually a band composition as it stands. After thirty-two bars one violin part joins in unison and eventually two male choirs. It was no doubt for this reason that Wagner personally recommended that this passage would make a good band transcription. In a letter to Friedrich Wilhelm Graf von Redern, dated Dresden, 26 June 1846, Wagner wrote,

> While I doubt that there are many pieces in my opera that are suitable for production as military music, I permit myself to draw your attention, however, particularly to one number which has gone exceedingly well on parades here in Dresden; I refer to the first section of the fourth scene of the second Act; it is in the style of a March with chorus ... that lends itself well to treatment as an effective piece for military band.

Wagner's use of the term 'military music' simply reflects the large band with woodwinds and brass and did not suggest a military style. Quite the contrary, in another letter Wagner specifically speaks of the style he had in mind.

> You think that my stage arrangement is inadequate to represent Elsa's bridal procession in the second act in conformity with the length of the music (as well as with the artistic effect I intended), and you suggest a courtly ceremony—as prelude to the actual bridal procession—with which I cannot agree at all. That is much too much ceremonial for the noble, naive simplicity of that time ...
>
> The particular atmosphere which my *Lohengrin* should produce is that here we see before us an ancient *German* kingdom in its finest, most ideal aspect. Here no one does anything out of mere routine and court custom, but in every encounter the participants take a direct and genuinely personal part; here there is no despotic pomp which has its 'bodyguards' (oh! oh!) and orders the 'people pushed back' to form a 'lane' for the high nobility ... I beg of you, for God's sake, take out that awful stuff with the masters of ceremonies, marshals, bodyguards, etc.: they must have no further place *here*. Let my *Lohengrin* be beautiful, but not ostentatious ...
>
> Elsa must—on the high ground before the palace—actually come to a stop. She is moved and affected, as if overcome by bliss. Only after 8 measures does she once more proceed very slowly toward the cathedral, sometimes, pausing, cordially and naively acknowledging greetings. Not only does it take shape *this way*, but it actually becomes what I intended it to be; namely, no march-like procession, but the infinitely significant advance of Elsa to the altar.[5]

My modern edition of this beautiful music includes some important changes when compared to the old edition which American bands used for so many years. First of all, the old edition left out some of the music, one of the two male choirs, which I cannot explain unless the former arranger was working perhaps from a piano score. Then, since this music in the opera connects with the stage action this processional for band lacks a final cadence. The older edition created a cadence but unfortunately, for aesthetic reasons, it was one bar short. I also wrote out the unusual turn which Wagner preferred and which I always found wasted much rehearsal time when it appeared only as a symbol.

The reader can see sample score pages and hear a performance at www.whitwellbooks.com.

---

5 John N. Burk, *Letters of Richard Wagner* (New York: Vienna House, 1972), 333ff.

Fanfares for 4 Trumpets

This work consists of three fanfares of various lengths for four natural trumpets and timpani, and is dedicated to the Bavarian King's 6th Chevaulegers-Regiment.[6]

Because of Wagner's close association with the King of Bavaria he was in a position where he could not refuse a request for a piece such as this.

Actually, he was very familiar with and often heard military band concerts and never had any aesthetic objections in doing so. He did, however, have musical objections, particularly in the case of German bands and their conductors and he criticized them strongly in his literary papers. It is worthy of note that on one occasion, during the Winter of 1858–1859 in Venice, he was quite delighted to hear an Austrian band perform arrangements of his music. He recalled this in his autobiography.

> Strangely enough, it was the thoroughly German element of good military music, to which so much attention is paid in the Austrian army, that brought me into touch with public life in Venice. The conductors in the two Austrian regiments quartered there began playing overtures of mine, *Rienzi* and *Tannhäuser* for instance, and invited me to attend their rehearsals in their barracks. There I also met the whole staff of officers, and was treated by them with great respect. These bands played on alternate evenings amid brilliant illuminations in the middle of the Piazza San Marco, whose acoustic properties for this class of production were really excellent. I was often suddenly startled towards the end of my meal by the sound of my own overtures; then, as I sat at the restaurant window giving myself up to impressions of the music, I did not know which dazzled me most, the incomparable piazza magnificently illuminated and filled with countless numbers of moving people, or the music that seemed to be borne away in rustling glory to the winds. Only one thing was missing that might certainly have been expected from an Italian audience: the people were gathered around the band in thousands listening most intently, but no two hands ever forgot themselves so far as to applaud, as the least sign of approbation of Austrian military music would have been looked upon as treason to the Italian Fatherland.[7]

A letter Wagner wrote at this time (24 October 1858) thanking one of these Austrian conductors reveals, more than the passage from his autobiography quoted above, his genuine appreciation.

> Honorable Conductor,
>
> I could not find you in the Piazza yesterday to thank you for the wonderful performance of the *Rienzi Overture*, so today I do this in this written form. I appreciated it very much that your musicians had noticed everything, had marked everything so well and brought everything out correctly. From the very beginning it was perfect, with the tempo entirely correct. [My only suggestion is that] four bars before the Allegro there should be more drums and very strong; that place is dull.
>
> Once again, the best thanks and the assurance that you have made it very enjoyable for me.
> Auf Wiedersehen!
>
> Yours faithfully,
> Richard Wagner

The reader can see sample score pages and hear a performance at www.whitwellbooks.com.

---

[6] In the Marine Band Library, Washington, DC, is a photocopy of a page of sketches, said to be brass fanfares performed at the time of the first production of the Ring in Bayreuth. The present writer found this page very difficult to read, but it appears to be simple quotations of now-familiar motives of the Ring.

[7] Ibid., 696.

Excerpts from the *Ring* for Band

With respect to Wagner and his associations with the regimental bands in Bavaria, we must mention that there was at least one band transcription, the scene of Brünhilde's Awakening from *Siegfried* in which he apparently had some involvement. During the latter part of the nineteenth century, the Hanover publisher, Louis Oertel, who published much band music, published a fifteen-minute band transcription of this music and the text at the beginning tells us that the score was 'arranged by Anton Seidl and Gottfried Sonntag under the supervision (*Aufsicht*) of the Master.' The text continues,

> This composition was arranged, with the approval and under the supervision of Richard Wagner, for the band of the 7th Bavarian Infanterie-Regiment, by Anton Seidl and Gottfried Sonntag ('Kg. Rechnungsrat a.D. in Bayreuth'). The new instrumentation [of this published version] was done by Oskar Junger, Kg. Obermusik-meister, 7th Bavarian Infanterie-Regiment 'Prinz Leopold' in Bayreuth.

This introductory text also includes an excerpt from a letter of Seidl to Sonntag which suggests that the original arrangement can be dated in 1878.

Of course our principal interest lies with the nature of the 'supervision' by Wagner. The fact that this transcription was done for a regimental band stationed at Bayreuth adds weight to this possibility of some participation by Wagner. So does the involvement of Anton Seidl, later a famous Wagnerian conductor, but at this time a copyist and disciple of Wagner.

The question is complicated by the fact that Oertel published not the Seidl-Sonntag-Wagner version, but a later one revised by Junger. Further, this score is only a three-stave condensed score with no list of the complete instrumentation—therefore, whatever set of parts one has, one is never completely sure if everything is complete.[8]

Another Seidl, unrelated to Anton, was responsible for three lengthy band transcriptions from the *Ring* which were published by Schott during the 1880s. This was Arthur Seidel, conductor and composer, who was born 13 April 1849 in Neisse and died 28 March 1910 in Breslau.

During the latter part of his life, Wagner accepted monies in advance from Schott with the promise of giving them future works to publish.[9] The present writer was told, while visiting the publisher in Mainz in 1977, that the engagement of Seidel to prepare the *Ring* band arrangements was an attempt on the part of the publisher to recoup some of the monies given the composer. The understanding at Schott, in 1977, was that Seidel had done these arrangements from the actual autograph scores, which disappeared during World War II. This seems reasonable, as the band scores (but not parts) were undoubtedly published *before* the orchestral score and parts.

Seidel prepared a '*Fantasie*,' on *Die Walküre*, *Siegfried*, and *Das Götterdämmerung*, each consisting of twenty minutes, or more, of non-stop music. Seidel had earlier published projects of this nature, but they tend to be traditional 'pot-pourri' works consisting of rapidly changing

---

[8] I am quite sure my set, now in Trossingen, is not complete.

[9] Wagner confirms this arrangement in his *My Life*, 803.

excerpts and melodies. What makes the *Ring Fantasies* so much more successful is that they consist of much lengthy portions of the music. On the other hand, in my opinion, each of the *Fantasies* contains about fifteen-minutes of beautiful, inspired transcription, with the rest suffering from awkward modulations, weak connection points, and some scoring which just doesn't sound well.

But this is not to detract from Seidel's accomplishment: he was making band transcriptions of music no one had ever heard and within these vast operatic scores he certainly found the right passages to transcribe. We must also credit Schott, whose aesthetic ideals prompted them to publish these gigantic band scores at a time when German military bands were already traveling full speed on their long decline down to the lowest popular repertoire.

Several large band libraries in the United States own copies of the Seidel transcriptions, including the Marine Band, Eastman School of Music, and the University of Illinois.

My frustration with the Seidel transcriptions led me in the Summer of 1988 to spend four months making my own band transcriptions of excerpts of music from the *Ring*. The reader can see sample pages and hear recordings for *Das Rheingold* (7½ minutes of music) *Die Walküre* (15 minutes), *Siegfried* (7½ minutes) and *Das Götterdämmerung* (15 minutes) at the website, www.whitwellbooks.com.

Reviews of the Whitwell *Ring* Excerpt Transcriptions

> Received your tape recording of the Ring today. Thanks very much. You have supplied the band world with another fine and practical arrangement. I should like to do it.
>
> Leon Bly, April 18, 1989
> Stuttgart, Germany
> Stuttgart School of Music

> Just a note to thank you for your *wonderful* Wagner tape. I really enjoyed it and was, as always, impressed by *your* ensemble and your musicianship.
>
> Larry Sutherland just did your edition of *Götterdämmerung* at the Wind Festival last weekend—fine job.
>
> Gregg Hanson, April 18, 1989
> Salt Lake City, UT
> University of Utah

> Just before leaving Chicago I slipped your Wagner Ring tape in my briefcase. I have just finished listening to the entire tape both sides. What a tremendous job you have done. Your band plays the arrangements exceptionally well. There are many sections I have never heard arranged for band. Did you do all the arrangements?
>
> Regardless, congratulations on one mighty fine tape.
>
> Ed Gangware, April 28, 1989
> Nashville, TN

I played your arrangement of Excerpts from 'Siegfried' on our Southeast United States Band Clinic Concert last week. It was truly outstanding in every way. It is a great transcription and without a doubt one of the most beautiful ones that I have ever heard. Dr. Frederick Fennell and Dr. Jay Julian were at the concert and they really did enjoy it as well. There was no question in anyone's mind that Excerpts of 'Siegfried' was truly beautiful.

You are very gifted, extremely talented and your transcriptions are some of the very best I have ever heard. I hope that every effort will be made to have them published so that the really fine collegiate bands will have a chance to play them. These arrangements have been long needed for the college repertoire and it would be unfortunate unless many of the university bands are aware of them. You may be sure that I will do everything possible to make the conductors aware of your marvelous transcriptions and your truly great talent.

John M. Long, Feb. 12, 1990
Troy, AL
Troy State University

Gruss seiner Treuen an Friedrich August den Geliebten bei seiner Zurückkunft aus England den 9. August 1844

Composed
Summer, 1844, for TTBB, large concert band

Source
BRD-Mbs: full score

Publication
Dresden, C. F. Meser [1844] for voice and piano
Samtliche Werke, 16, for TTBB only

First Performance
August 9, 1844

Wagner provides a very lengthy and interesting account of the origin and first performance of this composition. It is apparent in his account that Wagner remembered performing some additional music, which he refers to as the original version of the March from *Tannhäuser*. Whatever this was, it is lost.

I was to receive the gratification of another triumph in the summer, which, although it was of no particular moment from the musical point of view, was of great social importance. The King of Saxony, towards whom, as I have already said, I had felt warmly drawn when he was Prince Friedrich, was expected home from a long visit to England. The reports received of his stay there had greatly rejoiced my patriotic soul. While this homely monarch, who shrank from all pomp and noisy demonstration, was in England, it happened that the Tsar Nicholas arrived quite unexpectedly on a visit to the Queen. In his honor great festivities and military reviews were held, in which our King, much against his will, was obliged to participate, and he was consequently compelled to receive the enthusiastic acclamations of the English crowd, who were most demonstrative in show their preference for him, as compared with the unpopular Tsar. This preference was also reflected in the newspapers, so that a flattering incense floated over from England to our little Saxony which filled us all with a peculiar pride in our King. While I was in this mood, which absorbed me completely, I learned that preparations were being made in Leipzig for a special welcome to the King on his return, which was to be further dignified by a musical festival in the directing of which Mendelssohn was to take part. I made inquiries as to what was going to be done in Dresden, and learned that the King did not propose to call there at all, but was going direct to his summer residence at Pillnitz.

A moment's reflection showed me that this would only further my desire of preparing a pleasant and hearty reception for his Majesty. As I was a servant of the Crown, any attempt on my part to render an act of homage in Dresden might have had the appearance of an official parade which would not be admissible. I seized the idea, therefore, of hurriedly collecting together all who could either play or sing, so that we might perform a Reception song hastily composed in honor of the event. The obstacle to my plan was that my Director Luttichau was away at one of his country seats. To come to an understanding with my colleague Reissiger would, moreover, have involved delay, and given the enterprise the very aspect of an official ovation which I wished to avoid. As no time was to be lost, if anything worthy of the occasion was to be done—as the King was due to arrive in a few days—I availed myself of my position as conductor of the Glee Club, and summoned all its singers and instrumentalists to my aid. In addition to these, I invited the members of our theatrical company, and also those of the orchestra, to join us. This done, I drove quickly to Pillnitz to arrange matters with the Lord Chamberlain, whom I found favorably disposed towards my project. The only leisure I could snatch for composing the verses of my song and setting them to music was during the rapid drive there and back, for by the time I reached home I had to have every thing ready for the copyist and lithographer. The agreeable sensation of rushing through the warm summer air and lovely country, coupled with the sincere affection with which I was inspired for our German Prince, and which had prompted my effort, elated me and worked me up to a high pitch of tension, in which I now formed a clear conception of the lyrical outlines of the *Tannhauser* March, which first saw the light of day on the occasion of this royal welcome. I soon afterwards developed this theme, and thus produced the march which became the most popular of the melodies I had hitherto composed.

On the next day it had to be tried over with a hundred and twenty instrumentalists and three hundred singers. I had taken the liberty of inviting them to meet me on the stage of the Court Theater, where everything went off capitally. Every one was delighted, and I not the least so, when a messenger arrived from the director, who had just returned to town, requesting an immediate interview. Luttichau was enraged beyond measure at my high-handed proceedings in this matter, of which he had been informed by our good friend Reissiger. If his baronial coronet had been on his head during this interview, it would assuredly have tumbled off. The fact that I should have conducted my negotiations in person with the court officials, and could report that my endeavors had met with extraordinarily prompt success, aroused his deepest fury, for the chief importance of his own position consisted in always representing everything which had to be obtained by these means as surrounded by the greatest obstacles, and hedged in by the strictest etiquette. I offered to cancel everything, but that only embarrassed him the more. I thereupon asked him what he wanted me to do, if the plan was still to be carried out. On this point he seemed uncertain, but thought I had shown a great lack of fellowship in having not only ignored him, but Reissiger as well. I answered that I was perfectly ready to hand over my composition and the conducting of the piece to Reissiger. But he could not swallow this, as he really had an exceedingly poor opinion of Reissiger, of which I was very well aware. His real grievance was that I had arranged the whole business with the Lord Chamberlain, Herr von Reizenstein, who was his personal enemy, and he added that I could form no conception of the rudeness he had been obliged to endure from the hands of this official. This outburst of confidence made it easier for me to exhibit an almost sincere emotion, to which he responded by a shrug of the shoulders, meaning that he must resign himself to a disagreeable necessity.

But my project was even more seriously threatened by the wretched weather than by this storm with the director; for it rained all day in torrents. If it lasted, which it seemed only too likely to do, I could hardly start on the special boat at five o'clock in the morning, as proposed, with my hundreds of musicians, to give an early morning concert at Pillnitz, two hours away. I anticipated such a disaster with genuine dismay. But

Rockel consoled me by saying that I could rely upon it that we should have glorious weather the next day; for I was lucky! This belief in my luck has followed me ever since, even down to my latest days; and amid the great misfortunes which have so often hampered my enterprises, I have felt as if this statement were a wicked insult to fate. But this time, at least, my friend was right; the 12th of August, 1844 [sic?] was from sunrise till late at night the most perfect summer day that I can remember in my whole life. The sensation of blissful content with which I saw my light-hearted legion of gaily dressed bandsmen and singers gathering through the auspicious morning mists on board our steamer, swelled my breast with a fervent faith in my lucky star.

By my friendly impetuosity I had succeeded in overcoming Reissiger's smoldering resentment, and had persuaded him to share the honor of our undertaking by conducting the performance of my composition himself. When we arrived at the spot, everything went off splendidly. The King and royal family were visibly touched, and in the evil times that followed the Queen of Saxony spoke of this occasion, I am told, with peculiar emotion, as the fairest day of her life. After Reissiger had wielded his baton with great dignity, and I had sung with the tenors in the choir, we two conductors were summoned to the presence of the royal family. The King warmly expressed his thanks, while the Queen paid us the high compliment of saying that I composed very well and that Reissiger conducted very well. His Majesty asked us to repeat the last three stanzas only, as, owing to a painful ulcerated tooth, he could not remain much longer out of doors. I rapidly devised a combined evolution, the remarkably successful execution of which I am very proud, even to this day. I had the entire song repeated, but, in accordance with the King's wish, only one verse was sung in our original crescent formation. At the beginning of the second verse I made my four hundred undisciplined bandsmen and singers file off in a march through the garden, which, as they gradually receded, was so arranged that the final notes could only reach the royal ear as an echoing dream song.[10]

A leading newspaper in Berlin published a note on this performance and gives, perhaps, a more accurate count of the number of performers.

Under the direction of Reissiger & Rich. Wagner, 106 instrumentalists and 200 vocalists went to Pillnitz to serenade the King with a patriotic song composed by Wagner. The King spoke in the most appreciative terms of the excellent piece.[11]

This original band composition by Wagner is available in a modern edition from Dr. Ronald Johnson, Conductor, the Wind Symphony, The University of Northern Iowa, Cedar Falls, IA 50613.

---

[10] Richard Wagner, *My Life* (New York: Tudor, 1911), 330ff, 358.

[11] *Berliner Musikalische Zeitung*, 1844, Nr. 1.

Festgesang, *'Der Tag erscheint'* (Weihegruss)

Composed
May 1843, for TTBB, 4 horns, 4 trumpets, 3 trombones, and tuba

Source
Private Collection: full score, location not available to the public

Publication
Samtliche Werke (Mainz, 1970), 16

First Performance
7 June 1843, Dresden

The account which Wagner left of this composition, while rich in some details unfortunately is not clear with regard to the instrumentation used at the first performance. Was it an unaccompanied vocal work or one with brass instruments? Both versions survive in early sources.

> On the 7th of June of this year (1843) the statue of King Frederick Augustus by Rietschl was unveiled in the Dresden Zwinger with all due pomp and ceremony. In honor of this event I, in collaboration with Mendelssohn, was commanded to compose a festival song and to conduct the gala performance. I had written a simple song for male voices of modest design, whereas to Mendelssohn had been assigned the more complicated task of interweaving the National Anthem into the male chorus he had to compose. This he had effected by an artistic work in counterpoint, so arranged that from the first eight beats of his original melody the brass instruments simultaneously played the Anglo-Saxon popular air. My simpler song seems to have sounded very well from a distance, whereas I understood that Mendelssohn's daring combination quite missed its effect, because no one could understand why the vocalists did not sing the same tune that the wind instruments were playing.[12]

A letter written at this time to his brother, Albert, Wagner gives essentially the same information.

> On the 7th we had a grand festivity here, the unveiling of the monument to Friedrich August. A chant for men's voices—to be executed in the Zwinger—was ordered of me by the King. Mendelssohn had to compose the second one. My chorus, being simple, uplifting and effective, decidedly bore off the palm; whereas Mendelssohn's turned out both pompous and flat.

Another letter, of 13 July 1843, which Wagner wrote to his half-sister, Cacilie, gives us the size of the choral forces.

> Reissiger went off on holiday in the middle of May, leaving me practically on my own to carry out all the duties, both in church & in the theater, in addition to which I received a commission from the King to write a commemorative hymn for the unveiling of the memorial to King Friedrich August. Mendelssohn was also commissioned to write a piece. The overall control of the performance, which took place in the Zwinger, was

---

[12] Richard Wagner, *My Life* (New York: Tudor, 1911), 312.

entrusted to me. I assembled a choir of 250 singers from the local choral societies, & made a great name for myself, in that it was universally agreed that my own piece, which was straightforward & uplifting, knocked Mendelssohn's over-elaborate & artificial composition into a cocked hat.

Most books on the music of Wagner assume this festival song was unaccompanied, simply because Wagner mentions no instruments in his account in his autobiography. We know the version for male choir, trumpets, horns, trombones, and tuba which was published in the *Complete Works*, in 1913.

What, then, was the version sung at the original ceremony? To this writer there is first the matter of circumstance. Both Wagner and Mendelssohn write a work for 250 male singers for the same performance. Brass instruments are available and used for the Mendelssohn work. It does not make much sense that the Wagner version with brass was not also used. The fact that he refers to his music as 'simple,' still describes it, but should not be taken to mean unaccompanied.

The stronger argument is the music itself. This is not a brass accompaniment added later to a preexistent vocal piece. The brass parts here are sometimes independent, with non-harmonic notes not found at all in the vocal parts. Thirty-three bars from the end the brass ensemble has music for itself alone, the singers have a rest but what were they doing if the performance were sung *a cappella*?

Ludwig van Beethoven, Siegessinfonie

IN THE PRUSSIAN NATIONAL LIBRARY in Berlin there is a manuscript score for large military band of a composition known as the *Siegessinfonie*, or 'The Victory Symphony.' The cover page is in the handwriting of Beethoven and he wrote,

On Wellington's Victory
At Victoria, 1813
Written for Mr. Maelzel, Ludwig von Beethoven

One early critic, while acknowledging that this is a minor work of Beethoven, nevertheless observed, 'There is no mistaking the claws of the Lion.' And he is right for one immediately recognizes Beethoven. But more than that, Beethoven's heart was into the composing of this work. In his sketchbooks one finds him thinking out loud,

Wellington's Victory Vittoria, only God save the King, but a great victory overture for Wellington.
......
I must show the English a little what a blessing there is in God Save the King.
......
It is certain that one writes most prettily when one writes for the public, also that one writes rapidly.

The surviving score is in the hand of Beethoven's copyist but it contains numerous corrections in Beethoven hand, following his custom of careful proof-reading. On the first score page one also sees in Beethoven's hand the Italian tempo marking as well as a metronome indication: Allegro con brio 128 [followed by a half-note symbol].

Even though Beethoven knew he was composing a work to be engraved on a machine, he wrote as if he were composing for real players. One sees, for example, the usual 'natural' parts for trumpets and horns, whereas if he were thinking of writing for a machine he could have used chromatic parts for these instruments.

At the end of the score is another page containing Beethoven's sketches for the trumpet fanfares which open the later appearance of this music in the work for orchestra known as *Wellington's Victory*. The presence of this page confirms that after Maelzel failed in his original purpose he gave the score back to Beethoven for use in their next plan. The *Siegessinfonie* for band, by the way, became Part II of the *Wellington's Victory*, now arranged for orchestra.

The origin of this *Victory Symphony* for band is quite interesting. As Beethoven wrote on the front of the score, the composition was commissioned by the court composer in Vienna, Johann Maelzel (1772–1838), a name known to every musician today for his little chronometer for establishing tempi. Maelzel had created a brief period of public interest with his exhibitions of his Panharmonicon, a machine which must have been a cross between a music box and the vastly popular manufacture of nearly life-sized mechanical dolls in Europe. One of these instruments 'performed' several popular overtures, including one by Haydn. This instrument was sent to Boston where it received great attention, one critic exclaiming how wonderful it was to hear 'live' music. Whatever this was, it was lost at sea on the return trip to Vienna. Then there was a machine which performed something called 'The Burning of Moscow' which also blew smoke and snow out at the listeners.

To jump ahead in the story, Maelzel got in trouble with a machine advertised as a mechanical chess player, which in fact had a midget inside. Now he had no choice but to flee Vienna and he went to, of all places, Philadelphia, where he opened a store and lived for several years, enjoying the local interest in his having been a friend of Beethoven. Maelzel took with him a full size mechanical trumpeter[1] which played several concerti and which had shared the program in Vienna with the premiere of Beethoven's *Seventh Symphony*. Maelzel sold this trumpet player to someone in Philadelphia and as of 1877 it was still there and still being exhibited.

After a time Maelzel sailed for Havanna where his health began to fail. He was returning to Philadelphia when he died on board a ship off the coast of South Carolina in 1838.

Returning to the *Siegessinfonie*, it was apparently Maelzel's idea to capitalize on the news of the victory at Vittoria in Spain. Although Napoleon himself was not present, this was the first instance in which troops of Napoleon were defeated and it resulted in a general sense of relief throughout Europe. Beethoven must have been interested, not only because he regularly read newspapers, but because he no doubt clearly recalled trembling in a basement room on Ballgasse in 1805 when Napoleon was sending rockets into downtown Vienna.

One visitor to Maelzel's workroom at this time was the fine composer, and Mendelssohn's teacher, Ignaz Moscheles. He reported that in his conversation with Maelzel that the latter claimed he provided Beethoven with all the subject matter for the composition, including,

> how he should depict the horror of the battle and arrange 'God save the King' with effects of representing the hurrahs of a multitude. Even the unhappy idea of converting the melody of 'God save the King' into a subject of a fugue ... All this I saw in sketches and score, brought by Beethoven to Maelzel's workshop.

Regardless of whose idea it was, one does hear the famous anthem played in which two bars are set for band alone, the next two bars sounding like a great crowd shouting and making noise while the band continues underneath, and so on throughout.

It appears the original idea of Maelzel was to create a large Panharmonicon to perform Beethoven's music and then take it on a tour culminating in a great performance in London. In the end Beethoven wrote a score which demanded so many instruments [forty-four parts] that Maelzel was unable to build a machine large enough to perform it. I think he probably told

---

[1] An account from Philadelphia reads, 'The machinery of the trumpeter is contained within the trunk of the figure, and is worked by a steel spring which drives a revolving barrel, on which are pegs similar to those in a musical box; a bellows just below the neck of the figure furnishes the wind, and a valve with a steel tongue, which is lengthened or shortened by means of levers working on the pegs of the barrel makes the different notes.'

Beethoven that the problem was in raising enough money for the tour for in any case the idea was abandoned. As an alternative, Maelzel talked Beethoven into rewriting the Symphony for orchestra and adding a representation of English and French bands and fanfares as an introduction, thus the birth of the new work, *Wellington's Victory*. Beethoven finished this composition and one performance was given in Vienna, requiring a large number of friends to cover all the parts. Among those helping out was the famous string bass player, Dragonetti, and, of all people, Meyerbeer.

I scored the band version for a full modern band. The final note in the piccolo part probably cannot be played on the modern piccolo, but I wrote it in anyway to be as faithful as possible to Beethoven—whom by 1813 would not have heard it in any case.

The reader can see sample score pages and hear a performance at www.whitwellbooks.com.

Anton Reicha, Commemoration Symphony for Band

> You should come to our place to hear a concert next Tuesday.
> We will play a *quintetto* by Reicha.
>   *Les Employees*, Balzac, 1838

Anton Reicha (1770–1836) was the son of a civic wind player in Prague who died when Anton was ten months old and a mother who offered no encouragement. As a result he ran away to live with his uncle Josef Reicha, who had composed some fine wind ensemble music, and moved with him to Bonn in 1785. There, sitting in the small string section of the court orchestra belonging to the Elector Max, Anton became friends with another fifteen-year-old boy, Ludwig van Beethoven.

When the French armies of Napoleon captured Bonn in 1794 Anton fled to Hamburg, Paris and eventually to Vienna while trying to support himself by composition, teaching and playing. He arrived in Vienna in 1801 and apart from renewing his friendship with Beethoven, who arrived in Vienna in 1792, he did what every other aspiring young composer did upon arrival at this great center of music, he made an acquaintance with Haydn and took some lessons with Salieri and Albrechtsberger. One can imagine how inspired the now 24-year-old young composer was and years later he reflected in his autobiography.

> The number of works I finished in Vienna is astonishing. Once started, my verve and imagination were indefatigable. Ideas came to me so rapidly it was often difficult to set them down without losing some of them. I always had a great penchant for doing the unusual in composition. When writing in an original vein, my creative faculties and spirit seemed keener than when following the precepts of my predecessors.

Once again, in 1805, the armies of Napoleon interrupted his life and so Anton elected to return to try his luck in Paris. Here finally he made his permanent residence and by 1818 he was established as a professor at the conservatory. His students there included Berlioz, Liszt, Gounod, Chopin and Cesar Franck. He became a naturalized citizen in 1829, won a *Legion d'honneur* in 1835 and achieved the peak of Parisian recognition by being elected a member of the *Academie francaise*.

Before turning to the music of Reicha, I should like to quote a little-known and lengthy eulogy of him written by Berlioz and published in the *Journal des Débats*, 3 July 1836, the most important newspaper in Paris.

> The death of Reicha … could hardly be foreseen. Although he had already arrived at his sixty-sixth year, he had conserved a robust health, a juvenile vigor that an existence consecrated to tranquil works could not alter, totally exempt of the ambition and cares that even the most just brings in his wake. Of a naturally cold temperament, and given to observation rather than to action, Reicha quickly had recognized that the difficulties,

chagrins, disappointments of all kinds that the composer must necessarily encounter at each step, above all in France, before arriving at the exhibition of his works, were too great in number for the perseverance with which he felt himself gifted. Making his choice philosophically, he determined, therefore, early on, to profit by the occasion when it was presented, but not to lose his time nor his labor to cause it to happen, and above all never to be painfully attached to its pursuit. He wrote tranquilly what he pleased, accumulated work on top of work, masses, oratorios, quartets, quintets, piano fugues, symphonies, operas, treatises; causing some to be heard when his resources permitted; trusting to his star for the fate of the rest, and always tranquil in his pace, deaf to the voice of criticism, very little sensitive to praise …

He attached great value to his knowledge of mathematics. 'It is to this study,' he said to us one day during one of his lessons, 'that I owe having been able to succeed in making myself completely the master of my ideas; it tamed and cooled my imagination that earlier dragged me about madly, and by subjecting it to reason and to reflection, it doubled its strengths.' I do not know if this idea of Reicha is as correct as he believed and if his imagination gained much by this study of the exact sciences; perhaps the love of abstract combinations and mental games in music, the real charm that he found in solving certain thorny propositions which only served to make him deviate from his straight road by making him lose sight of the result for which he was continually reaching; to the contrary, did they damage a good deal of the success of his work, and did they make them lose something in melodic or harmonic expression, in purely musical effect, what they gained (if to be sure, it was gaining) in arduous combinations, in conquered difficulties, in curious works made rather for the eye than for the ear? However that may be, his first attempts that he had performed at Bonn received the most encouraging reception. Dating from that moment he abandoned himself more specially to the study of composition, with his colleague and childhood friend Beethoven. Still, the intimacy does not seem to have lasted long between the two great musicians, and probably the complete divergence of their ideas on certain important points of the art's poetics, must have been the cause. What makes me think so is that I often have heard Reicha express himself quite coldly regarding Beethoven's works, and to speak with a badly disguised irony about the enthusiasm which these created …

The desire to perfect his art and to profit by the counsel of J. Haydn caused Reicha to make the resolution of spending some years in Vienna near that great artist. Upon his arrival in Austria, towards the end of 1802, Reicha received, from Prince Louis-Ferdinand of Prussia, an amateur as zealous as he was distinguished, the same who perished some years later in the Battle of Jena, a flattering letter in which the Prince made the most brilliant offers to Reicha to entice him to come stay with him, and to teach him counterpoint. But Reicha preferred to sacrifice all these advantages to the one more precious to him, the society of Haydn …

From 1809 he accepted a professorial chair, and, in the doubly difficult art of teaching music, which is, at one and the same time, both an art and a science, he proved to be so superior that to fill his shoes seems to us today, if not impossible, at least terribly difficult. The most famous among his disciples, the one whose name, by its very celebrity, came the least naturally under my pen when I was speaking of students, is our great instrumental composer, an author besides of two dramatic compositions, where beauties of the first order shine forth, M. Georges Onslow. It is to be noted that, despite the apparent severity of Reicha's precepts, none of the living professors has been more prompt than he to recognize an innovation, even if contrary to all admitted rules, if a happy effect resulted from it, and he saw there the germ of progress. In considering how tight the diapers still are in which they would like, in the schools, to keep musical art, one must confess that this merit reveals, in one so gifted, a great honesty of talent and a reasoning ability of the highest order.

The 24 Woodwind Quintets

The well-known woodwind quintets were composed by Reicha between 1811 and 1820 for five professors at the conservatory, Joseph Guilou, flute; Gustave Vogt, oboe; Jacques Bouffil, clarinet; Louis Dauprat, horn and Antoine Henry, bassoon. Perhaps because such virtuoso wind playing was yet new to Paris, the concerts which featured these works became very popular in Paris and the mention of them by Balzac in one of his novels, given above, as 'local color' is a reflection of this. An encyclopedia of music by John Sainsbury published in 1825 gives an early review of these works, including a curious substitution of the English horn for the oboe.

> Reicha's skill has been shown in a variety of compositions, but especially in some admirable quintets, composed expressly for the flute, clarinet, cor Anglois, French horn and bassoon; these are performed frequently at *L'Ecole des Fils d'Apollon*, and, indeed, on all occasions when first-rate performers on the appropriate instruments assemble together.
>
> No description, no imagination, can do justice to these compositions. The effect produced by the extraordinary combinations of apparently opposite-toned instruments, added to Reicha's vigorous style of writing and judicious scoring, have rendered these quintets the admiration of the musical world.

Here we also find a rare contemporary portrait of Reicha,

> Reicha is still in the vigor of life, of middle stature, and most urbane manners, his general courtesy greatly endearing him to strangers, to whom he is uniformly obliging. He has often expressed to this writer his wish to write an oratorio for the English in the style of their favorite Handel.
>
> In private life he is cheerful and amiable; his favorite amusement is a game of tric-trac. His rooms are decorated with a profusion of elegant and curious articles, which have been presented to him by numerous individuals in public and private life, as testimonies of friendship and of the respect and admiration due to his genius and perseverance.

Ludwig Spohr also mentions in his autobiography hearing a rehearsal of these quintets while he was in Paris.

> Two days ago I heard two more quite new quintets of Reicha, which he wrote for the morning-concerts … They were played at a rehearsal, which appears to me to have been given solely for the purpose of fishing for more subscribers to the morning-concerts, among the numerous persons who were invited … It is sad to see what means artists here are obliged to resort to, in order to procure support for their undertakings. While the Parisians press eagerly forward to every sensual enjoyment, they must be almost dragged to intellectual ones …
>
> I found the composition of these two new quintets, like those I had previously heard at Kreutzer's, rich in interesting sequences of harmony, correct throughout in the management of the voices and full of effect in the use made of the tone and character of the different wind instruments, but on the other hand, frequently defective in the form. Mr. Reicha is not economical enough of his ideas, and at the very commencement of his pieces he frequently gives from four to five themes, each of which concludes in the tonic. Were he less rich, he would be richer. His formal sections also are frequently badly connected and sound as though he had written one yesterday and the other today. Yet the minuets and scherzo, as short pieces, are less open to this objection, and some of them are real masterpieces in form and content. A German soundness of science and capacity are the greatest ornaments of this master.

The Symphony for Band

I have never found, even in my days as a player, the famous quintets to be a moving experience for the listener. They have always seemed to me to have been intended as something fun to play, something to challenge the technical skill of the players. And yet they are major works, as long in duration as regular symphonies of that period, so he must have put some effort into composing them. Certainly, judging from his comments in his autobiography, his own aesthetic aims cannot be questioned.

> I have never been interested in writing for the popular demand. To enlighten the public has been my aim; not to amuse it ... Many of my works have never been heard because of my aversion to seeking performances ... I counted the time spent in such efforts as lost, and preferred to remain at my desk.
>
> I have become indifferent to all praise and criticism, being sufficiently rewarded when I instinctively feel I have achieved something worthwhile. If a good work is a failure, it is not the composer's fault, but the public's. It often happens that today a work is damned, tomorrow it is acclaimed. Was it not so with the works of Mozart? At first they were not understood, they were bitterly criticized, publishers refused them. But all of this has not prevented Mozart from reaching immortality.

We also noticed the following comment in his autobiography mentioning his unknown compositions, among which we assume the symphony for band to be.

> It is impossible to discuss my complete works here. More than a hundred have been published; about sixty are still in manuscript. Among the latter will be found my finest efforts.

In 1815 Anton Reicha, while living in Paris, produced an extraordinary *Symphony* for wind band, with optional possibilities for expanding the work to include two or more additional bands in *concertato* fashion. In his Foreword he says the music was composed for when there is a need to commemorate great men, great exploits, funerals of heroes and great men or to celebrate any important future event. This statement does not sound as if the Symphony were commissioned by a third party. Further comments in the Foreword speak of military associations and outdoor performance. Most likely his intent was to have music ready which might be used in one of the famous Parisian festivals which had been so popular with the public during the Revolution and continued on an irregular basis. The actual title in his own handwriting reads, *Music to Celebrate the Memory of Great Men and Great Events*.

I have read the view that the *Commemoration Symphony* was composed for use in the ceremonies associated with the reburial of Louis XVI and Marie Antoinette in 1815. That seems a distinct possibility, although I have found nothing in the national library in Paris which documents this and the autograph score itself appears to me to have never been used, as the paper is unused and without markings, finger prints and smudges, etc. Further more, the Foreword, in Reicha's own hand, discusses the purpose in writing this Symphony and nothing in his discussion in any way refers to the ceremony of the reburial of Louis XVI. But, even so, some part of this score may have been copied out and used as well on that occasion.

The major work performed at this ceremony for Louis XVI in Notre Dame was another band work, the great *Requiem for Louis XVI and Marie Antoinette* by Charles Bochsa, a work of some fifteen movements.[1] The *Requiem* by Bochsa contains really lovely music throughout and because it begins with a *Marche funebre* and concludes with a *recitative* and *Apotheose* I have always believed it to be a model for the Berlioz *Symphony for Band*. I should also point out that the first movements of both the Reicha and the Bochsa have a clear musical reference to the most famous funeral march of the French Revolution by Gossec.

The autograph score for the *Symphony for Band*, a work which is musically extraordinary in many ways, is even more remarkable for a very lengthy Foreword in Reicha's own handwriting in two languages, French and Gothic German.

> This work is composed to commemorate: 1st, the memory of great exploits; 2nd, the death of heros and great men; 3rd, to celebrate any important future event.
>
> The performance of this work must be assigned to a good conductor only, one who would be well advised to study the work thoroughly before having it performed.
>
> The place selected for the performance must be large and open (uncovered) and the orchestra must be at a distance of 50 steps from the audience.
>
> One must employ exactly the number of instruments indicated in the score for without them the piece will not produce a good effect. These instruments are: 3 piccolos, 6 oboes, 6 clarinets, 6 horns, 6 bassoons, 6 trumpets, 3 double-basses, 6 army drums and 4 small field-guns.
>
> The musicians must not be too close to each other, so that the sound gets more widely spread.
>
> The double-basses must not be replaced by other instruments as they are absolutely necessary (no other instrument can go so low), neither must the above mentioned number of instruments be increased, unless one more double basse or double bassoons are added.
>
> The drums must be located at about 100 steps behind the orchestra and there must be only 3 drums beating at a time in order to be able to take turns. The beating of the drums must be a muffled rolling, even when the orchestra is playing forte.
>
> The conductor must make sure that the drums are exactly starting and finishing in accordance with the time.
>
> It is advisable not to display the field-guns to the sight of the audience, in order to get more of an effect of surprise.
>
> The Marche funebre is repeated 3 times, the first time without drums or field-guns; the second time with drums but not field-guns; the third time with both drums and field-guns. It could also be considered to have one or two infantry regiments maneuvering, if there is enough room, in accordance with the march.

---

[1] A copy of the score and parts of this work can be found in the Whitwell Archiv at the Bundesakademie fur musik in Trossingen, Germany. Bochsa, then a highly respected composer in Paris got into trouble by developing a side income creating and selling phony autograph documents—autograph letters of Jesus, etc. He fled France, literally one step ahead of the police. Going to England with only the clothes on his back he managed in a brief period of time to work his way back up in society, becoming a director of the Academy of Music in London. Then, unfortunately, he got in trouble, some sort of swindle together with a nun, and had to flee again. Now he sailed to America, made his way to the west coast where he gave a concert in San Francisco and then on to Australia where he died, but not before composing a Requiem for himself. This is the same Charles Bochsa who made historic developments in the construction of the harp and wrote educational studies for the harp which are in the possession of every harpist today.

I can think of no specific ensemble composition before 1815 with such extensive notes regarding its performance, but then there were no earlier wind works of this scale. The first and most striking thing one finds here is the discussion of acoustics, especially his emphasis on the space between the individual players. I, too, believe that wind instruments need more space between players than string instruments in order for the tone to somehow come together before it leaves the stage. Reicha returns to this topic in his treatise on harmony and melody (Paris, 1824) where he wishes there were a means of measuring the exact amount of air actually set in motion by a tone. Such a measuring instrument, he believed, would allow a composer to determine how many musicians are necessary to fill a particular hall with sound and how far from the audience the musicians should be.

The other remarkable aspect of this Foreword is the attention given to the instrumentation. Before considering his discussion I need to first give the reader a description of the score itself. First of all, the score is a copy, a so-called 'Presentation Score,' one very carefully prepared for posterity, with careful script writing and with the musical notation perfectly aligned, etc. It is basically a score for *one* band and it is clear, visually and musically, that the work could be played by one band. The music for the possible addition of two additional bands is given in what in effect is a footnote. This music is condensed into three staves at the beginning but later this extra instrumentation is expressed in a numeric 'code.' In his Foreword Reicha also explains this code, as in the following example.

> In the lines for horns and trumpets, the digit '2' means that only 2 principal instruments must play, in other words the first of the 3 primo and the first of the 3 secondo. However in lines 8, 9, and 10 the digit '2' means that only the 2 primo ripieno must play.

When one writes all this out in the form of a full score, the result is music for one band with two additional bands entering and exiting for emphasis much like the concertato principle in the Baroque concerto. Indeed, Reicha's use of the word 'ripieno' in the above example, is precisely what these expanded parts would have been called in a Baroque concerto.

In his Foreword Reicha is clearly concerned that only the instruments in the score be used and, in view of his careful comments about acoustics, it seems clear that what he was concerned about was the instrumental color. In other words, when he says '2 clarinets' he means two *parts* played on the clarinet instrument, not two players. This is why in his Foreword he begins the instrumentation discussion by writing, 'One must employ exactly the number of instruments indicated in the score.' He does not say, 'the number of players are …' I make a point of this distinction because taken as a list of instruments this instrumentation represents a typical French infantry band of this period, with the exception of trombones. In the tradition of the military in the early nineteenth century these parts could be doubled, and frequently were in the case of the clarinets. The important conclusion, therefore, is that this is not a chamber work. It is a work for band.

The one exception which Reicha allows in his Foreword is his approval for the substitution of contrabassoons for the string bass if additional support is needed. This music was composed at a time when there was no adequate solution for the bass part in a wind band. One would expect at this time in a French work, especially if it were intended for use in a cathedral, the serpent. We may reasonably assume that Reicha's choice of the string bass was an aesthetic one, that is, he probably found the serpent sound unacceptable. This wind bass problem would remained unsolved until the invention of the modern tuba in 1835.

One will also notice that Reicha calls for a specific kind of small cannon and requires four of them. In the score these are numbered 1, 2, 3 and 4 in order for the composer to notate precisely when each particular cannon is heard. The effect he gets is an aleatoric one, as would be the case in a military environment, and not one in which they are heard in order. Since four cannons are rather impractical in a modern concert hall I have always used four single timpani, one placed in each of the four corners of the hall so that the listener hears them on all sides. This has proved tremendously effective.[2]

The first time I performed this work I used one player on a part with three full ensembles, which required three contrabassoons. The result lacked 'body' in the woodwinds as the modern brass and percussion rather overwhelmed them.

The next time I performed this work I tried to represent the original score in the center of the ensemble and used the non-French infantry modern instruments sitting on the sides and performing the 'ripieno' parts of the implied second and third bands. This idea failed utterly as the change in instrumental color as the secondary band entered and exited gave a total sound which was too far removed from 1815.

The third time I performed this Symphony I used the version now obtainable on my website (www.whitwellbooks.com). This time I concentrated on the fact that this work is basically a Symphony for band. I scored it for one modern band, so all the students could have the experience of hearing this remarkable music. The 'ripieno' parts I simply left out as they only double and that doubling cannot be fully appreciated by the audience unless the stage is of such a size as to allow real physical separation between all three ensembles. This final revision, in my judgment, is faithful to the style and the wonderful musicianship of Reicha in this composition is preserved.

There is a final question regarding this 'Presentation' score and that regards the movement called the *Marche funebre*. One writer has suggested that this movement is not part of the *Symphony* on the basis that it is the only movement with a separate title and the instrumentation is slightly different as it lacks flute or piccolo parts. Also Reicha mentions this movement apart from the rest when he comments in his autobiography,

> It was principally for the army that I composed this marche funèbre, which may be performed alone.

---

[2] This was the same time the famous Russian horn bands were touring in Europe, ensembles consisting of wooden 'trumpets' in varying sizes and in which each player played only a single pitch. Once in St. Petersburg the Kappellmeister, Sarti, was ordered to prepare a very large ensemble of these instruments and found that his court carpenters could not create a large enough instrument to produce several bass pitches. So the enterprising Sarti looked around until he found cannons which produced the required pitches.

On the other hand, Reicha in his own handwriting discusses this movement together with the other movements of the Symphony in the Foreword and it shares the four cannons with the last movement. In the presentation score as it stands, it clearly appears to be part of the Symphony, but it is possible that in giving the Symphony out to a copyist to prepare the presentation copy of the symphony Riecha may have just included this separate work as a means of preserving it. This might also explain why it is found in the score as the last of the four movements.

In the end, it is for the conductor to decide if this movement is to be performed as part of the symphony. The problem for me is the fact that this *Marche funebre* is very beautiful and I could never leave it out. In my modern edition I make it the third movement as it seems to musically follow the beautiful slow movement and because the *Poco presto* movement ends in such a powerful fashion that the *Marche funebre* would seem anti-climatic as a final movement.

The Commemoration Symphony for Band [duration ca. 20 minutes]

Adagio–Allegro
Adagio
Maestoso un poco adagio
Poco Presto

Adagio–Allegro. The first movement begins with great whole-note chords over rolling percussion followed each time by soft, mournful and even painful melodic fragments. The lengthy Allegro section contains much material, some imitative, some very lyrical together with *forte* cadences consisting of syncopated half-notes which will remind the listener of the first movement of Beethoven's *Third Symphony*. Both the Adagio and Allegro are written out in an extended repeat. Even this single movement taken by itself stands as the most powerful and exciting band work to this date in history.

Adagio. The second movement is a very beautiful theme and variations. The theme is very sad and perhaps nostalgic in character and some of the variations are challenging for the woodwinds. The first variation is strangely broken up, with soft rolling in the snare drum, with no snares, running continuously underneath. This is the side drum part which Reicha asks to be played behind the audience. This movement looks difficult but I have always been surprised that the woodwinds seem to play it with no difficulty.

Marche funebre, Maestoso un poco adagio. This Marche funebre has always seemed to me to have a kind of Handel quality, homophonic, noble and uplifting. It is a brief movement and at the end includes the cannons playing as members of chords, not as independent effects.

Poco Presto. The fourth movement is a movement of considerable length, but in the character of a fast dance style in the meter of $\frac{2}{4}$. It is lyrical, interesting and powerful.

The Reicha *Symphony for Band* can be heard, and sample score pages seen, at the website www.whitwellbooks.com.

The Reicha Symphony is an interesting composition. Your instrumentation sounds fine and is useful for the modern band.

>Wolfgang Suppan, May 2, 1987
>Graz, Austria
>Hochsuchule für Musik

The Reicha Symphony is a great work and it sounds like you have done a fine job with the arrangement for modern band. I shall purchase it as soon as I get a new budget in January.

>Leon Bly, Sept. 29, 1991
>Stuttgart, Germany
>Stuttgart School of Music

This is the first large-scale instrumental composition in the history of the band. There were some large works for band and chorus during the French Revolution, but the Revolutionary symphonies for band are musically insignificant and cannot be compared in any way with the Reicha. The style is of the period of Mozart through early Beethoven which makes it important in programming as the large band works which follow this one are distinctly Romantic in style. I recommend the composition very highly.

Hector Berlioz, Symphony for Band

When one requests to see the 'autograph' score of the great *Symphony for Band* by Berlioz in the National Library of France in Paris, what one encounters is a 'presentation score,' that is, a clean copy in the hand of his copyist, Rocquemont, with the exception of the first six pages which are in the hand of Berlioz.[1] There are no corners dirty from conductor's turning the pages, no pencil markings made by conductors and in general no evidence that this score was ever used for a performance.

On the other hand, one immediately notices that the cover, which is entirely in the hand of Berlioz, is quite different. It is dirty, torn and bent and has been attached with tape to the presentation score. Judging by this cover, it was torn from an earlier score which *was* used in performance. We wish we could see the previous score.[2]

The fact is, as is the case with other of his compositions, Berlioz seems to have made changes and corrections over a long period. We suspect, for example, that the torn and dirty cover now taped to the 'autograph score' currently in Paris was originally part of an earlier score which he took on his six-month tour of Germany in 1843, hence its much used appearance. Even assuming the copy in Paris today was made to replace, and perhaps make corrections in, the 'travel' version, nevertheless this 'final score' in Paris also has some additional changes, in red ink, made after it was completed. Not only that, but the sudden reappearance of the hand writing of Berlioz on page 71 and on pages 106 and 107 indicates that he was *still* composing as this 'final' copyist score was in progress. What was he doing?

One of these brand new passages includes the extraordinary abrupt shift (it can hardly be called a modulation) from B♭ to A major. This passage contains a reference to the 'Dresden Amen,' which we believe is a tribute to his friendly association with Mendelssohn during the German tour and the latter's *Reformation Symphony* which uses this cadence extensively. It is a most heart-lifting and thrilling four bars.[3] The other passage in the hand of Berlioz in this 'final' score is a strengthened final cadence. Here, while waiting for Berlioz to supply his latest changes, we can see the bored copyist was filling the margins of the score paper with doodles.

---

[1] Even the portion in Berlioz' hand is also a copy as can be seen by the alignment, etc. Another indication of this score not being truly an original autograph score is the fact it has no original page numbers. Some random pages do have numerical figures which have no relationship to the order of pages in this score.

[2] Berlioz, in letters of 1844, 1845 and 1851, as well as the printed schedule of the Exposition de l'Industrie concert of August 1844, contain information on numbers of players needed. No such information by Berlioz is this specific regarding the very first version.

[3] Mendelssohn and Berlioz did not get along well when they first met in Rome as young men. Subsequent letters before Berlioz' arrival in Leipzig on his tour make it clear that both men were nervous about this reunion. However they got along in splendid fashion, Berlioz mentioning that Mendelssohn treated him 'like a brother' during the month they were together in Leipzig.

The publication of this 'final' score by Schlesinger in the Fall of 1843 includes even more changes, though minor. And finally, the composer's famous treatise on instrumentation was published in December 1843, and it contains a quotation of this symphony. The manuscript for the treatise[4] contains autograph corrections on nearly every page and the subsequent published form has still further changes!

With this many changes made *after* the 'final' version was set on paper, one wonders how many changes were made earlier. Unfortunately all earlier scores were apparently destroyed, but from a variety of sources one does find a few clues which shed light on the earlier forms of this symphony. Since we began with the final version, we will proceed to consider the earlier forms of the score in reverse chronological order.

The most important change in the symphony before the German tour was the addition of the fifty-three bar choral part for the end of the third movement, which was done sometime before a performance of this version in Brussels in September 1842. We have one important clue regarding what the third movement was like before the addition of the choral finale, and this is found in a letter of 1840 by the famous French composer, Adolphe Adam. He reported that the entire third movement was constructed in four-bar phrases. Yet in the version we know today, one finds in the middle of this movement a long section of three-bar phrases, the character of which is a long vamp. I had always assumed the purpose of this section was merely to build momentum. Recently, however, I did a performance of this symphony in Germany in a hall in which the stage did not allow enough room for chairs for a large chorus. That posed a problem as I did not want the chorus to stand for the entire symphony just to sing a few bars at the end. The second and third movements are connected, so they can't just enter before the movement they sing. As I was walking around this German town thinking about this problem one day, it suddenly dawned on me that perhaps Berlioz had the same problem (early concert halls being smaller by today's standard), and that perhaps he added the long vamp for the purpose of marching in the chorus. I tried it and it was just enough time to bring in a large chorus (in two lines) and furthermore it was most dramatic from the audience perspective to have the chorus passing among them in the middle of the movement. By the way, the choral part was added by Berlioz himself to his pre-existent music, resulting in some places in more French than can easily be sung. It is much easier to sing in a modern translation in English.

The pre-choral score seen by Adam may be the same as the version of February 1842, in which the composer added for the first time the optional string parts. We are assuming the first version with strings was similar to the string writing in the 'final' version now in Paris. It may have been quite different, however, for we find that in a performance on 7 November 1842, Berlioz conducted the choir and band on stage and Habeneck conducted the strings in the pit. Indeed he advertised at this time that this was a symphony 'for two orchestra.'

---

4   Now in the Bibliotheque de Grenoble.

Perhaps an additional suggestion that the original version of the score with strings may possibly have been different from the string writing in the version we know is a letter to his sister, dated 5 February 1842, in which he mentions that he has 'just rescored (*que je viens de reinstrumenter*) the third movement,' a phrase which seems to go beyond merely the adding of doubling strings.

And before this version there is yet another which stands after the original, first form and before the one with strings. This intermediate version is mentioned by Berlioz in his autobiography in which he writes of making, 'my usual corrections and retouching' after the first version, but before the addition of string and choral parts. This version of the symphony was performed on 7 and 14 August and 1 November 1840 and one of the August performances was heard by Richard Wagner and prompted his famous observation that it was only this symphony for band which finally convinced him of the genius of Berlioz. We also know that the symphony originally had a different name from the one we know today, *Symphonie Militaire*. The second movement also had a different title, *Hymne d'Adieu*.

Well, what do we know of the very first version of this symphony? As is well-known, some form of this music was used at the first outdoor performance as the military performers marched to the performance site. But surely this early street version was different from the music we know today. Certainly the first movement, *Marche funèbre*, in the form we know today contains music which stylistically seems out of place as music to be performed while marching down the street.[5] We are thinking, for example, of the cries of terror in the unison woodwinds punctuated by the canon-like sounds of the great bass drum and timpani beginning in measure [240] and the soft, haunting trombone melody of the transition section in the recapitulation.

Indeed, there are again some clues that at least the street version was much simplified. In fact, Berlioz, in his autobiography, says exactly this, 'I thought that the simplest plan would be best for such a work.'[6]

Additional significant clues pointing to an original street score being very different from the version we know today are found in the testimony by two distinguished scholars, Prod'homme[7] and Pohl,[8] who had the opportunity to examine early materials which no longer exist. First, they both agree that the original instrumentation was quite different from the (indoor) version we know today, in particular being very heavy in percussion. Even more significant are the keys of the original natural horns given by Pohl. The natural horns in E♭, G and D would be appropriate for the second and third movement we know today. However, they would be impossible for the current first movement, which is in F minor. The implication of this is that the original first movement was probably in G minor, the alternative being that the horn players would have to walk down the street carrying five crooks on their arm.

---

5   The simplified version of the great forte unison trombone utterance of the first movement exists in some later scores and may reflect a special simplified form for use in the street.

6   *Memoirs of Hector Berlioz* (New York: Dover, 1966), 232.

7   J. G. Prod'homme, *Hector Berlioz* (Paris, 1927), 138.

8   Louise Pohl, *Hector Berlioz' Leben und Werke* (Leipzig, 1900), 140.

All things considered, not to mention simple logic, the available information suggests the first movement originally played by military musicians marching down the street was quite different from the first movement we know today.

This brings us to a tradition which, we believe, has caused many conductors to fail to appreciate this masterpiece. The first recording, decades ago, was made by a French conductor whose career was in the fields of military and popular music. He, no doubt taking the first movement title, *Marche funèbre*, literally, performed the first movement in his recording at a *very* slow pace as would be characteristic for a dirge. The resultant problem is that the melodic material of the first movement, consisting of long note values, taken together with a very slow tempo results in a performance which is tedious and boring.

I had a conversation with this French conductor in 1991, at a time when we were both working on an engagement in Italy, and, among other things, I found he appeared to have no knowledge of the original band works of Saint-Saëns, who is a very big composer in France. He said, for example, that he was unaware of the *Occident et Orient*. I asked him specifically if he had looked at the autograph score of the Berlioz Symphony and he said no. This is regrettable, for if he had, he would have seen that the first movement contains a metronome marking of quarter = 72, some twenty percent faster than his performance. Had he performed the movement at that tempo, the modern performance history of this masterpiece might have been quite different.

There is no evidence that Berlioz ever had in mind a slow, dirge-like tempo. For one thing, Berlioz tells us, in a letter to his father, that in the street performance, during which he conducted 210 military band musicians while walking backwards, that they performed not only the first movement six times but also the third movement six times. Well, if one imagines the soldiers marching at a funeral procession pace of 60 quarter-notes per minute or slower as characteristic of a dirge, then the third movement becomes musically impossible. And, conversely, one cannot imagine a circumstance in which the 210 walking musicians changed the speed of their walk eleven times during the procession in order to accommodate the differing tempo needs of the two movements.

A common tempo at which both movements might be walked and played while maintaining some musical logic for both might be one of about 72 quarter-notes per minute. Curiously, this is exactly what is written in the autograph score. Berlioz wrote in ink, at the beginning of the first movement in the surviving 'final' score, 'due Metr: de Maelzel.' But he did not originally notate in ink a number following this. What follows is 72, written in pencil, which may represent his adding this after some additional reflection. Scholars do not agree whether the 72 is in Berlioz' hand, but even if it is not one can still suppose it was added by someone familiar with the tempi used in performances which Berlioz conducted, for this particular score does not appear to have ever been used in later performances.

The significance of this metronome marking of 72 becomes more interesting because of another metronome marking, also indicating 72, and which *is* in the hand of Berlioz, in the second movement. In the second movement he gives 72 as the tempo associated with an *Andantino poco lento e sostenuto*. The first movement, where the tempo of 72 appears, carries the

Italian words, *Moderato un poco lento*. Leaving aside the fact that our modern metronome gives the 'Moderato' range as being 108–120 beats per minute (!), normally one *would* expect a general Moderato range to be somewhat faster than that of an Andantino. Did Berlioz originally have in mind an even faster tempo for the final indoor version of the first movement? Or did he perhaps consider that the limiting language following the Moderato, '*un poco lento*,' would bring the tempo down to something similar to the quarter-note = 72 of the Andantino in the second movement?

No matter how one analyzes this language, with accompanying tempo numbers, one fact remains very clear and that is that Berlioz never intended the final version of the first movement to be played slower than a metronome marking of quarter-note = 72. This will be perfectly clear to the modern conductor if he only proceeds as he always should, letting the melody itself determine the tempo, and dismisses from his mind any extra-musical thoughts of an actual funeral procession. This is all the more important because the music we perform today is clearly not the same music played in the streets of Paris in 1840.

Notes on Performance Practice

There are two fundamental challenges for the conductor in the first movement. First, since the melodies are written in long note values the basic themes have the potential to have a loss of momentum. But this is easily and immediately resolved by having the players add the dynamic markings which Berlioz assumed they would, that is crescendo in the first bar and a diminuendo in the second bar. This, together with the countermelody which should have crescendo and diminuendo in the opposite directions, since it begins a bar later, immediately gives the music a sense of surging momentum. This adding of crescendo and diminuendo should be continued throughout the movement as they are so characteristic of the melodic material itself. I find that fine players do this almost instinctively at the softer levels but often forget to continue to do this at the louder levels.

An important variant of this melodic principal is found at rehearsal letter F. Here the four-note figure in the woodwinds should be heard as a cry, thus each figure should begin with perhaps a *mf* volume followed by a diminuendo.

The other difficulty is the repetitive rhythm underneath the music. The trouble comes if the conductor follows the current tendency to elongate all wind pitches, which I call 'Brahmsifying,' a style inappropriate before the last quarter of the nineteenth century. Earlier, in both wind and string tradition, individual notes unattached by slurs were played shorter than the written version. If one has the students play these quarter-notes full value this line becomes very sluggish and tends to slow down. Playing as a light staccato prevents this. Equally important is playing a late sixteenth-note in the dotted figure, an early sixteenth-note again tends to make the figure dull and too heavy.

At rehearsal letter G the woodwind melodic lines again need much melodic shaping with crescendi and diminuendi. I find the accompaniment flute triplets sound better if they are played tutti, but very soft.

I believe a ritard. needs to begin two bars before rehearsal letter H, with H being *meno mosso*. The shock of rehearsal letter J should be accompanied by an *a tempo*.

Six bars after rehearsal letter R I begin slowing things up to prepare for one of the most dramatic moments composed by Berlioz, a man given to dramatic moments. At rehearsal letter S the woodwinds are clearly intended to be a great cry, with the cannons of war in the percussion each place where a *forte* is notated. When the bass drum and timpani join, as additional cannons, a mallet producing a sharp attack, like the report of a cannon, is needed.

Rehearsal letter T should be maestoso and give the listeners the impression that this is the end. But it is not, as the harmony in the sixth bar soon announces. The real final cadence is very powerful, but is followed by three soft notes. I have never felt confident that I understood what Berlioz was thinking here. It could be some Latin formula from the church, or it could be that he wanted the effect of the sound drifting off into space almost as if it were an echo. One thing is certain, if there is any volume to these three notes they will give the impression that the music is to continue.

One initial warning about the second movement, an accompanied trombone solo. Every trombonist looks at his part at home and concludes that it is so easy it requires no practice. The fact is, it is very difficult, requiring enormous stamina and I have seen many very fine players embarrass themselves in rehearsal.

The great cathedral bells, in character if not in pitch, which begin the second movement should be in the character of a recitative determined by the feelings of the conductor and not a matter of strict time. The sixteenth-note figure before the long tones should be played as one would if it were notated an eighth-note. This is a problem of notation and we can be sure Berlioz did not want a small note crushed into the great bell sound. I personally believe that this is an echo of the ancient association between music and dance. It has been my experience that no matter how this little note is notated and no matter what the tempo of the music, that it probably reflects the stamping feet of the dancer. If one lifts the left leg, puts it down rapidly while lifting and lowering the right leg, there is a natural interval in time in the subsequent sound. So, if one played the first two sounds crushed together, it would feel as awkward as trying to stamp the feet so fast that one falls off balance. And to perform the figure with a long pompous first note would be as awkward and a very slow lifting of the left leg before beginning move.

For the Andantino after rehearsal letter B it is important to remember that in earlier times the Andantino was a faster tempo than Andante, not a slower one. It is important that this music not drag.

At rehearsal letter E the solo trombone part can be left out for eight bars, to allow a much needed opportunity for the soloist to allow some blood to flow back to his lips. The soloist will always tell you, 'that's OK, I don't need to rest,' but in the concert he will.

In the final movement the basic march tempo which begins at the double bar is notated to be 'half-note music' and not 'quarter-note music.' The music will not take flight if the conductor conducts in four. However, there is a musically 'built-in' ritard. which begins four bars before rehearsal letter A, which is then slower and in four. The tempo at rehearsal letter A should be the tempo the conductor feels is correct for the music at rehearsal letter B.

Rehearsal letter E is a return to the alla breve style at the beginning of the movement. Rehearsal letter H is the music Berlioz added in order to bring in the chorus. For a performance with no chorus, the use of crescendo and diminuendo shaping of the three-bar figure helps develop momentum for what is otherwise a vamp.

I conduct alla breve at rehearsal letter M, with an allargando five bars before rehearsal letter N, where it is again alla breve. As at the beginning of the movement there is an allargando before rehearsal letter O, which is maestoso and in four. The third bar after rehearsal letter P is the quotation of the 'Dresden Amen.'

I consider it impossible to program anything after this composition.

Nineteenth-Century Italian Sinfonias for Band

The fact is we write a thing differently from the way in which we play it.
    François Couperin (1668–1733)

What Couperin means in the above statement is that what is on paper is not the music. What is on paper is only a symbol, a representative of the real thing and every fine musician understands that the goal is not to reproduce what is on paper but to perform the original ideas behind those symbols. But this is a very difficult concept for young musicians and conductors to act upon because we are trained in exactly the opposite philosophy.

A great many private teachers teach the student to perform what is on the page—exactly what is on the page. They do not ask the young student to speculate on what the composer was thinking. Then this method of teaching is given the highest official sanction when the student and his band attend a band contest. There, to do anything at all which is not on the page is a punishable offence. These kinds of private teachers are really teaching only the grammar of music and the contests give awards for good grammar, not for good music making.

The instruction for young conductors is very much the same. The emphasis is on the grammar and the distinguishing of the grammar with Roman numerals. This was exactly what Couperin had in mind, in another place, when he observed,

> Just as there is a difference between grammar and oration, so there is an infinitely greater one between music theory and the art of fine playing.

In the case of band repertoire, the young conductor then faces a contemporary literature in which the composer is fearful of trusting the conductor and thus fills the staves, and the space above and below them, with as many instructions as there is room to write. All the conductor has to do is what he has been trained to do—play what is on the page. But are the listeners moved?

Recently my wife and I attended a recital of compositions by Schubert, performed by Emmanuel Ax. It was a wonderful performance. In particular Mr. Ax gave a beautiful demonstration of the reality that in music Time consists only of the internal relationships of music traveling live through space, unrelated to the arithmetic symbols of time printed on the page. He, for example, made the most elegant and subtle rubato in cadences, allowing them the logic which the ear wants, and not the correctness the eye demands. He did a lot of things which were not on paper! *But here is the point*: while what he did was not on paper, it *was* in the *music*. It was the music itself which taught him what to do.

This caused me to reflect, after the concert, on the fact that today's band repertoire does not contain much sensitive music capable of teaching these things to the conductor and allowing him to grow as a musician from the experience of performing that repertoire. It is one of the primary reasons that, during my days as a full-time conductor, I used to program much pre-twentieth century music. Before the twentieth century the composer had trust in the performer and believed the ear of the performer would tell what was needed, sparing the time of the composer for writing small details of the music itself. For example, in the second movement of the Schubert great C Major Symphony there is a place in the score where one finds an *a tempo*, but nowhere before this is found the word ritard. Schubert assumed the performers would hear the ritard. in the music itself and he was only concerned with clarifying where the original tempo resumed. Thus, in this case, the burden falls on the ear of the conductor. He must, using only his ear, determine where the ritard. begins, and how much ritard. is appropriate, and in the process of finding exactly the right answer he grows as a musician.

This musical education which derives from the conductor having to discover the composer's meaning by ear, rather than by eye, is one reason I recommend the wonderful nineteenth-century Italian sinfonias to contemporary band conductors. They are very musical, something which makes them popular with the audience, but not all of that musicality is apparent to the eye. I was recently restudying one of these small masterpieces, the *Sinfonia*, '*La Corona d'Italia*,' by Sebastiano Vitaliti, which illustrates some of the kinds of musical problems which require the ear to solve, and thus contributes to the growth and musical experience of the conductor.

One of the first things one notices in this score is that almost all the dynamic marking are either ***pp*** or ***ff***, appearing to the eye as if the entire composition is either very soft or very loud. But the music is quite elegant and so this does not make sense. The first thing I thought of was Verdi's comment to Toscanini that no matter what he put on paper Italian orchestras would play ***mf***, therefore he would write ***ppp*** in order to get a ***p***.

But the more I began to hear this score in my head, the more I began to believe that these particular dynamic markings had nothing to do with loud and soft at all. For example, I began to believe that ***ff*** meant something like 'more enthusiasm,' the degree of which would be solved by the ears of the players and conductor and could, as a matter quite apart, vary considerably in degree of 'loudness.' This line of thought occurred to me in part because I reflected on the history of the Italian markings for tempo at the beginning of compositions. These began in Italy at the end of the sixteenth century and we see Praetorius exclaiming in 1619 that this is a pretty good idea and we should adopt this idea in Germany! But the problem is that they originally meant something more than tempo, as we can see in 1739 when Mattheson reminds his readers that 'Andante' means 'hope' and 'Allegro' means 'comfort.' By 1756 Leopold Mozart writes in his book that these Italian words have lost their meaning and should be ignored, putting one's trust in the music itself to communicate the correct tempo. The thought therefore occurred to me that perhaps these familiar Italian abbreviations for dynamics may also have originally had fuller, or even completely different, meaning in the late sixteenth century. Certainly we cannot assume (as I was told in college) that the famous Gabrieli *Sonata 'Pian e forte'* was the first time anyone played music with dynamics.

I hope the reader can see in this example how the solution is found in the ear of the conductor, and not by the eye looking at the score, and how in the process his musicianship profits.

Another example in this *Sinfonia* of a case where the ear must decide, in place of the eye, has to do with the appearance of a fermata sign. It occurs after a very strong, short and accented chord is repeated eight times in the meter of $\frac{2}{4}$. Then a rest for the entire band occurs and the rest has a fermata in all voices. It is what I was told as a student a 'Grand Pause.' I do not recall any teacher explaining what a Grand Pause is psychologically, but I was told that in the case of a unison rest under a fermata that the fermata meant one performed the duration in question exactly one half longer than whatever the duration is on paper. There are more secrets they did not tell me in school, that Mozart used a fermata symbol over the final double bar of a movement and that in Milano the bus stop signs have a fermata symbol. In both cases the fermata symbol means 'stopping place' and it could mean only this in the Vitaliti *Sinfonia*. But why is it there, and how long does one wait before resuming with the music, which is of a very soft anticipatory nature. It is the conductor's ear alone which must make this decision on behalf of all the listeners in the room and factors like the acoustics of the room and the size of the audience may enter into the solution.

On the other hand, Mozart and earlier composers also used a fermata sign to mean either a place for a cadenza or an *Eingang*. It would, in fact, be possible to do an *Eingang* in this place in the Vitaliti, making a very brief improvisation which prepares the new music and the new dynamic level.

In this composition the conductor must of course determine also what the initial Italian marking of Allegro mosso assai means and again only his ear can make that judgment. And then at the end, how much faster is Animato assai and the following Piu mosso? Do these latter increases in tempo cause us in retrospect to reconsider the original Allegro mosso assai? Or do we take Leopold Mozart's advice and ignore them all, letting the music itself tell us the correct tempo?

Finally, this *Sinfonia* is filled with beautiful and expressive melodies, none of which have any crescendo or diminuendo markings or accents on paper. But no conductor's ear will allow him to 'play what is on paper' in such music.

I hope the conductor can see how much growth is possible as well as the kinds of educational discussions possible with students in performing these original nineteenth-century Italian masterworks for band. I have made modern performance editions of several of these Sinfonias and they can be found on my website (www.whitwellbooks.com) where one can see sample score pages and hear performances is most cases.

Avallone, Vincenzo, *Sinfonia* 'Entrata in Napoli'
Gallo, Vincenzo, *Piccola Sinfonia*
Parmegiani, Gaetano, *Sinfonia*
Ponchielli, Amilcare, *Sinfonia* in F major
Ponchielli, Amilcare, *Sinfonia* in B♭ minor
Vitaliti, Sebastiano, *Sinfonia*, 'La corona d'Italia'

The evening ended with an appropriate bang with a great performance of Sebastiano Vitaliti's composition, 'Sinfonia, La Corona d'Italia.' The charged, operatic piece had the audience mentally dancing through 19th century Italy and left them applauding Whitwell and the Wind Ensemble.

Daily Sundial, review, Dec. 7, 1989 by Ben Eshbach

I have listened with attention to the Vitaliti symphony—it is excellent.

> Luigi Lettiero, Jan. 15, 1990
> Rome, Italy
> Professional Symphony Clarinetist

Special Memorial Compositions for Band

Because the band is able to function outdoors there has been a very long tradition for using it to provide funeral music. For this reason the band's repertoire has been enriched by compositions known to all band conductors, such as the Berlioz *Symphony for Band* and the Brahms *Begräbnisgesang* for band and choir.

In addition, all band conductors know the work discussed separately in this series, the *Trauermusik* by Wagner, composed to accompany the return of the remains of von Weber to Germany. Less well-known are two similar compositions, the Filippa *Marcia funebre* written to accompany the remains of Rossini to Italy and the Halvey *Marche heroïque* to accompany the remains of Napoleon back to France.

Filippa, Giuseppe, *Marcia funebre per il trasporto delle ceneri dell'immortale Maestro Gioachino Rossini da Parigi nel Tempio di S. Croce in Firenze.*

> The Filippa really impressed me … it is a work I have to play.
> Leon Bly, Sept. 29, 1991
> Stuttgart, Germany
> Stuttgart School of Music

This original band composition was composed for the return of the remains of Rossini to Florence, Italy. Compared with the Wagner *Trauermusik*, this *Marcia funebre* is much more intense, dramatic and operatic. I regard this as a very fine composition.

Rossini died in 1868 and his service was performed in the Trinity Church in Paris, with his *Stabat Mater* being sung by the chorus of the Conservatory. He was buried in the *Pere Lachaise* cemetery in Paris near the remains of Chopin.

But the Italians wanted their great countryman back and so in 1887 his remains were transported to the *Basilica di Santa Corce* in Florence, Italy, in a ceremony which attracted six thousand people. There he lies near the remains of Galileo, Machiavelli and Michelangelo.

Sample pages of my modern edition of this *Marcia funebre* score, together with a recording, can be found on my website (www.whitwellbooks.com).

Fromental Halevy, *Marche heroïque* (1840) for the return of the remains of Napoleon to Paris for band

Jacques-François- Fromental -Élie Halévy (27 May 1799 – 17 March 1862) was a French composer remembered mainly for his opera *La Juive*, which was praised highly by Mahler and Wagner. After studying at the Conservatoire with Cherubini he became an active choral conductor, composer and was elected to the *Institut de France* in 1836. His son-in-law and former student was the composer Georges Bizet.

The *Marche heroïque* was composed for the great occasion when the remains of Napoleon were returned to Paris on 14 December 1940. A great procession carried the remains across Paris in the fashion of the great processions of the French Revolution. Indeed one of the features of this Marche are long pauses filled only by the sound of a resonating gong, which was the central feature of one of the great compositions of the Revolution, the *March lugubre* of 1790 by Gossec. One newspaper reported on the use of the gong, as it is also used by Halvey, as 'the notes, detached from one another, break the heart, pulling at ones insides.' Another newspaper wrote that the sound of the gong 'filled the soul with religious terror.' These accounts reflect the fact that the large gong had never before been heard in Paris and this great public sensation caused it to be imitated in later band compositions, such as the *Requiem for Louis XIV* (1815) by Bochsa.

One observer of this solemn procession was the writer, Victor Hugo, who gave his impressions as follows.

> The whole possesses a grandeur. It is an enormous mass, gilded all over, whose stages rise in a pyramid atop the four huge gilded wheels that bear it ... The actual coffin is invisible. It has been placed in the base of the carriage, which diminishes the emotion. This is the carriage's grave defect. It hides what one wants to see: that which France has reclaimed, what the people are awaiting, what all eyes were looking for—the coffin of Napoleon.

Sample pages of my modern edition of this *Marche heroique* score, together with a recording, can be found at www.whitwellbooks.com. On the same site one will also find the *Four Marches for the Marriage of Napoleon* by Paer.

Amilcare Ponchielli (1834–1886), *Elegy on the Death of Garibaldi*

Ponchielli was a famous nineteenth-century Italian opera composer whose opera, *La Gioconda*, with its famous 'The Dance of the Hours,' is still in the international repertory. He also served as the conductor of the Cremona Civic Band, for whom he composed more than seventy original works and an equal number of transcriptions.

Giuseppe Garibaldi (1807–1882), whose popularity, his skill at rousing the common people, and his military exploits are all credited with helping to make the modern unification of Italy possible. He traveled widely, including a six-month residence in New York City in 1850–1851.

I regard this *Elegy* by Ponchielli to be one of the great band compositions of the nineteenth century. It is filled with dramatic effects, some almost extraordinary in character, and yet the general style is operatic. It is very musical, with haunting melodies.

Sample pages of my modern edition of the *Elegy* score, together with a recording, can be found at www.whitwellbooks.com. In my Whitwell Archiv in Trossingen one can also find a copy of another original band composition by Ponchielli, the *Marcia funebre* for Manzoni.

Leon Karren, *Symphonie funèbre*, for band

This lyric and dramatic one-movement symphony was composed by Leon Karren, a distinguished band conductor of the French *Division de Brest*. A large number of his compositions were published in Paris, ca. 1881–1907, including works for solo instruments and band and band with chorus.

Sample pages of my modern edition of the *Symphonie funèbre* score can be found at www.whitwellbooks.com.

Wilhelm Wieprecht (1802–1872), *Trauermarsch*

Wieprecht certainly personified the growth and development of military music in Germany during the first half of the nineteenth century and in his desire to improve the repertoire of the military band, he composed a large number of original compositions, not to mention numerous arrangements, for his concerts in Berlin.

Berlioz, who was touring Germany, heard a performance of this composition and spoke of it in his autobiography.

> The concert ended with a very fine and well-written funeral march, composed by Wieprecht, and played with only one rehearsal!!

I have had reports from performances of the *Trauermarsch* from Wisconsin to Australia and everyone seems to find it an exceptional composition.

Sample pages of my modern edition of the *Trauermarsch* score, together with a recording, can be found on my website, www.whitwellbooks.com.

Wilhelm Wieprecht (1802–1872), *Festmarsch on Themes of Beethoven*

Between 1840 and 1860, a period when orchestras were just making a transition from being private aristocratic ensembles to becoming ensembles giving concerts before the public, the bands in Europe were performing outdoor concerts before thousands of listeners. Many ordinary listeners first heard the music of Beethoven and Wagner in such concerts. In the case of Beethoven entire symphonies were transcribed for band and sometimes two symphonies would be heard on a single concert!

This *Festmarsch* was composed as a memorial to Beethoven by Wieprecht. It is an original composition by Wieprecht but it is based on themes from the *Piano Concerto in E-flat* (Nr. 5) by Beethoven.

Sample pages of my modern edition of the *Festmarsch* score, together with a recording, can be found on my website, www.whitwellbooks.com.

Special Variation Collections for Band

During the Baroque Period the ability to perform extemporaneous fugues was a basic skill for Protestant organists in Germany. The great interest in hearing these organists, in particular Bach, set the stage for keyboard players in the Classical Period to perform variations on popular melodies in public as part of their recitals. This, in turn, resulted in numerous publications of variations for all instruments and for ensembles during the nineteenth century.

I would like to bring to the reader's attention three original nineteenth century sets of variations for band which are of unusual interest. It has been my performance experience that each of these have attracted wide interest in the public.

Amilcare Ponchielli (1834–1886), *Carnevale di Venezia, Variazoni per Banda*

Ponchielli was an important nineteenth-century Italian opera composer whose opera, *La Gioconda*, with its famous 'The Dance of the Hours,' is still in the international repertory. At the same time he also served as the conductor of the Cremona Civic Band and enjoyed putting on his uniform and conducting in public. For this band he composed more than seventy original compositions of all kinds and an equal number of transcriptions of opera and orchestral music.

The folk melody, 'the Carnival of Venice,' was the subject of perhaps more nineteenth-century sets of variations than any other melody. Because Ponchielli was a gifted composer and musician these variations for band are particularly musical. Unlike the familiar variations for piano or various solo wind instruments, with their endless triplets, the emphasis here is developing a different musical character in each variation. The composition consists of a lengthy original introduction and a Finale which encompass fourteen variations and with a total performance time of about fifteen minutes.

These particular variations are not easy and one is amazed that a small town band, composed of amateurs who all had other full-time jobs, could have been capable of performing a work with such technical demands.

The Ponchielli *Variations* are available in my modern edition and sample pages and a recording can be found on my website, www.whitwellbooks.com.

Siegfried Ochs (1858–1929), *Variations on a German Folksong, 'Kommt ein Vogel geflogen.'*

Siegfried Ochs studied music at the Royal School of Music in Berlin where he was a student of the famous violinist, and friend of Brahms, Joseph Joachim. He founded the Berlin Philharmonic Choir and specialized in the performance of early music.

His *Variations on a German Folksong*, the children's song, '*Kommt ein Vogel geflogen*,' was apparently originally published for band. Later the work was arranged for piano by Busoni and in an arrangement for orchestra it has been widely performed by community orchestras.

The composition first presents the folk melody in a simple setting and it is then followed by twelve variations, each in the style of a familiar composer. Some of these will still be familiar to almost any musician today, such as the parody on Wagner's *Tannhäuser* with its famous contrapuntal scales. The quartet for horns in the style of Mendelssohn's *Midsummer Night's Dream* and the 'Strauss Waltz' are particularly precious. The German military march which concludes the composition is the grandmother of all familiar marches. Following is the complete catalog of these variations.

Theme
Var. 1, in the style of J. S. Bach; 'a simple melody with learned counterpoint, closing like an Organ Fugue'
Var. 2, in the style of a Josef Haydn string quartet
Var. 3, in the style of Wolfgang Mozart, 'a clarinet solo'
Var. 4, in the style of a Viennese Waltz of Johann Strauss
Var. 5, in the style an operatic finale by Giuseppe Verdi
Var. 6, Parody on the Garden scene of *Faust* by Charles Gounod
Var. 7, Parody on *Lohengrin* and *Tannhäuser* by Richard Wagner
Var. 8, in the style of a Ludwig van Beethoven violin Sonata
Var. 9, horn quartet in the style of *Midsummer Night's Dream* by Felix Mendelssohn
Var. 10, in the style of Johannes Brahms' *Hungarian Dances*
Var. 11, in the style of Jacob Meyerbeer and the 'Blessing of the Daggers' of his *Hugenots*.
Var. 12, Finale, in the style of a German Military March

The Ochs *Variations* are available in my modern edition and sample pages and a recording can be found on my website: www.whitwellbooks.com.

Wilhelm Mejo, *Variations on 'Gaudeamus igitur'*

> The Mejo *Variations on 'Gaudeamus igitur'* really impressed me ... it is a work I have to play.
>
> Leon Bly, Sept. 29, 1991
> Stuttgart, Germany
> Stuttgart School of Music

This composition was published by Breitkopf und Härtel in 1844 as *Variations sur un Thème favori für Harmoniemusik*. Mejo was a composer and teacher in Chemnitz, Germany, where in 1833 he founded the Robert Schumann Philharmonic. Aside from the use of the famous university song, 'Gaudeamus igitur,' which Brahms also used in his *Academic Festival Overture*, one of the valuable aspects of this composition is that it is very close to the Classical Style, something very rare in original large band works.

The Mejo *Variations* are available in my modern edition and sample pages and a recording can be found on my website: www.whitwellbooks.com.

On the Five Whitwell Symphonies

I COMPOSED MY FIRST WORK, a piano concerto with band, when I was aged eighteen and a student at the University of Michigan. The score no longer exists[1] but as I recall it was filled with the enthusiasm of a young student who had been hearing great masterpieces for the first time. Consequently, stylistically it ran the gamut from Bach to Wagner—as my friends quickly pointed out. There was one melody in particular which several students pointed out was identical with a melody in the second movement of the Berlioz *Requiem*. This is something all composers of diatonic music fear, that they will think of some melody only to find later that it had been used by some earlier famous composer. In this case the interesting thing was that at age eighteen I am quite sure I had never heard even a recording of the Berlioz *Requiem*. Nevertheless, into the trash the score went.

It was more than thirty years before I thought of composing again, this time at the urging of my friend Frederick Fennell. I had recently heard one of those extraordinary madrigals by Gesualdo and so I decided to make a paraphrase on it. The result I felt was not good enough to put my name on it, so I gave the composer's name as Solil la Qui. There had been a series of much discussed articles in the *Instrumentalist Magazine* under the name of Solil la Qui and in one issue the editor even published an anonymous photograph identified as the non-existent writer. I reasoned that if the non-person had published articles, and a photograph, he deserved to have written a composition.

For several decades I memorized and conducted new compositions of the most complicated nature, and premiered more than forty of them, and observed their almost universal failure to communicate with the listeners. One composer expressed his lack of concern, observing that in two hundred years listeners would understand his music. Subsequently, I decided that should I begin to compose in earnest my goal would be to compose music which communicated to the listener in the most simple and direct way possible.

DAVID WHITWELL, SYMPHONY NR. 1, 'THE VIENNESE LEGACY' (1987)

i. Chaconne
ii. Adagio

When I was serving as Associate First Horn in the US Air Force Symphony Orchestra and Band, in Washington, DC, I frequently had the occasion to perform authentic background music in one or another of the famous hotels where political dinners were held. It could be quite interesting, as on one occasion when I was able to observe a vibrant conversation between Harry S. Truman and John F. Kennedy, but at the same time I never forgot that I

---

[1] One melody alone survives as the beginning melody of the second movement of my fourth symphony.

was not a guest but rather an anonymous, unseen musician in the balcony. And in spite of this ignominious status the performance often required considerable skill, as performing quantities of Strauss Waltzes I had never even heard with no rehearsal.

All this came to mind after I had been conducting in Europe when one bitterly cold day in Vienna, late at night, I saw a solitary horn player, poorly dressed for the weather, struggling in the face of the strong wind and snow with his horn case on his back. This poor musician had no doubt been performing some festive music at the Hofburg, helping provide entertainment music for the aristocrats of Vienna who were now riding home in their chauffeured limousines. It was thinking of him that brought this music to the surface and at the time I thought of it as the 'dark side' of the Viennese waltz. The two movements are a continuous development of a single waltz melody.

Sample score pages of this Symphony and a recording can be found on my website, www.whitwellbooks.com.

Reviews of Symphony Nr. 1

I have listened to your Symphony *several times—Congratulations David*!!
 I like it very much indeed. As I have told you several times—I consider you the most talented student I *ever had*. But I did not know of your *talent as a composer*.
   William D. Revelli
   Ann Arbor, MI, Nov. 8, 1987
   University of Michigan

Thanks for your compliment of sharing your performance of your own 'OPUS ONE' with me.
 To me it was first class all the way—in concept, in execution and in listening. How on earth have you kept your talent as a composer under a bushel for so long!! Congratulations!
   Mark Hindsley
   Urbana, IL, Nov. 11, 1987
   University of Illinois

I certainly enjoyed hearing your symphony. The trouble is that I like the work; the first movement is especially good. Now what do I do with a 'Post-Brahmsian' composition written in 1987?
 I hope you don't mind my 'joshing' a little. The symphony, especially as an Opus One, is really very good. It fills a void in the wind band repertoire and therefore is a very valuable work for student organizations.
   Leon Bly
   Stuttgart, Germany, Nov. 12, 1987

I have given your 'Opus 1' at least a dozen hearings. I've played it in the morning, in the evening, driving to and from. I really like it. It is outstanding. Being a work of traditional content doesn't detract a bit. I find myself drawn to the work more every time I hear it. You have a wealth of ideas in the *Chaconne*. And the order of their succession is perfect. I've played it for several friends and they all agree on the unique quality of the work as a whole. No one failed to notice the depth of feeling in the chorale-portion of the *Adagio*. The lyricism is absolutely heart-warming!
   Robert Bailey, professional trombonist
   Minneapolis, MN, Oct. 19, 1988

Thanks for the tape of your Symphony. I enjoyed listening to it, even so you say it sounds like old music; but it is written so perfectly well for a combination of wind instruments, so it really sounds! My sincere congratulations.

    Karel Husa
    Ithaca, New York, April 12, 1989

DAVID WHITWELL, *SINFONIA DA REQUIEM* (1988)

i.	*Requiem aeternam*	(Rest eternal)
ii.	*Tuba mirum*	(The trumpet shall sound)
iii.	*Dies Irae*	(Dreaded Day, Day of Ire)
iv.	*Lacrymosa*	(Mournful day)
v.	*Libera me*	(Deliver me from everlasting death)

In 1968 my wife and I moved to Vienna in order for me to study conducting at the famous Akademie für Musik. We both felt that if we were going to live in Vienna we wanted to live *in* Vienna, right in the middle and not out in the 25th district. We were fortunate to find a small apartment on Kärtnerstrasse just one block and a half from the great cathedral, Stefansdom, which is the heart of the city.

From the first moment I stepped into this apartment I had a strong feeling of the presence of Mozart. Of course I immediately attributed this to the basic excitement of being, on my first trip to Europe, in the city of Mozart, Haydn, Beethoven, Brahms and Mahler. But this feeling of the presence of Mozart in this apartment continued for the entire year. Of course when my mind was otherwise involved in perhaps conversing with my wife, or studying scores, etc., the 'Mozart Effect' was not apparent. But in moments of reflection the feeling returned. It was always there.

Twenty years later, in 1988, I read a new small book by Robbins Landon called *The Last Year of Mozart's Life*. In this book he had reproduced a map of central Vienna dating from about the time of Mozart's death. In these old European cities the basic blocks of building remain the same but the streets tend to change names over the centuries. It was, therefore, only when I saw this older map that I realized that my apartment was in the same building and on the same floor as the apartment in which Mozart died! The reader will understand the utter sense of shock as I thought back on those feelings of 1968. Indeed for some weeks I had the circumstances of the death of Mozart constantly on my mind.

To free myself from this obsession I decided, as a kind of exorcism, to write a Requiem for Mozart, who did not have one performed when he died. Fortunately I was on sabbatical the Spring of 1988 and could devote myself completely to the composition of this, my second symphony, the *Sinfonia da Requiem*. There are a number of curious things about this work, beginning with the fact that the act of composition was almost without a sense of labor. Indeed some movements came to me faster than I could write them down. As an inexperienced composer I found this rather startling but I attribute it to the fact that my feelings were so unusually focused. It is when the feelings are not engaged that composition becomes difficult.

The performance of this *Sinfonia da Requiem* has always had a strong impact on the audience, especially in concerts throughout Europe. I attribute this to the music drawing upon the listeners' own love of Mozart and thoughts of his early death. Indeed, on more than one occasion I have turned to face the audience at the end of a performance of this work in Europe to find numerous audience members crying.

Sample score pages of this Symphony and a recording can be found on my new website, www.whitwellbooks.com.

Reviews of Symphony Nr. 2

Surely one of the best things of the evening was the sound of this work, characterized by an impressive power in its most emphatic moments. The American ensemble took advantage of the open gallery of the Cloister, to create pleasant stereophonic effects by locating the trumpets and trombones on the sides of the flight of steps that hosted spectators. The saxophone soloist [Bill Wilson] in the *Lacrymosa* created a very beautiful and successful effect, while in the *Libera me* (with the sky imperturbably perturbed) a tranquil melody of conciliation and thanksgiving was lifted up to the divinity.
Brescia Oggi (Italy), July 15, 1989

In the *Sinfonia da Requiem*, composed in memory of the last days of the great composer, Mozart, allowed the composer, David Whitwell, to place himself into the very moving last days of Mozart, who, as is well-known, composed a Requiem on his deathbed which, however with superhuman effort, he was not able to finish. Whitwell rendered the tragic and hectic of those last December days of almost 200 years ago in a grandiose manner. In the next to last movement, the 'Lacramosa,' the public experienced a wealth of tone and rhythm after an earlier movement, the 'Dies Irae,' the trumpets, horns, and trombones captured a defiant reaction against the deadly disease. In the final movement, the 'Libra me,' a measured movement, besides a monumental finale the heartache of the composer over the all too early death of the talented Mozart was expressed. The audience experienced the real ability of this orchestra where it was able to produce the finest nuances of tone at the softest dynamic levels.
Markgrafler Tagblatt (Germany), July 19, 1989

The Requiem was then performed a full orchestra strength, a Mass which was composed by Whitwell after he had occupied himself intensively with the last years of Mozart. In addition to the four parts of the Catholic Liturgy (Introitus, Dies irae, Tuba mirum and Lacrymosa) there sounded a fifth movement, a 'Libera me,' which is to be found first in Verdi. Also reminiscent of Verdi was the dramatic power of the Dies Irae movement, which captures the terror of the Last Judgment with musical means.
Badische Zeitung (Germany), July 19, 1989

On the Five Whitwell Symphonies 133

The *Sinfonia da Requiem*, the second piece of the evening, was composed by the conductor of the ensemble, David Whitwell, in honor of and to commemorate Mozart. The five movements are constructed in the formal manner of the Requiem Mass, with the first movement featuring the brass. The 'Tuba Mirum' can be compared to a funeral march which received an almost dramatic character through punctuation and tonal repetition.

Rhythmically, the 'Dies Irae' was fascinating by the colorful use of lively timpani. The 'Libra me' impressed with its full, round brass sound

> *Sudkurier* (Germany), July 18, 1989, appearing also in
> *Schwabische-Zeitung* (Germany), July 18, 1989

The *Sinfonia da Requiem* was the most expressive and important composition on this concert and a substantial composition. We admired both the transparent instrumentation, with much solo playing, as well as the use of the full range of the wind orchestra and found the work very challenging musically.

> *Gemeindeblatt* (Bozen, Italy), May 16, 1991

Just a brief note to tell you how much I enjoyed your *Sinfonia da Requiem*. It is absolutely the best writing for winds that I've heard in 20 years! Bravo!

> Prof. Jerry D. Luedders, Oct. 24, 1988
> California State University, Northridge
> Chair, Music Department

I listened to it in my office yesterday, and again last night at home. I happen to be a sucker for Romanticism, so I enjoyed it very much. I don't think you need apologize for the harmonic language. There is so much garbage written in contemporary language that good music using any language is welcome. Congratulations.

> Dr. William Toutant, Nov. 9, 1988
> California State University, Northridge
> Dean of Fine Arts

Thank you for the tape of your Opus Two, *Sinfonia da Requiem*—which is indeed a very fine work. I have listened to the tape several times and am convinced you have a real talent for composition. I do hope some publisher will publish it if you are so inclined. It can be a most worthy addition to the band's repertoire. Congratulations!

> William D. Revelli, Nov. 18, 1988
> Ann Arbor, MI

Thank you for your great composition. I had a deep impression in hearing the *Sinfonia da Requiem*.

> Wolfgang Suppan, Nov. 22, 1988
> Graz, Austria, Hochschule fur Musik

I am amazed, impressed and proud of you.

> Mark Hindsley, Nov. 27, 1988
> Urbana, IL

This is a very moving concept, and I thought your players performed with love and obvious respect and affection for you.

> Tim Reynish, Dec. 1, 1988
> Manchester, England
> Royal Northern College of Music

Congratulations. Your Requiem is truly beautiful. Such mastery for a second composition—the counterpoint, the gorgeous part-writing, the clean, clear forms, the wonderful colors and voicings and, of course, the deep understanding of the instruments—a most moving and genuine experience. It reveals your many years of study and devotion to your craft. All music, every minute. Beautiful. Have your started Op. 3 yet?

> Ted Hegvik, Dec. 11, 1988
> Philadelphia Orchestra
> West Chester, PA

My heartiest congratulations to you for such a fine work. It has pathos—emotion and passion—musicality and heart—qualities almost unheard of in today's works for wind instruments. I was moved by the music and look forward to the day when I can study the score.

I felt the first movement set the scene very well; the second prepared me for the real excitement of the third (probably my favorite); the fourth is a necessary calm; and the final movement pulls it together for a very satisfying close.

Serious band conductors will be in your debt for this composition. It adds a much needed quality (for lack of a better word) to today's repertoire.

> Gilbert Mitchell, Dec. 31, 1988
> Alexandria, VA
> Former Conductor, US Army Band

To put it mildly I am delighted with the composition. In my opinion, it is not only a worthwhile work, but it was beautifully performed.

I hope that you have found a publisher for the number. It is worthy of publication. There is so much mediocre band music published today that this is like a breath of fresh air.

> George S. Howard, Dec. 31, 1988
> San Antonio, TX
> Former Conductor, USAF Band

I thought you might like to hear from a performer of your work. I first performed the *Sinfonia da Requiem* under the direction of Mr. Ronald Johnson, on Dec. 6, 1988. My part was bass drum.

This composition evoked many emotions in me, even at the time I was actually playing it ... I felt triumph, despair, but most importantly a sense of hope, even in its sense of finality.

I was on the verge of tears during the moment between the last chord and before the audience began applauding.

Thank you for giving me a chance to be a part of such a wonderful, beautiful expression of yourself.

> Kate Wilson, April 3, 1989
> Cedar Falls, IA
> Student, University of Northern Iowa

Enclosed is a program of the first complete performance of your *Sinfonia da Requiem* in Europe. I played three of the movements already in February for a conductor's clinic, where it was enthusiastically received. We used four of the movements for a couple of concerts at the 17th Harrogate International Music Festival in England. The work got a lot of very positive comments after the performance here in Stuttgart and the students really enjoy playing it.

> Leon Bly, April 18, 1989
> Stuttgart, Germany
> Stuttgart School of Music

I have your *Sinfonia da Requiem*. I have waited so long for the music and now that I have it I am filled with joy. I thank you for it.

In the Spring I will perform this work at the Pfarrkirche in Bozen and in the Cathedral in Brixen, which will be a live broadcast on the Italian National Television.

> Gottfried Veit, Sept. 3, 1990
> Bozen, Italy

During the past month I have listened to many tapes and reviewed many scores in my search for the repertoire I wish to program with the National Music Clinic Conference in Philadelphia next February, 1991.

During my search for the band's repertory, I have listened and listened to the tape you kindly sent me of your *Requiem Symphony*. This is truly 'my kind' of music and I truly love it.

Hence, I write you to ask if you can provide me with parts and score. I am anxious to program it and believe it would be received with great enthusiasm by the audience.

> William D. Revelli, Sept. 7, 1990
> Ann Arbor, MI

I had the opportunity to hear this work daily while on tour with the Wind Ensemble in Europe. The composition was met with unbridled enthusiasm by every audience and I grew to appreciate the work more and more with each performance. This reaction is not always the case with new compositions.

> Jerry D. Luedders, March 1, 1991
> Northridge, CA
> Chair, Music Department

Thank you for all you did for us at the CBDNA Conference. In special congratulations to your deep feeling composition in honor of Mozart. We get fine inspirations through this work.

> Wolfgang Suppan, March 4, 1991
> Graz, Austria
> Hochschule fur Musik

The performance of your *Sinfonia da Requiem* was the greatest success and will long be remembered by the players and the large audience.

> Gottfried Veit, May 20, 1991
> Bozen, Italy

> Maestro Fulvio Creaux, Conductor of the Band of the Guardia di Finanza of Rome will soon conduct your *Requiem Symphony for Mozart* and he will send you a tape of it. Before the end of 1991 also in Brescia in our Teatro Grande, the *Sinfonia* will be played. They are already studying it.
>
>> Giovanni Ligasacchi, July 4, 1991
>> Brescia, Italy

> By separate post I have sent you a cassette tape with the last concert of the Gazzaniga Town Band which performed your *Symphony in Memory of Mozart*, which I enjoy very much.
>
>> Marino Anesa, August 3, 1991
>> Soronno, Italy

> We all love your 'Sinfonia de Requiem' and look very much forward to the performance in two weeks!
>
>> Felix Hauswirth, Nov. 17, 1991
>> Cham, Switzerland

DAVID WHITWELL, SYMPHONY NR. 3 'MEDITATIONS ON HAMLET' (1989)

i. 'When churchyards yawn, and Hell itself breathes out'
ii. 'Thoughts Beyond the Reaches of our Souls'
iii. 'Good Night, Sweet Prince'

This Symphony came to mind after I attended a performance of Shakespeare's famous play. Although the symphony was never intended to reflect the play itself, the music came to mind after three lines of text seemed to stay with me. The lines associated with the second movement, 'thoughts beyond the reaches of our souls,' seemed to me to require the natural voice and so I tried to use singing in a natural way, not as an effect as one usually finds in band music. Surely it is a reflection on American music education that in the premiere the faculty, other students and public were absolutely astounded that band members could sing.

Only the last movement, with its little Renaissance march, has a more direct association with Shakespeare.

Sample score pages of this Symphony and a recording can be found on my website, www.whitwellbooks.com.

Reviews of Symphony Nr. 3

> My husband and I would like you to know how very much we enjoyed your composition you shared with us Friday night.
>
> We appreciate the fact that you dared to dignify it with noble simplicity while enriching it with moving harmonies.
>
> It truly gave us an experience 'beyond the reaches of our souls.'
>
>> George & Fern Gaines, Oct. 24, 1989
>> Northridge, CA
>> Members of the audience

Congratulations for your *Symphony Nr. 3*!! It is a beautiful piece—I would like to play it next year with my band here in Zug. I think they should be able to handle it—its not too difficult I think! I would like to conduct the European premiere.

> Felix Hauswirth, December 19, 1989
> Cham, Switzerland

Thank you for sending me the tape of your new *Symphony Nr. 3, 'Hamlet.'* I really do like it and I plan to program it in the future.

> John M. Long, Feb. 12, 1990
> Troy, AL
> Troy State University

DAVID WHITWELL, *SYMPHONY OF SONGS* (1990)

i. Song of Faith
ii. Song of Tranquility
iii. Song of Freedom

This Symphony came to mind after a period of reading about the lives of my ancestors as they traveled West from Virginia to Tennessee during the eighteenth century. Perhaps for genetic reasons, I found it very easy to close my eyes and put myself among them and the consequent various emotions seemed to become the music of this Symphony in the most natural way.

Sample score pages of this Symphony and a recording can be found on my website, www.whitwellbooks.com.

Reviews of Symphony Nr. 4

> Your Symphony of Songs was a beautiful composition as the melodic idea were most impressive.
>
> > Tony Mazzaferro, March 23, 1990
> > Fullerton, CA
> > Fullerton College

> David, your 4th *Symphony* is beautiful!
>
> > Felix Hauswirth, May 1, 1990
> > Luxembourg

> I wish you could know how much pleasure your gift has brought me. I really enjoy Classical music and Rachmaninoff, Beethoven & Dvorak are old friends of mine! Now I am happy to list Whitwell among them—your symphony is an absolute delight. There are no ho-hum parts to be endured while waiting for the good stuff!
>
> It is full of sweet harmony and satisfying crescendos. I love it and congratulate you on a beautiful composition.
>
> Thank you, thank you, thank you.
>
> > Bessie Shimmon, May 6, 1990
> > Modesto, CA

I received the tape of *Sinfonia* Nr. 4. It is a beautiful composition as your others, which would be worth of being printed and sent through all the world.

> Giovanni Ligasacchi, May 12, 1990
> Brescia, Italy

As I love romantic style music, I very much liked the music on the cassette. I congratulate you with your *Fourth Symphony*—beautiful harmony and lovely melodies.

> Egil Gundersen
> Skien, Norway

Congratulations on your new symphony. I listened fascinated to this noble and colorful music. Do you think we could play this symphony?

> Wolfgang Suppan, May 17, 1990
> Graz, Austria

Thanks for the tape of your fourth symphony. The symphony is very nice, and Ilona likes it very much. You have given the band world another collection of lovely melodies and emotional music.

> Leon Bly, May 21, 1990
> Stuttgart, Germany

Thanks very much for sending a recording of your fourth symphony, 'A Symphony of Songs.' It is a beautiful work and one that I will get to in the hope of performing it in the near future.

> John P. Paynter, May 24, 1990
> Evanston, IL
> Northwestern University

I think your Symphony Nr. 4 is the best thing you've done yet. I particularly liked the first movement. You amaze me! I didn't know you wanted to be a composer. Have you wanted to be one all your life and postponed it until now?

> Frank Battisti, June 15, 1990
> Boston, MA
> New England Conservatory of Music

Thanks for the tape. Very impressive. Somewhat like an English Shostakovich.

> H. Robert Reynolds, June 19, 1990
> Ann Arbor, MI
> The University of Michigan

I like your *Symphony of Songs* very much.
> Gottfried Veit, Oct. 10, 1990
> Bozen, Italy

David Whitwell, *Sinfonia Italia* (1991)

 i. Dawn on Monte Rosa
 ii. Sacro Monte
 iii. La Visione

During the Winter of 1990–1991 I was invited to serve as the President of the Jury for an international piano contest in Italy, which was a very interesting musical experience. One round required a short work of the pianist's choice by either Liszt or Scribian. Needless to say I heard a number of compositions which I am sure few people alive have ever heard. Another round demanded a Beethoven Sonata of the applicant's choice. Since I knew all these sonatas my evaluation of the students was rather immediate and unalterable. Nevertheless I often found myself not in conformity with the rest of the jury. The jury consisted of ten well-known European piano teachers and myself, being intended to be a 'normal listener.' We voted like Roman emperors, with our thumbs. No written comments, little discussion and then either thumbs up or down. If the majority was thumbs down the student, who may well have spent months on this repertoire and flown from around the world at his own cost, was immediately eliminated and indeed disappeared. In several cases I found myself embarrassed when the vote was ten thumbs up and one thumb down, or vise versa. In the case of an extremely musical young lady from Finland who played a Beethoven sonata on a level of any world artist I found myself with the only thumb up in the air. I later asked one of the other members of the jury, an Argentinean, to explain this. 'I don't understand,' I asked, 'this young lady was very musical!' 'Oh,' said my friend from Argentina, 'but a piano competition has nothing to do with music!'

 It was not these experiences in the theater which resulted in the music of this symphony, but rather my free time there which allowed my hiking in the mountains of the area west of Milano.

 Monte Rosa is the highest mountain in Italy, a very large and imposing sight in all respects.

 Sacro Monte refers to a small local shrine in the mountains near Varallo. It consists of a series of tableaus of life-size figures carved by local artists depicting the final days of Jesus. When I visited it was in disrepair with the figures covered in dust, all of which added to a sense of the ancient. While walking around this outdoor shrine I heard distant church bells. These are heard again in this movement together with the singing of the village faithful (represented by the unison singing of the audience). Each time the audience sings they first hear the pitch in the orchestral chimes, followed by unison band members playing the pitch and rhythm to be sung, for example dotted quarter-note, eighth-note and half-note: *Do-mi-ne*. It is quite amazing, for genetic reasons, how easily and confidently the audience performs this (I do cue them). I also try it once before the beginning of the symphony, mostly because announcing to the audience that we are going to rehearse seems to engender great excitement. Having done so, I then play the symphony non-stop. In other words, it would be aesthetically wrong to play the first movement and then stop to rehearse.

 Sample score pages of this Symphony and a recording can be found on my website, www.whitwellbooks.com.

Reviews of Symphony Nr. 5

I thank you for the score of 'Italia.' It is a very interesting work, specially for Italy.

>Giovanni Ligasacchi, Feb. 19, 1991
>Brescia, Italy

I received the tape of the *Sinfonia Italia*. It is a very important work, which makes honor to you.

>Giovanni Ligasacchi, Juy 4, 1991
>Brescia, Italy

I appreciated very much your composition and I made a copy that I registered in the archives of our Consorso Valsesia Musica.

The descriptive musical speech is at the same time evocative and meditative, is supported by an excellent instrumentation, and makes your work interesting and qualified. I hope I can perform it.

>Giancarlo Aleppo, August 14, 1991
>Grignasco, Italy

Thanks for the tape of your fifth symphony. I am amazed at how rapidly you turn out the symphonies and still maintain such fine quality. (Just be careful not to write a tenth symphony unless your ancestry can be traced to the Soviet Union.) This symphony certainly captures the spirit of Italy.

>Leon Bly, Sept. 29, 1991
>Stuttgart, Germany
>Stuttgart School of Music

PART III
On Performance Practice

General Principles of Early Performance Practice

bona fides

My interest in the performance practice of early music began with my PhD dissertation on the early symphonies of Mozart, which provided me with a broad background in pre-Classical music, in particular the early stages of the sonata form, the uses of chromaticism and non-harmonic tones in Mozart and most important the influence of the new Italian styles. I want to acknowledge in particular my studies in early music with Fr. Russell Woolen of Catholic University of America in Washington, DC. Father Woolen not only discussed in depth the music on the page, but trained us to examine carefully the marks found in the margins of manuscripts. It was this training which allowed me to discover several important details in the Mozart, *Gran Partita*, K. 361, which had been overlooked by earlier scholars. Among these, two in particular were the discovery that the circular smudge on the bottom stave of the Romance was a blot from Mozart's measure count at the end of the previous Minuet, which brought to an end a century-long debate on whether this was one composition or two shorter ones which had been bound together, and my calling attention to the small '1' (one) and first ending bracket in the final written out bar of the Adagio of the Romance which indicates this bar should be omitted the final time, before the jump to the coda.

During the time I was a student at the Akademie für Musik in Vienna (1968–1969) I was invited by Karl-Heinz Füssel, of Universal Edition, to participate in the creation of a new Urtext Edition of the Mozart piano sonatas. As part of my assignment to prepare the initial draft of the first seven sonatas, I had the opportunity to discuss notational problems with Christa Landon, an authority on Schubert and with Alexander Weinmann on questions associated with early Viennese publishers. Among my discussions with many other Viennese musicians I particularly treasured those with the library staff of the Vienna Philharmonic, men who were living catalogs of information on Viennese traditions.

During my two-year residence in Salzburg I had the opportunity to have discussions with such scholars as Ludwig Finscher of Frankfurt, the world's authority on the Classical Period string quartet as well as the numerous directors of music collections in various European libraries. Some of these studies resulted in publications in the *Mozart/Jahrbuch*, *Music & Letters* and the *London Musical Times*.

During the 1970s when the new Harmoniemusik repertoire was being discovered I was invited to work with a number of professional octets in Europe, during which, of course, I had many discussions with these players on the subject of Classical Period performance practice. Among the groups I worked with there were those of members of the Vienna Symphony, one of the Stuttgart Radio Orchestras, the Brabant Orchestra in The Netherlands, the State

Philharmonic in Brno and faculty ensembles from conservatories in Germany, The Netherlands, England, Switzerland and Peru. In the US I had similar discussions with an octet from the Los Angeles Philharmonic and with professionals at a Chamber Music Festival in Santa Fe.

In addition I had the opportunity to discuss performance practices as a guest lecturer in conservatories in Austria, Belgium, Bolivia, Brazil, Chile, China, England, Germany, Hungary, Israel, Italy, Korea, The Netherlands, Peru, Portugal, Russia, Switzerland and Taiwan.

Why is knowledge of performance practice important to the performer?

The first and most important answer is to learn to be musical. Musicality is not taught in conservatories. Early in the twentieth century a modern style of performance evolved, at first as a reaction to late nineteenth-century Romanticism. Bruce Haynes, professor of the early oboe at the Royal Conservatory at the Hague and at the University of Montreal, described the modern style as 'Prudish, the musical equivalent of "political correctness,"… impersonal, mechanical, literal, correct, deliberate, consistent, metronomic and regular.'

> Modern style is the principal performing protocol presently taught in conservatories all over the world. Its spirit is summarized by a succinct piece of graffiti found in the bathroom of an American conservatory: 'Chops, but no soul.'[1]

The American critic, Richard Taruskin, characterizes the apparent modern goal of just playing exactly what is on paper as the 'aural equivalent of an Urtext score. This seems to be most characteristic—dare I say it?—of English performances.'[2]

Haynes describes these modern performances which sound like just 'running through' the composition as leaving the impression that 'no one is home.'

> When parameters like dynamic nuance, individual note-shaping, rubato, agogics and note placing, pauses, beat hierarchy and emphasis are regularly present in one's performance, they act like windows into the soul. It's pretty difficult to do all these things while maintaining a distant, mechanical persona … A kind of neutral 'run-through' (with windows closed and nobody home).[3]

I can't count the number of performances I have heard when it seemed no one was home! That is not the goal of music, that is the antithesis of music!

And that can't be the goal a musician should aim for. The goal which fine musicians aim for, and that which is missing when 'there is no one home,' is found in accounts by earlier musicians. For example, Roger North in describing the violinist, Nicola Matteis, recalled,

---

[1] Bruce Haynes, *The End of Early Music* (Oxford: University Press, 2007), 49.

[2] Richard Taruskin, 'The pastness of the present and the presence of the past,' in *Authenticity and early music*, ed. N. Kenyon (Oxford University Press, 1988), 137–207.

[3] Haynes, *The End of Early Music*, 113.

> I have seen him, in a good humour he hath held the company by the ears with that force and variety for more than an hour together, that there was scarce a whisper in the room, tho' filled with Company.[4]

Quantz, who spoke of the 'inner feeling—the singing of the soul,' wrote,

> If musicians are not themselves moved by what they play, they cannot hope for any profit from their efforts, and he will never move others through their playing, which should be their ultimate aim.[5]

The reader should not conclude that what Quantz described is simply a romantic style of playing, for he is describing that which was the goal of musicians for a very long time.

I believe it can be said that most of the individual topics of performance practice all contribute to the musical effect described by Quantz, as well as heard in great artists today. It was the performance practice of the Baroque and Classical Period which laid the foundation for all later serious music and which contributed to something written on paper being turned into music. The study of these principles directly affect one's musicality. For example, to name only one, agogic accents are much a part of what shapes melody, but they are nowhere found on paper.

Second, knowledge of performance practice is very important if our goal is to have the composer speak to us as an individual. This was already a concern in 1739 as we can see in an observation by Johann Matheson.

> Those who have never discovered how the composer himself wished to have the work performed will hardly be able to play it well. Indeed, they will often rob the thing of its true vigour and grace, so much so, in fact, that the composer, should he himself be among the listeners, would find it difficult to recognize his own work.[6]

We have also mentioned in chapter one Croce's emphasis on the value of communicating with great minds. Without a basic knowledge of performance practice we would fail to have all the information needed to make this experience possible.

Finally, it is a matter of literacy. Some of the idioms discussed below are very widely known and to conduct a performance without knowing about or observing one of these can raise eyebrows. More than once I have heard such an omission in a concert by a 'famous' conductor and thought to myself, 'I can't believe he doesn't know that!' At work here is a matter of simple ego, we are so sure our instinct is right that we see no need for further study. We think everyone must hear a musical solution as we do. I recall that when I was studying with Eugene Ormandy, a man too busy to have ever made a study of early performance practice

---

[4] Roger North [1728] *The musical grammarian*, ed. M. Chan and J. C. Kassler. (Cambridge University Press, 1990), 271.

[5] Johann Joachim Quantz [1752], *Treatise on Flute Playing*.

[6] Johann Matheson, *Der volkommene Capellmeister* [1739], translated by Robin Stowell, in *The Early Violin and Viola* (Cambridge, 2001), xiii.

and at the same time had a very sensitive musical ear that he could ordinarily trust, he asked me if I had any idea why he was so often criticized in the press for his lack of knowledge of Baroque style.

General Principles

No one can know for sure all the truths of performance practice followed by musicians two centuries earlier. For one thing, music, being a live experience itself, is always fluid, always changing. The famous singing teacher, Pier Francesco Tosi, wrote in 1723 that 'Musick in my Time has chang'd its Stile three times.'[7] And a musician who performed with the violinist, and friend of Brahms, Joachim, complained, 'To play with the Old Man is damned difficult. Always a different tempo, a different accent.'[8]

Nevertheless there are now some generally agreed upon principles regarding the performance of early music. The following suggestions, both in general and in individual idioms, are ones which from more than fifty years of experience I firmly believe in and recommend. Any performance practice ideas which I arrived at I always tested in my own performances, for in the end it is the ear which gives one confidence in all musical solutions. It is a practice I recommend to the reader; let your own ear be the judge.

On Incomplete Notation

Nearly all the music we associate with the Baroque and Classical Periods was composed by men who were permanent employees of some court. Furthermore, their music was often written in great haste, at the demand of their aristocratic employer. As a result these composers often did not bother to place their own names at the top of the score, since everyone knew them, and we should add that after the parts were copied out, the original autograph scores were often discarded, their purpose having been served. Even as late as the great nineteenth-century Krommer Harmoniemusik works, all but three of the scores are gone.

In addition, the shared experience between composer and performers resulted, as a matter of saving time, in leaving many details for the individual performer to finish. It was the players who finished the score, but they did not always write their additions on their part. Dennis Libby explains this well.

---

[7] Pier Francesco Tosi, *Observations on the Florid Song*, trans. Galliard, 1743., 112.
[8] Robert Philip, 'Brahms's musical world: Balancing the evidence,' in *Performing Brahms: Early evidence of performance style*, ed. M. Musgrave and B. D. Sherman. (Cambridge University Press, 2003), 362.

The performer's contribution to a piece of music in performance was not regarded as post-compositional but as the final stage in the act of composition itself. It follows that it was not the composer's score but the performed music that embodied the finished work of art, one that was both fluid—varying with each realization—and ephemeral, not directly recoverable. The concept of performance as work of art can be seen as the central principle of this musical practice.[9]

It was for this reason that we find at the end of the famous book by Quantz on flute performance an engraving which contains this phrase, 'Performance is the vital principle in composing.'

The occasions when performers did write their additions and changes on their parts, of course, have become one of our most important insights into performance practice. Among the things frequently left to the player to finish were articulations, dynamics and a certain amount of improvisation. Even nomenclature, the title of the composition, or the names of the movement, are sometimes missing, which can result in problems in identification. For example, a set of four string parts by Haydn were for years assumed to be a quartet until Robbins Landon discovered horn parts associated with them which then proved they were part of an unknown symphony.

Finally, there is the problem which remains today that the composer, even if he had the time to write everything he could on paper, is faced with a notational system incapable of representing many things, in particular feelings. It was for this reason that the sixteenth-century philosopher, Vincenzo Galilei, observed that the player's goal toward the composer should be to communicate 'not only what he says but often what he wished to say.'

And, of course, in earlier periods when improvisation was so prevalent, we will never be able to completely recreate ancient performance. This is made clear in a report by the French diplomat, and gamba player, who reported on hearing Frescobaldi perform in 1639.

> Although his printed works give sufficient witness to his ability, one has to hear him in person improvising toccatas full of contrapuntal devices and admirable inventions in order to fully appreciate his profound knowledge.[10]

These kinds of problems require the one who creates a modern score from older parts to make a variety of judgments on the details of the score. In published editions of earlier works this person's name is frequently not given, only the original composer's name and the publisher. Therefore one has to have the confidence, where confusion is found, to overrule what appears on paper. Again, the performer's ear must judge, or as Schumann once said, 'If it sounds good, it can't be bad.' To be more precise, it is the genetic understanding of music, together with our relative near relationship to even seventeenth-century composers, which should offer the modern ear some confidence in making these judgments.

---

9 Dennis Libby, 'Italy: Two opera centres,' in *The Classical Era*, ed. N. Zaslaw (Prentice-Hall, 1989), 16.

10 A. Maugars, *Response faite à un curieux sur le sentiment de la musique d'Italie* [1639].

Time and Placement

Because music is music only when it is live, music exists in time. But time does not exist, it is man-made and from time to time nations agree to make small changes to bring 'time' into synchronization with the earths rotation, etc. When modern notation was invented by Church mathematicians the element of time was not included, because the Church was trying to maintain the argument that music was a branch of mathematics. Thus in our notational system the rhythmic relationships are based on an arithmetic relationship with other notes and not as independent expressions of time. There was no official commentary by the Church on tempo or any other aspects of time for centuries. Indeed for the very complicated, and mathematical, proportional system of the early Renaissance Church music to work, there could be no variation in the initial time, other than the mathematical multiplications of it.

With the beginning of the Renaissance most composers began to write, as Monteverdi requested, 'music of the beat of the heart, not of the hand.' In the sixteenth century, the nobleman, Giovanni de' Bardi, in comparing the old medieval style of singing with the modern Renaissance style observed,

> The singer may contract or expand the time at will, seeing that it is his privilege to regulate the time as he thinks fit.[11]

From this time on, time became more and more an expression of feeling, once again, after centuries of Church pretense, fulfilling the true role of music as a special language to express feeling. During the twentieth century when the complex academic music once again demanded that 'time' dominate feeling, many composers once again wrote music requiring arithmetic precision but not feelings. I pass over the invention of the nineteenth-century metronome as few musicians use it other than to check an initial speed. Beethoven advised it was only good for the first few bars,[12] as did Bruno Walter,[13] and Berlioz wondered if it were even possible for a musician to 'maintain this rigid uniformity for more than a few bars.'[14]

Music is not an arithmetical expression of time. Music is an expression of feeling, which cannot be measured in time. For this reason musicians from the fifteenth to the twentieth century felt very free to vary the time within the phrase or within the measure according to the demands of feeling. Specialists in early music call this practice 'Placement,' meaning the placement of what comes next according to psychological time and not chronological time.

'Rubato' is a familiar term to most musicians, but the practice was much broader in use than mere rubato. When for example within a bar one voice improvised the other voices simply waited before going on until the improvisation was completed or indicated the return of ensemble motion. No account of this delay appears on paper. This practice of Placement

---

[11] *Discourse on Ancient Music and Good Singing*.

[12] Quoted in Erich Leinsdorf, *The Composer's Advocate* (New Haven: Yale University Press, 1981), 165.

[13] *On Music and Music-Making* (New York: Norton, 1957), 43.

[14] His essay on conducting.

is particularly important at internal cadence points, allowing a full and satisfying resolution before beginning the next phrase. Actually we do this all the time and no one would ever notice. Suppose you had at the end of a phrase in slow common time the following music.

In order to get a resolution which has time to resolve we would often conduct this bar: half-note, quarter-note, and a release by a lift or cut-off, and then the pick-up to the next phrase. But we would have then conducted a $\frac{5}{4}$ bar, even though it is $\frac{4}{4}$ on paper. Grainger, in the second movement of his *Lincolnshire Posey* actually writes $\frac{5}{4}$ for the second bar of every phrase in order to ensure a full resolution. He was afraid that if he wrote $\frac{4}{4}$, band directors would conduct $\frac{4}{4}$, thus cheating the resolution and creating an awkward feeling.

Dear reader, the great musicians practice Placement all the time in small degrees, because they understand we cannot allow Time, in the sense of the quarter-notes marching by, to adversely affect our communication of feeling with the listener. Please feel free to do this whenever your ear tells you it is necessary and that without doing so the music would become artificial sounding. No apologies are necessary. Exception: In a music competition, of course, one cannot do this, for music competitions have nothing to do with music.

Music and Movement

Because instruction in music in the modern universities is founded on the late Medieval perspective of music as rational concepts, including mathematics, rather than on its true origin as an expression of the feeling–experiential nature of man, we have come to think of the primary role of the conductor as being also mathematics-related—he gives the metrical 'beats.' But it is far more accurate to say the conductor expresses the *duration* of the beat. That is, the conductor is a personification of the *movement* of music through time. One might go further and say the conductor is a modern symbol of the ancient relationship between movement and music.[15] Movement itself is a form of communication, which, of course, is what the conductor above all engages in. Therefore, to understand both the evolution of conducting and the artistic function of the modern conductor, one must begin with the consideration of movement itself.

One might suppose that the close relationship between movement and music begins in the fetus, where *both* hearing and movement develop in the inner ear. Therefore it should be no surprise to find the earliest of early men using movement as a form of communication long before the earliest speech. Lower animals, of course, also use movement as a means of com-

---

[15] Shortly after writing this, the author attended a solo dance recital by the great Mikhail Baryshnikov. It was interesting to observe not only numerous hand and arm movements which are identical to those of conductors, but also various relationships between movement and music. In particular, these included the correspondence of movement with melody, the obvious correspondence of tempi with emotion, and, of course, form.

munication, in particular with regard to mating ritual. Since musical communication also dates before speech, we must imagine the association of music and movement as not only a natural one but one understood quite early. Curt Sachs, in his discussion of dance in primitive societies, notes,

> Whether we speak of individuals or of entire tribes, peoples, and races, their melodies and dances must always be closely related. For both are determined by the same impulse to motion.[16]

Franz Liszt, in his extensive writings on the music of the Gypsies, also wrote of the earlier societies with regard to singing and dance.

> Dancing, being inseparable from music, lends itself naturally to singing; especially among primitive nations. Civilization eradicates and stifles this tendency by increasing the measure of what is expected from each art; and thus compelling it to adopt an isolated position, in order to become perfect. The union however always persists, until by degrees divorce becomes quite compulsory. Thus it happens that, in several countries (not by any means the least civilized) a custom survives of accompanying certain portions of the dance by choruses, interspersed with couplets, partly recited and partly sung by the principal dancer. In Poland, a neighboring country, the Krakowiaki and the Tropaki present examples, some of which have become quite celebrated in the history of national music.[17]

The association between movement and music is documented in the oldest extant literature. For example, a stone relief from the Assyrian Empire (750–606 BC) pictures two male harpists who are dancing while playing. The lyric poets of ancient Greece, who flourished during the sixth and seventh centuries BC, were poets who sang their works in public performance. Athenaeus reports that while they performed with few facial expressions, they were active with their feet, 'both in marching and in dance steps.'[18]

The most interesting ancient medium which combined music and movement were the Greek choirs, because what we know of their movements suggests they were used specifically to express, or amplify, the emotions of the music they sang. We first find reference to the Greek choral movements in a poem by the lyric poet, Alkman, in which he complains that he is too old and weak to *dance* with the chorus.

The Roman writer on oratory, Quintillian, goes so far as to suggest that motions can only be really learned through music.

> For, as we know, different emotions are roused even by the various musical instruments, which are incapable of reproducing speech. Further the motion of the body must be suitable and becoming, or as the Greeks call it *eurythmic*, and this can only be secured by the study of music.[19]

---

[16] Curt Sachs, *World History of the Dance* (New York: Norton, 1937), 183.

[17] Franz Liszt, *The Gypsy in Music* (1959), 292.

[18] Athenaeus, *Deipnosophistae*, I, 22.

[19] Quintillian, *The Education of an Orator* (Institutio Oratoria), I, x.

Through the years I have often thought about the relationship of movement and music, but both of them are so difficult to describe in words. I have noticed that the movement of just walking helps to clarify musical problems I might be having and somehow movement plays a role in confirming memory.

Because of the long association of movement and music, one sometimes, especially in earlier music, finds music which is clearly related to dance. An obvious example is a thirteenth-century *Estampie* found in the British Library.[20] Here in the seventh and eighth bar we have a cadence with repeated pitches, where the dancers bow and curtsy and then resume their original posture. Recognizing this tells the conductor that the seventh bar is performed stronger and the eighth bar pulls back somewhat.

There is a very familiar eighteenth-century cadence in which the key to interpretation is also found in the dance movements it imitates and which we will discuss below under 'Cadences.' Also, in the specific compositions discussed below, in the Mozart *Gran Partita*, K. 361 and the *Partita*, K. 388, the reader will find examples of interpretation based on movement on the opera stage.

Finally, there is a great conducting aid which Frederick Fennell told me about which is based on a visualization of movement. Ordinarily to begin a composition a conductor gives one preparatory beat in the time of the forthcoming music, no more and no less. This is easy enough for an orchestra to see when the meter is duple, for the natural up and down movement of the arm clearly shows the tempo. But in a work in a triple meter, which is conducted in one beat per bar, the difficulty is in giving one preparatory beat which prepares the appropriate length of the first bar. So Fennell told me that he stands on the podium, starts hearing the music silently in his head and imagines a great wheel rotating counter clockwise in the speed of the music, that is one revolution per bar. Then, when he feels ready, he just 'grabs' the bottom of the imaginary wheel and it carries his arm and baton up in exactly the length of preparatory needed to created the down-beat of the first bar, allowing the orchestra to come in with confidence.

The Music is Not on the Paper

For reasons which we will discuss below, conservatories today, in their emphasis on technique and data, teach students to think of music as something which exists on paper. But this is simply not true, as Haynes points out.

---

[20] Harleian 978.

152 On Performance Practice

> We normally like to think of the composition as the written object, because it has a fixed, stable form. We talk about the 'music' on the stand. But the notes on the page aren't a composition; in fact, they aren't music at all … Musical meaning doesn't exist until the moment of 'reception,' the moment a piece is performed and heard.[21]
>
> ……
>
> It is amazing that anyone could mistake a piece of paper for music.[22]

Not only is the music not on paper, that has never been the case. When K. P. E. Bach observed, 'It is possible, through different kinds of delivery, to make musical passages sound so different that they are scarcely recognizable,'[23] he was not making a complaint, he was describing the present tense of music-making. One can find such testimony throughout the Baroque and Classical Periods.

> François Couperin:
> Just as there is a great distance between grammar and Eloquence, there is the same infinity between notated music and music played well.[24]
>
> Johann Quantz:
> The success of a piece of music depends almost as much on the players as the composers.[25]
>
> Wolfgang A. Mozart:
> [The performer should play] so that one believes that the music was composed by the person who is playing it.[26]

There is even documentation from 1687 of a cantor in Flensburg who was dismissed because he 'had performed the same pieces repeatedly without introducing anything new.'[27]

What were these performers expected to add to the composition? Certainly not to recompose, except in accepted places for improvisation. They were expected to turn those lifeless dots on paper into present tense, living music by the addition of the one thing which the composer could *not* write on paper, feelings. And this is largely what Mahler meant when he made his famous comment, 'The important things in music are not found in the notes.'

So, why do conservatories fail to teach 'the important things'? Why do we accept musical performance without feeling?

---

21 Haynes, *The End of Early Music*, 22ff.
22 Ibid., 25.
23 *The Art of Keyboard Playing* [1753]
24 *L'Art de toucher le clavecin* [1717].
25 *The Art of Flute Playing* [1752].
26 Letter of 1778.
27 John Butt, *Music Education and the Art of Performance in the German Baroque* (Cambridge University Press, 1994), 17.

Modern Style: Chops, but no Soul

During the late nineteenth century, while musical performances were in general filled with feelings, there is no question that some artists, conductors in particular, went too far and began changing the actual composition by adding instruments, especially percussion, but even entire wind bands, to earlier scores. This led to a strong reaction leading to a new aesthetic in the twentieth century: play only what is on paper. This has the effect of taking the performer, especially his contribution of feelings, out of the performance. We can see this very clearly in a German *Lexikon* by Hermann Mendel published in 1882. Speaking of performance he requires two things of the performer:

1. A complete understanding of the notational signs employed by the creative artist.
2. The technical skill to 'execute' what the [signs] indicate.[28]

That sounds very much like the goals of the modern conservatory, doesn't it?

But it was after World War I that Modernism became the dominating style. The conductor, Arturo Toscanini, whom some called the 'New Puritan,' a believer in playing only what was on the page, was a leader as was, of course, Stravinsky, who was always saying music consists of B♭s and C♯s and nothing else. One observer quotes Stravinsky's envy of the military band leader, 'who keeps a revolver strapped in a holster by his side, and a notebook in which he marks a player's mistakes, for each one, sends him to jail for a day.'[29]

Bruce Haynes characterizes the twentieth-century Modernism's concerns as,

> Accuracy and good intonation, literalism in reading scores, automatic tempos and limited personal expression. Music reduced to audible mathematics, functioning like an automaton.
>
> ......
>
> But the problem is that if you spend hours working on playing in tune and together, you can't expect an inspired concert—you can expect a concert that is in tune and together.[30]

How many of us grew up sitting in rehearsals in which that was the sole object? And, of course, the phenomenon of the high school music festival is the epitome and goal of that kind of thinking—playing exactly what is written. These are not contests in music, they are contests in grammar.

But while the philosophical objectives may be Modern, this kind of playing is not. Haynes quotes the seventeenth-century Mattheson complaining that his German singers, in distinction with the Italian and French, 'sing very decently and rigidly, as if they had no interest in the content and had not the least interest in … the proper expression.' Thomas Mace bemoans, in 1676, musicians who 'take much Pains to Play their Lessons very Perfectly,' but lack life

---

[28] Quoted in Clive Brown, *Classical and Romantic Performing Practice* (Oxford University Press, 1999), 631.
[29] Timothy Day, *A Century of Recorded Music: Listening to Musical History* (Yale University Press, 2000), 187.
[30] Haynes, *The End of Early Music*, 50, 62.

or spirit. John Mason, in 1748, compares players with the worst of lawyers reading a deed, 'a flat, dull, uniform tone of voice, without Emphasis or Cadence, or any Regard to Sense or Subject.'[31]

Johann Quantz, in his famous eighteenth-century book on flute playing, writes,

> Poor delivery is when everything is sung without warmth, or played at the same level without alternation of Piano and Forte ... One contradicts the Emotions that should be expressed, or executes everything in general without sensitivity, without Emotion, without being moved one's self, so that the impression is given that the musician is singing or playing as an agent for someone else.

Or, as mentioned above, in the style of 'no one being at home.' But this was never a style, this was always just bad performance. And, in my view, that is all it is today.

To document the fact that this kind of performance remained at the heart of the Modern Era, Haynes cites two recordings of the Bach BWV 565, one by Leopold Stokowski, conducting an unnamed orchestra, and the other by Esa-Pekka Solonen conducting the Los Angeles Philharmonic in 1999, and concludes,

> To judge from these two recordings, we have lost much in substituting Modern style for Romantic style ... Stokowski's version is quite moving, and his players play as if they are committed to the music. Salonen is icy by comparison; the musicians do not seem to be involved and tend to play mechanically but with great precision.

We have lost much indeed and the great keyboard player, Wanda Landowska, saw it coming at the beginning of the Modern Period.

> If I am not mistaken, Romanticism is departing with a noisy farewell ... Let us not emulate those fashionable hosts, of whom Shakespeare speaks, who take leave negligently of the departing guest. Let us bow down, very low. Romanticism gave us strong emotions and unforgettable ecstasies; it awoke in us unbounded ideas and supreme flights of fancy; it flattered our palate with tart and bitter fruit, which seemed so good after an overabundance of sweetness; it brushed our skin with the coarse caress of a wild beast. May all the centuries to come look with full respect and envy upon its grandeur, which is still hovering sovereignly.[32]

Well, the twentieth century and Modernism is concluded so let's add up the score. At the end of a century, what have they left us? The Modernists have contributed an enormous stack of scores which had one performance only, because no one wanted to hear them again. And how many of those post-WWII scores are still in the repertoire? Can you name five? Even the 'great masters' are invisible; who plays Stravinsky or Schönberg any more?

---

[31] Ibid., 62.

[32] Quoted in Denise Restout, *Landowska on Music* (Stein and Day, 1964), 54

General Principles of Early Performance Practice 155

And what has been the cost of this repressive Modernism? Audiences for all kinds of Classical Music have diminished to two percent of the population in the US. Orchestras are dying. There remain only eleven 'good music' radio stations in a nation of more than three hundred million people. Not finding feeling in the concert hall the audience has turned to pop music, music of no substance or importance, but which does communicate feelings.

It is time to return feelings to Classical Music. Let's bring down the curtain on Modernism and take those scores and recycle them (the libraries do not want them) and save half the trees on the planet.

Once more with Feeling!

Just as one can find a record of bad performance in all periods, so one can find in all periods writers complaining the musicians are not going beyond the page to express themselves. Galilei warned the sixteenth-century player,

> And let it not come into your mind to try to defend yourself with the silly excuse of some who say they did not feel called upon to do more than that which they found written or printed.[33]

There is no more remarkable, indeed startling, testimonial to the importance of the performer's emotional role than a following passage in which Galilei wonders if the fact that the lute cannot sustain a pitch hinders emotions. The lutanist answers that the instrument most capable of this is the organ, but he has found on the contrary that such virtuosi of the organ, such as Claudio di Correggio and Gioseffo Guami,

> not by failure of their art and knowledge but by the nature of the instrument, have not been able, cannot, and never will be able to express the harmonies for *affetti* like *durezza, mollezza, asprezza, dolcezza*—consequently the cries, laments, shrieks, tears, and finally quietude and rage—with so much grace and skill as excellent players do on the lute.[34]

This is the essential problem in the performance of older music, converting the left hemisphere of the brain data form of older music into a live, right hemisphere experience for the performer and public. To put this problem another way, not only is Beethoven dead, but the music he left behind is written in a notational system entirely devoid of symbols for the emotions.

But since music only exists as music in the present tense, it is essential that this transformation take place if the listener is to be able to understand Beethoven. To perform the notes as they appear on paper will not accomplish this. The performer must take what Beethoven left, contemplate what Beethoven actually felt when he wrote those representations of music on paper, internalize these insights, engage his own emotions and use *these* in his performance

---

[33] Vincenzo Galilei, *Fronimo* (1584), trans. Carol MacClintock (Neuhasen-Stuttgart: Hanssler-Verlag, 1985), 83.
[34] Ibid., 87.

before the public. Quintilian, the first-century Roman teacher of oratory, was right on the mark when he said, 'We must be moved ourselves before we attempt to move others.'[35] It is as close to Beethoven as we can get. It is the performer who can make Beethoven live, not the notes on paper. This principle is one of the oldest known to us. Plato, in his list of requirements needed to be a music student, he included 'The ability to inspire through music.' In performance, he says, the performer is 'not in his right mind,' his soul is in ecstasy. And thus it has always been with fine performers. K. P. E. Bach, who spoke of 'playing from the soul, and not like a trained bird.'

> Musicians cannot move others unless they themselves are moved; it is essential that musicians be able to put themselves in each emotion they wish to rouse in their audience, for it is by showing their own emotion that they awaken sympathy. In languishing, sad passage, they languish and grow sad. That is visible and audible.[36]

By the way, Charles Burney once visited K. P. E. Bach in his home and later recalled,

> After dinner, … I prevailed upon him to sit down again to a clavichord, and he played, with little intermission, till near eleven o'clock at night. During this time, he grew so animated and *possessed,* the he not only played, but looked like one inspired. His eyes were fixed, his under lip fell, and drops of effervescence distilled from his face. He said, if he were to be set to work frequently, in this manner, he should grow young again.[37]

Johann Quantz, in his book on the art of flute playing, models his description of the fine player after Cicero's description of the fine orator.

> He must himself achieve a state of excitement if he is to evoke emotions in his listeners.

For those musicians who have not thought of the music of the court of Frederick the Great, including K. P. E. Bach, as being all that emotionally powerful, they might be surprised that Quantz's contention that emotional variety must be developed even at the level of a single bar.

> At each bar you should adopt a different Emotion, so to speak, being now melancholy, now gay, now serious, etc., as such changes are most necessary in music. They who can master this ability are not likely to lack applause from their listeners, and their playing will always be *touching*.

One can find many descriptions of musicians, especially during the Baroque Period, which testify to their contributions in adding their feelings to the score. And I believe it has always been the same for composers as well. Great composers have technical skill, but they are not thinking of their skill when they compose. They are thinking of some deeply personal feelings they need to express. Wagner writes,

---

35 Quintillian, *The Education of an Orator* (Institutio Oratoria), VI, ii.
36 K. P. E. Bach, *The Art of Keyboard Playing* [1753].
37 Charles Burney, *The present state of music in Germany …* [1773], II, 270.

Those like myself look neither to the right nor the left, neither forwards nor backwards. Time and the world are nothing to us. Only one thing matters to us and determines our actions, namely, the necessity to release what is within us.[38]

I believe Bruce Haynes was quite correct when he stated, 'Emotions might be called the meaning in music.'[39] Meaning is not found in Roman numerals written under chords, only grammar is found there. Meaning and the emotions are found in the heart.

It is time to draw down the curtain on the twentieth-century Modern style, which has been so costly to the history of serious music, and once again return the art of music to its only real purpose, a special language for the communication of feelings.

---

[38] Quoted in Walter Salmen, *The Social Status of the Professional Musician from the Middle Ages to the 19th Century* (Pendragon, 1983), 270–271.

[39] Haynes, *The End of Early Music*, 168.

Classical Period Performance Idioms

Cadences

Ritard Indications

Adagio used to mean ritard.

During the Baroque Period it was not unusual to see the word Adagio used to mean ritard., as one often sees, for example, in the music of Handel. Usually this is found in places where no other reasonable meaning could apply, such as a one-bar notation where it would be most unlikely to have a new tempo for only one bar. A typical example is this passage from the first movement of the Hautboisten *Concerto da camera*, HRD Fü 3741a, Nr. 29.

pp meaning ritard.

Where are the ritard. symbols in Mozart? With more than six hundred autograph scores extant, never once, in any score, do we see 'rit.' in his handwriting. Mozart's music was performed during his lifetime by the finest players in Europe, the orchestras of Vienna, Paris, Prague and London. Is it reasonable to suppose that all those fine players, performing hundreds of scores, never ever made a ritard. anywhere in performance? It is out of my field, but I don't recall seeing any ritardandos in Haydn scores either.

The word is not seen much in the Baroque Period either, but Robert Donnington has expressed his belief that ritardandos were played, added by the players when the chord movement suggested it. This could be the answer, for in the last, great C Major Symphony of Schubert, in the second movement, there appears after a long cadence '*a tempo*,' but he never wrote ritard., or *meno mosso* beforehand. It appears he assumed the players would ritard. the cadence and his main interest was to indicate where things returned to the original tempo.

And then there was the mechanical music box made by Père Engramelle, ca. 1775. There had been a considerable interest in music boxes in the eighteenth century and composers like Handel, Haydn, Mozart and Beethoven wrote works for them. But Engramelle developed a machine which could record piano performances very precisely and among the works he recorded the endings are clearly ritarded.

So the tradition in performance was there, but why didn't Mozart ever write 'rit.'? I believe that when Mozart wrote **p** or **pp** in the final bars of a composition it meant ritard. If you look at the end of the first movement of the *Piano Concerto*, K. 488, one of the big symphonic concerti of the Vienna period, for example, you see a typical big, forte, churning orchestral ritornello bringing the movement to an end, following the cadenza. But then, the final bar, a single bar!, is marked **p**. To the eye it looks like a printing error. It is like running into a wall. The music consists of a simple cadential figure which is repeated and I think it means just drifting off into space, as it ritards.

Consider the slow movement of the C Minor *Partita*, K. 388, one of the greatest of all Mozart works. The Andante begins with lovely music of a kind of domestic tranquility in nature. The exposition section ends with two isolated eighth-notes, strongly accented with a vertical stroke. It says, 'that's all!,' or 'the End!,' or something of that feeling. Then comes an extraordinary development section, melancholic and disjointed. Mozart begins the first theme, but stops in the middle. And it just hangs there in the air. He begins again, and stops with the melody incomplete, again hanging in the air. And again a third time. Clearly his mind was somewhere else, somewhere melancholic, sad and contemplative. We can't know what he was thinking about, but his mind was far away. When he decides to begin the recapitulation he writes *da capo*, then changes that to a *D.S.*, by creating his own symbol for it. His mind was still not back in the present tense. When you come to the end of the recapitulation the listener, and the players, are changed. This is no longer a graceful Andante; listeners and players have experienced that haunting and melancholic development section and that has changed the atmosphere. So to end with another two accented eighth-notes, 'that's all!,' would seem to have the effect of saying he wasn't serious about that earlier music, or it is a joke. He knew he could not do that, so he takes away the accents completely and goes to the opposite extreme, making the two eighth-notes **pp**. But to play these two notes suddenly *pianissimo* is like a whisper which also makes no sense. But if the two notes are ritarded it has the effect of allowing the listeners to release the withheld emotions—it becomes the musical equivalent of a sigh. The first time I tried this I was conducting at an adult chamber music festival in Santa Fe and the players were all professional people who had known this composition all their lives. When I did this ritard. in the first rehearsal, they were amazed and cried, 'That's right! How did you know to do that?!' It confirmed, for me, the very natural solution I felt.

A similar, and very difficult cadence, is found at the end of the Adagio in the Mozart *Gran Partita*, K. 361. Here Mozart ends with a simple cadential figure which is played three times, twice at the *p* level with the third time marked *pp*. Now, if you have fine players and you strongly insist, in rehearsal you *can* get the ensemble to play the third figure the text-book one-half the volume of the first two. But it never happens in concert, for the players after this very long, slow and intense movement just have nothing left by the end. I have never heard a performance where the last figure was truly *pp*. But if Mozart meant ritard.—and we can assume he wasn't writing the world's first 'fade-out ending'—then, like the cadence in the K. 388, a real allargando allows the listener time to release the pent-up emotions. And the result is beautiful and elegant, as we would expect from Mozart. Following is a very simplified version, which anyone can handle on the piano, where I add two fermata signs to indicate how I conduct it, that is to say, I really ritard. the last two beats of music.

I feel quite sure I am right about this new conjecture. Look at the ending of the Romance movement of the *Gran Partita*, K. 361. There is the final harmony, which is then repeated three times now marked *pp*. Below I will discuss the possibility that in some cases the staccato dot in Mozart meant an accent and this is a likely example as Mozart has already gone to the trouble to write the first two repetitions short through the notation itself. So one could make the case that this cadence was intended to be soft, but a certain increased conviction. But it could still do this while the *pp* adds the ritard., which again allows for the release of tension.

By the way, there is that strange measure in the *Partita*, K. 388, one bar before the closing section of the second movement. A single bar written with spaced individual sixteenth-notes marked (this bar alone) *piano*. Conductors have tried to make this one bar *piano* but then, at best, it only adds a sort of mystery for no apparent purpose. The music before this bar has a more rousing, almost county dance quality, during which the conductor and musicians inevitably feel the need to play a bit faster because of the leaping dance-like figure. But the bar after the one in question is the beginning of a necessarily tranquil closing section. If this single bar marked *p* were now taken to mean a ritard., like little cat's feet become more and more spaced, then it serves perfectly to bring the tempo back from the country-dance to the calm closing. I think it is the only solution for a bar which otherwise looks so strange on paper.

Well, now let's talk about the Italian language, which is not only the one written, but one Mozart spoke after two residences in Italy. When I consult my Cassell's *Italian–English Dictionary* (1967), the one used by all university people in the US, under the word *'pianissimo'* I find two meanings given. Not designated 'Nr. 1' and 'Nr. 2,' but just simply two meanings, both indicated as adjectives. One reads, *'very slowly.'* Pianissimo: Very slowly! A tempo definition! The other meaning, of course, is 'very softly.' Very slowly, it is exactly what I have contended Mozart meant in these various cadences!

If one then goes a few lines further down, one discovers the word *'piano'* is given a series of single word definitions: softly, gently, *slowly*, quietly. Slow? Did any teacher ever tell you the little **p** could mean *slow*? It does present an interesting question regarding all those slow movements of virtually every second movement of every Classical Period symphony and concerto. We have been taught to think of this as a *soft* movement, following the normal *forte* first movement. But if the **p** meant instead *slow*, then it raises the possibility that there could be a greater range of dynamic change, soft and loud, within this slow movement and not a more restricted expression because one is obligated to keep everything soft.

And finally, this alternative definition of **p** and **pp** continues today among everyday Italian speakers. If one enters a room filled with people engaging in noisy conversation and one protests, *'piano, piano,'* it is taken to mean 'calm down, calm down,' not to mean continue the conversation softly. Calm down. Slow down. That is what we should hear Mozart speaking to us in those cadences marked **p** or **pp**.

Standard ('Stair-step') Cadence

One of the most common cadences of the Classical Period has it roots in military band music of the Baroque. In the military form, shown below, the *Schellenbaum*, or 'Jingling Johnny' played on the fourth beat where the band has a rest. The concept of a standing army was reinitiated during the Baroque Period making it possible to teach the troops coordinated marching to music. So new was this idea, there was a fear that a single quarter-note rest might cause people to get out of step, hence the addition of the Schellenbaum, a pole holding an Islamic crescent on top, from which were draped numerous bells, which was crashed heavily against the ground on that rest.

The widespread interest in central Europe during the eighteenth century in the so-called 'Turkish musik' is well known. This, another branch of military music, caused this military cadence to become a very familiar one in indoor music. In its appearance in a regular Classical composition, there was a performance practice which included three rules:

1. The first beat is performed the strongest, with each succeeding beat played softer, hence the description 'stair-step' cadence.
2. The dotted figure on beat two was invariably double dotted.
3. The quarter-note on the third beat was played half its written value.

Rule number one was self-evident as the first beat of the cadence was always also the downbeat. Mozart, nevertheless, often drops an octave on the second beat to reflect this greater definition of the first beat of the cadence.

Standard Macro Meter Dance Cadence

Beginning with the music of the late Classical Period in central Europe one begins to find more and more use of macro meter. This practice is familiar to everyone with respect to the Scherzi, the third movements, of the Beethoven symphonies. They are written in a $\frac{3}{4}$ meter but every four bars constitutes the true single 'measure,' so that every fourth bar is a downbeat. They are, arithmetically in $\frac{12}{8}$, so why did he not write them that way? The reason was for ease in reading; those Scherzi in $\frac{12}{8}$ would have so many ligatures it would be hard to find the note heads. Actually Beethoven employed this practice very frequently in his music, which is very important for conductors to know in order that they do not conduct the wrong meter. The first movement of the Fifth Symphony, for this reason, should be conducted in four, not in the meter on paper.

Mozart also did this from time to time. In the *Gran Partita*, K. 361, for example, there are two minuets. One is an old style minuet conducted in three, but the other is a new style minuet and should be conducted in four (a macro bar).

It is this macro meter 'feel' which we find in another very common cadence of the Classical Period. Consider, for example, this cadence at the end of the first movement of the *Gran Partita*, K. 361.

First, it should be mentioned, as will be discussed below, that the final half-note was intended by Mozart to be played as a quarter-note. The critical thing in this cadence is the fact that the final down-beat should be felt not on the last bar, but on the second bar from the end. That is where the piece ends, with the following two quarter-notes being a kind of reflex action, very much like the feel of the stair-step cadence. The present cadence, however, was not military in origin but was a familiar dance cadence, which would have been recognized by the audience of the time. The first beat of the second bar from the end, the true final note, is where the (male) dancer bows to his partner. The third beat of this bar he raises up to standing position and the final bar he swings his arms to the side, with palms open as if to say 'There we are!'

The final six bars should thus be conducted as if it were in the meter $\frac{4}{2}$, in the example shown below as one such measure followed by three beats of an incomplete final bar. To perform the final quarter-note as the strongest, or even making it a half-note or longer, is to emphasize what used to be called a feminine beat, which has the effect of the listener expecting the music to continue.

Fermati

As Stop Sign

In earlier music the fermata sign was sometimes used to mean simply 'stop here.' Thus it made perfect sense to Mozart to put a fermata sign over the final double bar of nearly all movements. It was probably intended for the copyist, but in any case there was no intention that anything be held or extended. Following this tradition, it makes perfect sense in Milano that all the bus stops have the picture of a fermata sign on the sign which gives the name of the bus, etc.

Here is an example of a Baroque Hautboisten Gavotte, which has a fermata in the second bar. The fermata sign in this example does not call for any kind of improvisation. It is similar to a 'Grand pause,' but would not be held nearly as long.

I think the suggestion here is that the first three beats represent the dancers bowing and curtsying to present themselves, then a slight pause where the fermata sign is, followed by the dance proper. In this case the first two bars might be *meno mosso* with the third bar *a tempo*. The Thoinot Arbeau *Orchésography* of 1588 describes the dance movement corresponding to the first two bars.

> At the commencement … you must pre-suppose that the dancer, holding the damsel by the hand, makes the *reverénce* … To perform the *reverénce*, you will keep the left foot firmly upon the ground and bending the right knee take the point of the toe behind the left foot, removing your bonnet or hat the while and bowing to your damsel and the company. After the *reverénce* is completed straighten your body and replace your bonnet, then bring your right foot forward and place it beside the left.[1]

As Improvisation Sign

1) *Cadenza*

The appearance of the fermata sign familiar to most musicians is the one usually found in the first movements of concerti of the Classical Period. Typically found just before the final orchestral ritornello, the fermata sign is found over a tonic chord in the second inversion. During the Classical Period it was expected that the soloist would improvise, using the musical materials of the first movement. A valuable list of the eighteenth-century expectations was given by Türk.[2]

1. The cadenza should particularly reinforce the impression the composition has made in a most lively way and present the most important parts of the whole composition in the form of a brief summary or in an extremely concise arrangement.
2. The cadenza, like every extempore embellishment, must consist not so much of intentionally added difficulties as of such thoughts which are most scrupulously suited to the main character of the composition.
3. Cadenzas should not be too long, especially in compositions of a melancholy character.
4. Modulations into other keys, particularly to those which are far removed, either do not take place at all—for example in short cadenzas—or they must be used with much insight and, as it were, only in passing. In no case should one modulate to a key which the composer himself has not used in the composition.
5. Variety is necessary if the attention of the listener is to be held. Therefore as much of the unexpected and the surprising as can possibly be added should be used in the cadenza.
6. No thought should be often repeated in the same key or in another, no matter how beautiful it may be.

---

[1] *Orchesography* (New York: Kamin Dance Publishers, 1948), 79ff.
[2] D. G. Türk, *Kurze Anweisung zum Generalbassspielen* (Halle, 1791).

7. Every dissonance which has been included, even in single-voiced cadenzas, must be properly resolved.
8. A cadenza does not have to be erudite, but novelty, wit, an abundance of ideas and the like are so much more its indispensable requirements.
9. The same tempo and meter should not be maintained throughout the cadenza … The whole cadenza should be more like a fantasia which has been fashioned out of an abundance of feeling, rather than a methodically-constructed composition.
10. Even though the cadenza has been carefully written out and memorized, it should be performed as if it were merely invented on the spur of the moment.

The above description reflects the extent to which the concerto had become much more of a public event than it had been in the Baroque Period when such works were performed for select guests in palace rooms.

The Baroque cadenza was played as part of the final cadence, on the next to last harmony (dominant) and was much shorter, for singers and wind players that which can be done in one breath. The idea was for the artist to have the opportunity to make a final reflection on the feeling of the movement.

A comment by Castiglione, in his famous book on the art of the courtier,[3] suggests that the basic style of the Baroque cadenza may have been known already in the Renaissance.

> When a musician is singing and utters a single word ending in a group of notes with a sweet cadence, and with such ease that it seems effortless, that touch alone proves that he is capable of far more than he is doing.

2) *Eingang*

The *Eingang*, a term given the practice by Mozart,[4] was a generally brief improvised passage for the purpose of leading into the next material. And for this reason, it is usually played by the player who has the melody in the following music. Mozart often used this device in places where he seemed concerned that the following music, either in tempo or in style, might be too abrupt for the listener. The *Eingang* is recognized by the appearance of a fermata over a dominant or substitute dominant chord. It is essential that the conductor recognize the distinction in harmony between the cadenza and the *Eingang*. There are many recording which have been made of Mozart concerti where a cadenza is played where Mozart intended only an *Eingang*. Mozart often wrote out *Eingänge* and one can see an example in the Romance movement of the *Gran Partita*, K. 361.

Speaking of the *Gran Partita*, the first movement requires two *Eingänge*, one where the fermata is found thirteen bars from the end. Since this fermata occurs on a tutti *forte*, but is followed by a mysterious, *piano* passage, perhaps the *Eingang* in the first clarinet should be something which begins the transition to a softer dynamic level, so that it is not so abrupt.

---

3 Castiglione, *The Courtier*, trans. George Bull (New York: Penguin Books, 1967), II, 145ff.

4 Mozart coined the name, but I have seen the practice in Baroque music.

The other *Eingang* comes at the great *forte* climax at the end of the beginning Largo. Since this *Eingang* is followed by an entirely new section with a new tempo, it is possible to hear a rather bravo improvisation by the clarinetist, reflecting the loud climax. I prefer an *Eingang* more in the spirit of the Baroque, one which reflects back on the character of the Largo as a whole. I would suggest, for example, the following one which brings back the very first solo passage in the clarinet's first entrance in ②. This one, it seems to me, is contemplative, even nostalgic, and makes an elegant connection with the Molto Allegro, which is, let us remember, also at the *piano* level.

Inexact Notation

For the modern performer there are general problems which cause constant difficulties. One is the fact that many basic rhythms have only one form of notation, but numerous realities in performance. Consider the dotted eighth-note connected to a sixteenth-note, which in faster tempi can be played as two sixteenth-notes separated by an eighth-rest and in slow tempi the figure can become almost a triplet with a long second note. Taste is the only rule.

A more difficult example of this same rhythm is in compound meters where you find connected under a ligature an eighth-note, a dotted eighth-note followed by a sixteenth-note. This is a very difficult rhythm to perform accurately, as one can see in its appearance in the Vivace of the first movement of Seventh Symphony of Beethoven where no orchestra plays it correctly; they settle for turning the meter into $\frac{4}{8}$.

Shortening Notes

Another very important problem in modern performance is an apparent lack of knowledge of the fact that the general style in the eighteenth century consisted of shorter note values than is appropriate in the second half of the nineteenth century. It would be going too far to characterize the basic eighteenth-century style as staccato, but it tended in that direction. Even in keyboard performance if one had four quarter-notes on paper one created a space between the notes.

> The ordinary movement consists in lifting the finger from the last key shortly before touching the next note.[5]

---

5   F. W. Marpurg, *Anleitung zum Clavierspielen* (Berlin, 1755, 2nd edition 1765), I, vii, 29.

It is not clear just how 'staccato' the Classical Period style of playing was, or where this style originated. Some musicians in Austria told me that they are convinced that the origin was in folk-music and I have heard, high in the alps, some amateur instrumentalists playing everything really staccato. Bruce Haynes believed this style had its origin in the Baroque instruments which required 'much less pressure in embouchure, breath, touch or bow, can be stopped and started more easily.'

There must have been a few musicians during the Classical Period who played the much more legato style we use today, for Quantz mentions it in disapproval calling the notes glued together 'like a hurdy gurdy.'[6] Certainly today you hear wind players connecting everything, probably thinking the result is more 'symphonic,' but I call it 'Brahmsifying.'

So when did we begin to play earlier music like Brahms? I was told by some distinguished members of the Vienna Philharmonic that this happened shortly after the opera house was first opened in 1869. Apparently the kind of stone used for the interior of the hall, together with the paint, made the winds sound very shrill. After a few years of complaints the hall was repainted and there was some improvement. The winds, nevertheless, found that by lengthening everything the effect was lessened. These same Philharmonic players also taught at the Akademie für Musik and so the story goes their students moved across Europe teaching the new style.

The shortening of a note value in the Viennese Classical tradition can be seen in a very important rule: If a note is followed by rests until the next bar line, that note is played half its value. Often this was just shorthand for the scribe. Imagine four eighth-notes, then a bar line, then a quarter-note, with the five notes under a slur. Clearly strings or winds would play this as a group of five eighth-notes under a slur, even though the last note appeared as a quarter-note. But it was quicker for the scribe, and easier to read, if he wrote a quarter-note for otherwise after the bar line he would have to add an additional flag on the note stem and an additional rest.

Generally, however, the quarter-note after a bar line was played half its written value in order to prevent overlapping with another voice which enters. Here is a clear example, I think, by Mozart in the exposition section of the first movement of the *Gran Partita*. One can see here, in my abbreviated score, that if the clarinets played a full quarter-note as their final note, it would overlap the entering bassoons and obscure their entrance. I might mention that in this same passage in the recapitulation Mozart remembered the problem and this time he notated the final note as an eighth-note, the way the players would have played it even though it appears as a quarter-note.

---

6   Johann Quantz, *The art of flute playing* [1752].

Lengthening Notes

An important example of lengthening a note is found in the double-dotting, a style which continued well through the Classical Period in Vienna. Indeed the performance practice authority, Clive Brown, believes the double-dotting tradition can be traced through the nineteenth century and into the twentieth.[7] An important example of double dotting is found in the first measure at the beginning of the *Gran Partita* of Mozart. If one does not double dot here, then the third note takes on a strong 'bump' effect, with almost a syncopated feel, whereas the double dotting achieves a smooth and elegant beginning.

The early music authority, Bruce Haynes, writes at length in protest to those players whose goal is to play exactly what is on paper, which he calls Urtext style.[8]

> To play literally 'as written' from the page, Urtext style, would thus—paradoxically—be to play *not* as written, as it would overlook the shorthand messages embedded in the notation and assumed to be understandable.

He is thinking of such things as changing the tempo within a movement, based on feeling and chord changes; note shaping, pauses and two things which he includes under the definition of agogics, which we will discuss below. Here, for Haynes, these include prolonging and making stronger the first of a group of notes in faster passages to clarify the metric groups and delineate figuration, a practice most players do today. He also includes the rhythmic freedom to distinguish melodic ideas. A perfect example can be seen in 9 of the Wagner *Trauermusik*. Here one needs to stretch the two sixteenth-notes in order to make them lyrical. To play them as written gives them an instrumental quality. I regard this as a very important practice.

Another place where one needs to feel free to define, usually to lengthen, a note are those places where a note of small value lies just before a whole or half-note in a motive suggesting an announcement, or perhaps the ringing of big bells, the musical representation of 'Ta-Ta!' I have a firm conviction that the feeling behind this figure is once again related to movement, to the movement of feet in perhaps a Spanish dance. Try, with both feet together on the floor, lifting the left leg and then in rapid succession returning the left foot to the floor, lifting the right leg and returning the fight foot to the floor. I think, in terms of movement, you will find a natural 'feel' for the speed of this dance pattern. The sounds your feet make, in that natural movement, are the sound, I believe, that composers feel in writing this pattern. So, for me, in the following example, whether the composer wrote either version, I ignore the appearance on paper and play it the same way, in the speed of that dance step.

---

7 Clive Brown, *Classical and Romantic Performing Practice* (Oxford University Press, 1999), 8, 9, 11, 625.
8 Haynes, *The End of Early Music*, 109.

Inequality

Finally, a word on the practice known as inequality, a subject for which the reader can easily find additional information. Basically, this was a very frequently employed Baroque technique to relieve the dull quality of repeated notes on the same pitch. The composer wrote the regular eighth-note version because it was easier than adding an additional note with flag and the triplet symbol. I don't suppose any composer ever thought it would be played as written. I bring up this topic only because in the Baroque Hauboisten band repertoire there are some movements written in imitation of march music, or perhaps in quoting familiar march music. Playing these kinds of passages as written is deadly, but applying inequality allows them to take flight as the reader can seen in the following example.

Traditional seventeenth-century march pattern, as written:

Traditional seventeenth-century march pattern, as performed:

ACCENTUATION

Agogic Accents

Agogic accentuation refers to the emphasis of important melodic notes. It is clearly understood in language, where the right hemisphere of our brain adds the emotional definition to the sterile left brain vocabulary in order to establish meaning. Take a sentence like, 'I am going to go buy a hamburger.' If you repeat this each time emphasizing a different word the meaning of the sentence is dramatically changed. 'I am going to go *buy* a hamburger' (as opposed to getting a free one). 'I am going to go buy *a* hamburger' (as opposed to buying two or more), etc. The same idea using pauses creates new meanings. 'What is this thing called love?' 'What, is *this* thing called love?' 'What is this thing called, love?'

This agogic principle of emphasis may be very old. It is easy to imagine early man, before language when he was making only vowel-like utterances, making some small distinctions through his right brain choice of emphasis on a single vowel sound, such as 'oh,' 'Oh!,' or 'Oooooh.'

Later, when man had developed a spoken language, but still before the development of written languages, he surely continued in this same right hemisphere control of meaning, for we still do this today—we carry this from early man. And so we come to Homer, that immortal blind Greek poet, the author of the *Iliad* and the *Odyssey*. These epic stories were created before the advent of the written Greek language and were so passed down in an oral tradition for some two centuries until there was an available way to write them down. They were passed down by an extraordinary kind of performer called a Rhapsodist, one who was called a musician, never an orator and never a singer in the modern sense. The Rhapsodist delivered these epics from memory before audiences and, according to Plato's book *Ion*, named for a Rhapsodist, in which Socrates has a discussion with an actual Rhapsodist, they were creating strong emotional reactions in their listeners.

> SOCRATES. I wish you would frankly tell me, Ion, what I am going to ask you: When you produce the greatest effect upon the audience in the recitation of some striking passage, such as the apparition of Odysseus leaping forth on the floor, recognized by the suitors and shaking out his arrows at his feet, or the description of Achilles springing upon Hector, or the sorrows of Andromache, Hecuba, or Priam,—are you in your right mind? Are you not carried out of yourself, and does not your soul in an ecstasy seem to be among the persons or places of which you are speaking …?
>
> ION. That proof strikes home to me, Socrates. For I must frankly confess that at the tale of pity my eyes are filled with tears, and when I speak of horrors, my hair stands on end and my heart throbs.
>
> SOCRATES. Well, Ion, and what are we to say of a man who at a sacrifice or festival, when he is dressed in an embroidered robe, and has golden crowns upon his head, of which nobody has robbed him, appears weeping and panic-stricken in the presence of more than twenty thousand friendly faces, when there is no one despoiling or wronging him;—is he in his right mind or is he not?
>
> ION. No indeed, Socrates, I must say that, strictly speaking, he is not in his right mind.
>
> SOCRATES. And are you aware that you produce similar effects on most of the spectators?
>
> ION. Only too well; for I look down upon them from the stage, and behold the various emotions of pity, wonder, sternness, stamped upon their faces when I am performing: and I am obliged to give my very best attention to them; for if I make them cry I myself shall laugh, and if I make them laugh I myself shall cry, when the time of payment arrives.[9]

We can no longer know exactly what the Rhapsodists were doing in terms of their vocal technique,[10] but I am always reminded of the Rhapsodist when I look at our oldest European music notation, those ninth-century neumes, which no one today knows how to transcribe. Those characters do not look like meter or beats to me, so much as symbols to indicate *performance*, the pitch of individual syllables. And if they are a system of symbols to indicate, not *what* to sing, but *how* to sing certain syllables then the information which came down from that remarkable early scholar, Roger Bacon (1220–1292), may be a clue to confirm that explanation for the nuemes. He made the very interesting observation,

> For accent is a kind of singing; whence it is called accent from *accino, accinis* [I sing, thou singest], because every syllable has its own proper sound either raised, lowered, or composite, and all syllables of one word are adapted or sung to one syllable on which rests the principal sound.[11]

---

9   Ion, 534, c - 535e.

10 Whenever I hear ancient Chinese opera, with its extremely wide tessitura and great variety of vocal sounds, I wonder if it is the last remnant of the old vocal production of the Rhapsodist.

11 *The Opus Majus of Roger Bacon*, trans. Robert Burke (New York: Russell & Russell, 1962), I, 259.

If there was a system such as Bacon implies, where 'every syllable has its own sound,' then one can imagine the *text* of the Odyssey 'composing' the music for itself.

There are a few more references we should consider. The sixth century AD Greek writer, Paulus Silentiarius, wrote a poem in honor of a deceased lyre player, which mentions an interesting reference to music being the origin of grammar.

> Damocharis passed into the final silence of Fate; alas! The Muses' love lyre is silent: the holy foundation of Grammar has perished.

Guido of Arezzo, in his eleventh-century *Micrologus*, the first modern notation system to follow the neume system, mentions another vocal characteristic we carry from ancient man, the fact that we often have an unconscious raising of the pitch of the voice in states of fear or excitement. Guido adds a curious and very interesting psychological observation.

> We often place an acute or grave accent above the notes, because we often utter them with more or less stress, so much so that the repetition of the same note often seems to be a raising or lowering.[12]

By the way, it is in this treatise that we find the earliest reference to a ritard. at the end of a composition.

> Towards the ends of phrases the notes should always be more widely spaced as they approach the breathing place, like a galloping horse, so that they arrive at the pause, as it were, weary and heavily.[13]

In the *Compendium Musices*, of 1552, by Adrian Coclico, a treatise written to train boys to sing in Church, we again find a reference to placing specific music under a specific syllable.

> When he has learned these things clearly and rapidly, he will then begin to sing, not only as [the music] is written but also with embellishments, and to pronounce skillfully, smoothly and meaningfully, to intone correctly and to place any syllable in its proper place under the right notes.[14]

The final two references to this connection known to me come from the sixteenth century. Tinctoris (1435–1511) makes an incredible definition, 'A melodic interval is the immediate connection of one syllable after another.'[15] And, finally, Erasmus (1466–1536) writes,

> The accent can justifiably be called, as it was by some ancient grammarians, the soul of the word.[16]

---

[12] *Hucbald, Guido and John on Music*, trans. Warren Babb (New Haven: Yale University Press, 1978), 139.

[13] Ibid., 175.

[14] Adrian Coclico, *Musical Compendium*, trans. Albert Seay (Colorado Spring: Colorado College Music Press, 1973), 6.

[15] Tinctoris, *Dictionary of Musical Terms*, trans. Carl Parrish (New York: Free Press of Glencoe, 1963), 17.

[16] 'The Right Way of Speaking Latin and Greek,' [1528] in Ibid., XXVI, 422ff.

Because the above discussion spans more than 2,000 years we cannot know for certain what the earliest practice was with regard to using pitch, or music, to clarify meaning. What we are left with today is the agogic accent principle which, if not genetic, is in any case a very natural tool in performance to express meaning. But only if one uses it. As we have noted above, Music is not a thing, it is an act, it is something we do. How we place an agogic accent, or emphatic lingering, within a melody distinguishes our own individual interpretations of the music on paper.

But what if you elect to perform and add nothing in the way of agogic accents? Bruce Haynes compares the written form of the music to a cookbook and therefore observes that if one does nothing in shaping the melody, then instead of making a cake one is eating the cookbook.

Can one go too far? The Modernists of the twentieth century thought so and, believe it or not, the Vienna Conservatory in the early 1960s formed a *Stilkommission* which had among its goals the elimination of the 'agogic freedom of the Liszt-school.' With the Modernists School, of course, the pendulum swung too far in the opposite direction giving us a century of pretty dull music making.

On Ornaments

The reader will find there is a long history of the discussion of ornaments. Indeed, Johann Mattheson in the seventeenth century already complained,

> In the past our learned musicians have compiled whole books ... on nothing but vocal ornaments.[17]

We will not repeat the most familiar of these practices, but do want to make two observations. First, we often have had students tell us that their private teachers have told them that all eighteenth-century trills are upper-note trills. That is not correct. Baroque trills are very clearly upper-note trills, but Classical Period trills are without question main-note trills in principle.

We also want to mention the portamento, which is not familiar to wind conductors. The portamento is an unbroken slide from beneath to the note to be accented and which was used extensively in the nineteenth century by singers and string players.[18] Beginning in the 1930s it was identified as a characteristic of the Romantic style and thus retired by the Modernists. For wind conductors I should like to point out the use of written out portamento in the fourth movement of the *Suite Française* by Darius Milhaud. The written out portamento in the bass instruments in 43, and in similar places, reflecting a chill going up the spine, should be on the fast side, with no noticeable changes in pitch, that is a smooth slide.

---

[17] Johann Mattheson, *Der vollkommene Capellemeister* [1739], II, 14, 50–51.

[18] I have a recording of the last castrato made about 1904 which employs this frequently. I also have a recording from the 1920s of Ormandy, as a violinist, adding the portamento to increase emotion. He continued to use this frequently as a conductor.

The other portamento is the melodic one in ▨, and especially after ▨. This one is purely melodic, and is a painful cry. It should be performed very slowly, without pitch distinction and with a crescendo.

Finally, the slur mark, which appears first described in 1619 by Praetorius for the purpose of designating related groups of notes appears in Germany by the time of Bach to have taken on a new meaning. There is some indication in the late Baroque through Brahms the slur had taken on the meaning of a diminuendo.[19]

Written Accents

Before any kind of articulation was added to notes by writing, the wind instruments were practicing articulation through the pronunciation of syllables, known as syllabication,[20] which may be yet another remnant of the above discussion on the treatment of syllables through pitch. It was essential in the performance of the early cornetto, which was played from the side of the mouth and thus inaccessible to the tongue. The famous sixteenth-century book on cornetto improvisation by Dalla Casa includes pages of music with syllables underneath for the player to practice before getting to the actual repertoire of the book. A modern example is that of a nineteenth-century English flute teacher who taught the student to say the word 'territory' while playing four eighth-notes slurred two by two on paper. The sound of 'territory,' in my twenty-first century English, suggests that the result was that the first eighth-note was slightly louder and longer than the remaining notes, with the third eighth-note being slightly louder than numbers two and four.

This last example reminds us of the thirteenth bar of the oboe in the Adagio in the Mozart *Gran Partita*, K. 361. First I should remind the reader that this figure is really the only true consistent appoggiatura used by Mozart, everything else is generally intended to be grace notes. As I suppose all musicians know, the appoggiatura slurred to an eighth-note and two sixteenth-notes was intended always to be performed as four sixteenth-notes, with the first two slurred, with the first note accented. Mozart wrote it this way, and not as four sixteenth-notes, as that was one of the few recognized ways to indicate an accent. Four sixteenths written would be played two slurred and two tongued, but without an accent. A noticeable proof of this can be seen in ▨ of the Adagio where he writes four sixteenth-notes. When this material returns in the recapitulation one can see that Mozart first wrote in the oboe a G appoggiatura above the staff. Then he remembered he did not want an accent on this figure, so he crosses out the G appoggiatura and replaces it with a regular G, now part of four written out sixteenth notes.

To return to ▨ and the similarity with 'territory,' one can see in the principal oboe two appoggiaturas, one written as an eighth-note with one slash through it and the next one with two slashes through it. Mozart was not always entirely consistent in the matter of the number

---

[19] Haynes, *The End of Early Music*, 107.

[20] The only examples still in use are the double tonguing and triple tonguing on the trumpet.

of slashes, as one can see in the basset horn in ⟦14⟧ and in ⟦23⟧. Again, returning to the oboe in ⟦13⟧, the result of course will be two slurred sixteenth-notes, with the first one accented and two tongued ones, followed by two slurred ones and two tongued ones. But we can't help wondering if in writing first an eighth-note with one slash, rather than two slashes as in the following figure, he meant that the first of the eight sixteenth-notes is longer than the fifth one (with two slashes). Perhaps this is 'territory' on some earlier German word.

Mozart is also not entirely consistent in the use of the remaining familiar accent symbols, the *fp* and *sfp*.[21] Generally these kinds of mistakes in Mozart I attribute to the speed in writing this secondary data while his head is racing ahead with new melodic material. He was surely bored with this level of calligraphy, as one can see in the beginning of the *Gran Partita* when he went back later to fill in the horn parts. Here, with stems going the wrong way, we recognize speed and not thought.

While we do not know the difference Mozart had in mind between *fp* and *sfp*, it is clear that neither one had anything to do with dynamics. The *fp* was an accent at the established dynamic level and not like the modern *fp* which means really a *forte* dynamic level and a *subito piano*. One can see in the fifth bar of the fourth Variation of the Theme and Variations movement in the bassoon, Mozart very clearly writes the first eighth-note *forte*, as the climax of the previous crescendo; the second eighth-note *piano* to reestablish the piano level; and then a *fp* on the third eighth-note, which is clearly an accent at the *piano* level.

Staccato as Accent

One sometimes reads that early man must have had greater acuity in all his senses as a matter of survival. You have to be able to smell the tiger outside the cave even if you can't see him. Certainly, considering our noisy industrial environment, where our brain turns off our awareness of so much we do not need to hear (those 220 lights, for example), early man must have heard more. I am beginning to think early composers heard something we have failed to hear.

When I was living in Vienna, in 1968–1969, and working for Universal Edition on their project to publish an Urtext edition of the Mozart piano sonatas, I was preparing a draft of one of the sonatas and came to a passage where Mozart in his original autograph score had written a diatonic line of eight eighth-notes. The first two or three had staccato dots, very clearly notated. Then the next several had increasingly more elongated marks, with the pen scratching downward somewhat. The final three had marks which looked more like the stroke mark. For my copy I made them all staccato, reasoning that Mozart was always bored doing this sort of 'after composing' calligraphy and that as he speeded up the pen movement gradually turned into a more vertical mark, and that there was no musical evidence whatsoever that suggested that the articulation in these particular eight notes should change. My boss said, 'No! the last three are stroke accents!' After some argument, he sent me to have a discussion with Christa Landon, who lived in Vienna and was then becoming the recognized author-

---

[21] See the eighteenth bar of the third Variation of the Theme and Variations movement, where both *sfp* and *fp* are used in the same bar.

ity on Schubert. In the course of that discussion she made the statement that for Mozart the staccato dot was an accent, the smallest kind of accent available to him. This opened up the possibility that Mozart recognized a kind of progression in the vehemence of the articulation, graduating from staccato to the stroke.

After this discussion it occurred to me that since we know that Mozart used both *fp* and *sfp* at the *piano* level, a symbol calling for a still softer accent at the *piano* level would be something of considerable sensitivity.

Further thought made me come to believe that there is something in staccato performance we may have overlooked with our diminished sense of hearing contributed by the modern world. Take the vowel 'Lu' [any vowel will work] and sing legato quarter-notes at an andante tempo. Now if you make a note staccato the missing material has to come off the back side of the note, otherwise you could never align the pitch with other parts. So now sing 'Lu' the same speed but make it staccato. Now that half or so of the length has been taken away, the brain curiously concentrates not on the length left, or even the pitch, but now only on the attack. It sounds now accented and you can't prevent this brain-aural effect. A colleague I had try this observed,

> I can't make myself sing a short 'lu' and have it sound as smooth as the long, even though I'm quite convinced my tongue is doing the same thing.

So it does appear that staccato is *heard* as an accent.

I gave no further thought to this until 2010 when I was making modern scores from a vast set of parts in a German Baroque Hautboisten band library. In this collection there were a couple of movements which had in the upper left hand corner, underneath the tempo designation, the word, 'Staccato.' Since, as we know, the music of the Baroque and Classical Period was played more detached, approaching staccato, than we play today, I began to wonder what would be accomplished by the term 'staccato' when everything was already spaced? The only reasonable answer I could think of, two centuries later, was to make the performance accented.

In looking through this same Baroque collection, I found an example which I think comes pretty close to proving the point. This case[22] involves the pyramid principle, known to choral conductors since the fifteenth century, in which the brain tends to exaggerate upper partials thus requiring the conductor to adjust for more bass and less top in order to make the listener think he hears what the eye sees in the score. Here we have repeated octaves where according to the said principle the listener will hear the upper octaves louder than the lower ones. So the composer for this manuscript places the dots over only the lower notes, apparently to give them accents, with the result that the listener will perceive the accented lower pitches as being at the same dynamic level as the upper pitches. Surely here one can see no other reason for these dots on only the lower octave.

---

[22] BRD Fü 3741a, Nr. 8, first movement.

Another example[23] from this same collection shows a single bar with dots in all voices. Here the musical logic makes much sense as accents, and one can see no purpose for a single bar of staccato in this busy movement.

In doing a little research to see if anyone else mentioned this use of the staccato dot I found only one reference, but it is a striking one. In the 1905 edition of the *Elson Dictionary of Music* one finds,

> The staccato mark is sometimes used merely as an accent mark as may be seen in the closing theme of Beethoven's *Sonata Pathétique*, first movement, and in much other modern music.[24]

And, sure enough, there they are.

So, with this practice apparently documented from the late Baroque until Beethoven it certainly seems possible that Mozart may have also used the staccato dot to mean an accent. I find it difficult to suggest that in Mozart every dot over a note means an accent and not staccato, but it *is* possible that that is what he had in mind.

---

23 Ibid., Nr. 25, fourth movement.
24 *Elson's Music Dictionary* (Boston: Oliver Ditson Company, 1905), 5.

In any case, here is an example, taken from the end of the Romance movement of the *Gran Partita*, K. 361, which I believe is a good candidate for a place in Mozart where the dot means an accent and not staccato. In the next to last bar, we see the **pp** which we contend means a ritard. Mozart has already written 'staccato' in the notation, but writing eighth-notes instead of quarter notes. So, since the notes on paper are already a written out staccato, what would be the point in adding a staccato dot? But the dot here could mean a sensitive little accent. In terms of conducting, these eighth-notes are not notes which jump up into the air as if staccato. These eighth-notes have a kind of tenuto, a heavier downward feeling.

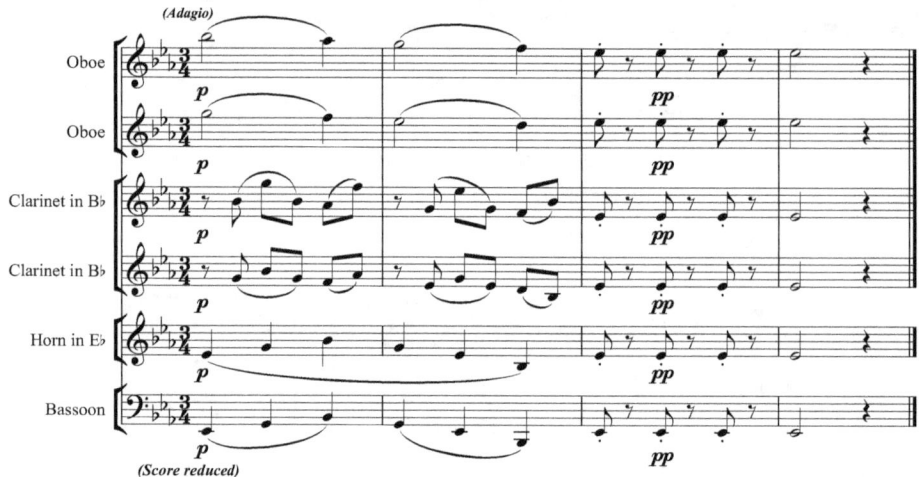

Tempo and Dynamics

Tempo

For many conductors, tempo begins with that Italian word in the upper left corner of the music page. This tradition began in the early years of the seventeenth century and was intended to communicate character, as for example in the case of *grave*, rather than tempo. By the second half of the century, Johann Mattheson reports that *allegro* meant *comfort* and that *andante* meant *hope*! Most conductors will be surprised at this and that is because, as Leopold Mozart reports in 1756 in his famous book on violin playing, the Italian terms had already lost their meaning. That being the case, he recommended that performers should ignore them and instead discover the tempo of a composition through the study of the music itself, giving some helpful suggestions on how to do this.

In spite of the ubiquitous metronome, with actual numbers assigned to these Italian words, as Leopold Mozart pointed out in 1756, as tempo indications these terms have no true meaning. Nevertheless, if you hand a new score to a young conducting student, the first thing he will do is look to see what is written in the upper left corner. If he sees Allegro, as an example, he immediately makes sweeping judgments about the composition, although he has yet to even glance at the actual music.

How have we come to place so much importance on something which had already lost its meaning in 1756?

During the countless centuries of music history before notation, tempo must have been a subject of concern only with regard to dance music. All other solo performance would no doubt have always consisted of performance dictated by feeling. One can imagine that feeling also determined even dance tempi until such time as there were known and repeatable dances which would have tended toward a narrow range of recognizable tempi.

We have no way of knowing much about tempo with respect to the medieval two- and three-part scores, that is in the sense of individual performances. But, given the Church's role in turning music into a branch of mathematics, it would seem reasonable to guess that the notation did not anticipate internal tempo changes, such as rubato, no matter how much 'feeling' the clerical singers were attempting to add to the music. In fact we may suppose it was their frustration in trying to be musical in a rigid mathematical system which helped lead to the extensive improvisation in church music.

This aspect of tempo must have become even more problematic in Renaissance church music as it became notated for four, five and more parts. Certainly with proportions, in which the music rapidly became, through diminution, faster (smaller note values), the very mathematical complexity must have made tempo as we use the term irrelevant after the beginning. In some extant examples there quickly accumulate so many ligatures that it seems impossible to believe anyone could have actually sung the music. Some therefore consider these to be mere 'educational examples' of the mathematics in question and not intended to be sung. But some music of this kind was sung and it was a real concern for working church music directors like Michael Praetorius in the sixteenth century. He feared the conductor might end up beating so fast that,

> we make the spectators laugh and offend the listeners with incessant hand and arm movements and give the crowd an opportunity for raillery and mockery.[25]

We suspect, therefore, that because of the notation itself, together with the Church background of making music be an expression of mathematics, rather than of emotion, that for most of the Renaissance performers probably no longer thought of tempo as an expression of feeling.[26] But by the sixteenth century a change was in the atmosphere and it came from Italy. Certainly we can hear the desire to write with stronger emotions in the music of di Rore, Monteverdi and Gesualdo.

But the Italians were also beginning to break down the regimentation of tempi, at least this seems clear in Praetorius' *Syntagma Musicum* (1619), which he wrote as a kind of introductory treatise for the purpose of introducing the Italian style to Germany. When discussing various signatures at the beginning of compositions, Praetorius finds there is no longer agreement

---

[25] *Syntagma Musicum*, III, 74. A facsimile of the original German publication has been printed by Bärenreiter Kassel, 1958. The page numbers we cite, therefore, are from the original print.

[26] Please do not read this as meaning that Renaissance music was devoid of feeling!

among the Italians. He suggests that the slower common time signature is used in madrigals and the faster alla breve sign is used in motets.[27] However, he has noticed that in *all* the compositions of Gabrieli, he uses only the alla breve sign. In the works of Viadana, he finds the alla breve sign in compositions with text and the common time sign in instrumental works. His own opinion, agreeing with what he has found in the works of Lassus and Marenzio, was that,

> the common time sign should be used for those motets and other sacred compositions which have many black notes, in order to show that the beat is to be taken more slowly … Anyone, however, may reflect upon such matters himself and decide, on the basis of text and music, where the beat has to be slow and where fast.

His last sentence is revolutionary, for we can see that the question of tempo has now passed from the composer to the performer.

In concerti, where madrigal and motets *styles* are found, it is necessary to change tempo. Here, instead of using the common time and alla breve signs, Praetorius suggests it might be better to employ the new practice of using Italian words, such as adagio, presto, etc.[28]

Praetorius clearly reflects[29] a level of rubato never mentioned in earlier treatises. For this practice he makes two general rules, first that a performance must not be hurried and second that all note values must be observed. Then he adds a comment that demonstrates how dramatic the revolution in the approach to tempo was. The conductor can now decide for himself changes in tempo with are entirely uncalled for in the score.

> But to use, by turns, now a slower, now a faster beat, in accordance with the text, lends dignity and grace to a performance and makes it admirable … Some do not want such mixture of [tempi] in any one composition. But I cannot accept their opinion, especially since it makes motets and concerti particularly delightful, when after some slow and expressive measures at the beginning several quick phrases follow, succeeded in turn by slow and stately ones, which again change off with faster ones.

This apparent new freedom among the Italians is confirmed by the many similar Baroque recommendations to the performer to feel free to vary the tempo. The whole story of the Baroque Period, music history texts notwithstanding, was a fervent attempt to return emotions to music, after fifteen centuries of their being discouraged by the Church. And so the very nature of these recommendations reflect a prior regimentation in the concept of tempo, which the Baroque composers seemed eager to destroy. The very practice Praetorius discusses above, relative to the freedom of the performer to make his own decision on tempo, had been mentioned four years earlier, in 1615, by Frescobaldi.

---

[27] Ibid., 48ff.

[28] Ibid., 51.

[29] Ibid., 79ff.

> These pieces should not be played to a strict beat any more than modern madrigals which, though difficult, are made easier by taking the beat now slower, now faster, and by even pausing altogether in accordance with the expression and meaning of the text.[30]

We wish to emphasize that the reason for this new freedom in tempo was to aid in the expression of emotion. One feels this clearly in Monteverdi, as well as his concern about the old style of rigid tempi, when he pleads that his song must be 'sung to the time of the heart's feeling, and not to that of the hand.'[31] And we find exactly the same plea by Giovanni Bonachelli in 1642.

> In accordance with the feeling one must guide the beat, sensing it now fast, now slow, according to the occasion, now liveliness, and now languor, as indeed anyone will easily know immediately who possesses the fine manner of singing.[32]

By 1676, the great English critic, Thomas Mace, seems to suggest that this new freedom now also included decisions on the tempo of larger formal sections of the music. If, he says, the music falls into sections, these may be played,

> according as they best please your own fancy, some very briskly, and courageously, and some again gently, lovingly, tenderly and smoothly.

He then continues with the same recommendation to the performer we have seen above.

> Beginners must learn strict time; but when we come to be masters, so that we can command all manner of time, at our own pleasures, we then take liberty ... to break time; sometimes faster and sometimes slower, as we perceive the nature of the thing requires.[33]

This new Baroque style of leaving to the performer, not the composer, the decisions regarding tempi in performance helps us understand what might otherwise seem to the modern reader a rather extraordinary incident involving Haydn in London. Haydn brought new symphonies with him for his second trip to London and when he went to the first rehearsal and, *as conductor*, sought to give the tempo for a manuscript work never before seen by the orchestra, he was immediately over-ruled by the 'Leader' who considered it *his* job to set the tempo. There must have developed some conflict for it carried over into a debate in the local newspapers. One who defended Haydn's right to set the tempo of his own music was the famous Charles Burney.

---

30 Girolamo Frescobaldi (1583 – 1643), *Toccatas and Partitas*, Book I.
31 *Madrigali guerrieri et amorosi* (Venice, 1638).
32 Giovanni Bonachelli, *Corona di sacri gigli a una, due, tre, Quattro, e cinque voci* (Venice, 1642).
33 Thomas Mace, *Musick's Monument* [176] (Paris: Editions du Centre National de la Recherche Scientifique, 1966), 429, 432.

> There is a censure leveled at him ... for marking the measure to his own new composition: but as even the old compositions had never been performed under his direction, in this country, till the last winter, it was surely allowable for him to indicate to the orchestra the exact time in which he intended the several movements to be played, without offending the leader or subalterns of the excellent band which he had to conduct.

During the nineteenth century we again find famous composers arguing for freedom in tempo, as we see, for example, in a letter by von Weber to the music director, Praeger, in Leipzig.

> The beat must not be like a tyrannical hammer, impeding or urging on, but must be to the music what the pulse-beat is to the life of man.
> There is no slow tempo in which passages do not occur that demand a quicker motion, so as to obviate the impression of dragging.
> Conversely there is no presto that does not need a quiet delivery by many places, so as not to throw away the chance of expressiveness by hurrying ...
> Neither the quickening nor the slowing of the tempo should ever give the impression of the spasmodic or the violent. The changes, to have a musical-poetic significance, must come in an orderly way in periods and phrases, conditioned by the varying warmth of the expression.[34]

And Richard Wagner complained that the 'conductor-guild' of his time dictated that there should be no tempo modification in the music of Beethoven, a view he attributed to the 'incapacity and general unfitness of our conductors themselves.'[35] This attitude is still very strong in Europe, where it is presently heard in the advice that with regard to the master composers one should play only 'what they wrote.'

Finally, after Brahms conducted his own *Fourth Symphony* with the famous Meiningen Orchestra he wrote Joseph Joachim complaining, of things not notated in the score, 'In these concerts I couldn't make enough slowings and accelerations.'[36] And anyone who has heard the extant recording of Mahler playing at the piano a transcription of his own *Fifth Symphony* will have been astonished to hear tempi, and tempo alteration so radical as to be virtually unrecognizable in the score.

After reading all these similar comments by really great musicians, we hope the reader who is a musician will pause to contemplate on the degree which the twentieth century has taken something away from him and given it back to the composer. Or have we performers just lost sight of something?

The most serious consequence of the Church's decision to make music a branch of mathematics, as a part of its campaign against the emotions, was the creation of the modern notational system by church mathematicians. Adhering to the Church dogma, they created a notational system without a single symbol which has anything to do with emotion or feeling.

---

34 Quoted in Felix Weingartner, *On Conducting* (New York: Kalmus), 41.

35 Wagner, *Prose Works*, IV, 336. The present writer, as a young conductor, once received a brutal tongue-lashing from Eugene Ormandy for creating a slight, brief cadential ritard. while conducting the Philadelphia Orchestra in the first movement of Beethoven's *Fourth Symphony*.

36 *Johannes Brahms im Briefwechsel mit Joseph Joachim* (Berlin, 1908), II, 205.

Having to notate music with such an incomplete system forced composers to seek other, less effective, means of communicating with performers, such as the language at the beginning of the score. Couperin makes these same points in the preface to his *L'Art de Toucher*.

> Not having devised signs or characters for communicating our specific ideas, we try to remedy this by indicating at the beginning of our pieces, by some such word as Tenderly, Quickly, etc., as far as possible the idea we want to convey.

The most familiar form of this practice to musicians is, of course, what Praetorius calls in 1619, 'the new practice of using Italian words, such as *adagio, presto*, etc.' For musicians today these Italian words convey tempo, but originally they were intended to reflect character, not speed.[37] It will be quite surprising for the reader to see how Johann Mattheson (1681–1764) defined some of these familiar terms.

> An *Adagio* indicates distress; a *Lamento* lamentation; a *Lento* relief; an *Andante* hope; an *Affetuoso* love; an *Allegro* comfort; a *Presto* eagerness.[38]

Whatever the original intent of these words were, their meaning had already become lost, according to Leopold Mozart, by 1756.[39] The importance of this truth can be seen clearly in his son's music. Wolfgang Mozart, in his beautiful and ethereal *Ave verum corpus*, has written music in common time which is performed by virtually everyone today at a tempo of quarter-note = 140, yet Mozart calls this Adagio! Leaving aside his comment to his sister that in his life he had never written a really slow movement, this example clearly demonstrates that whatever adagio meant to Mozart, it meant something beyond a reference to tempo.

Things were made a bit more confusing during the Baroque by the French vocabulary used in place of the Italian terms. In particular, the word, 'Movement,' by which, according to Mattheson, the French meant 'what the Italians commonly indicate only with some adjectives such as: *affettuoso, con discrezione, con spirito*.'[40]

In other words, Movement meant the emotional quality and did not refer to speed or tempo. It is in this sense that when we speak of the 'First Movement,' or 'Second Movement,' in a Mozart symphony, for example, we are reflecting the original intent which was 'first emotion' and 'second emotion.' There may have been more correspondence of such terms with tempo than we might think today. We have known Europeans who say 'First tempo' and 'Second tempo' when referring to the two principal tonal areas of the exposition section in the sonata form in Classical symphonies.

---

37 Only a few, such as 'grave,' today carry a character association.
38 Johann Mattheson, *Der vollkommene Capellmeister* (1739), trans. Ernest Harriss (Ann Arbor: UMI Research Press, 1981), II, xii, 34ff.
39 See his violin treatise.
40 Mattheson, *Der vollkommene Capellmeister*, II, vii, 7.

With this in mind we can understand the title of a book quoted by Mattheson, *Les mouvements differents sont le pur espirit de la Musique*.⁴¹ Mattheson himself says movement is a 'spiritual thing,' not a physical thing, and depends not on 'precepts and prohibitions,' but 'feeling and emotion.' To find the correct movement, the performer must 'probe and feel his own soul' as well as 'feel the various impulses which the piece is supposed to express.'⁴² The ability to correctly find the movement, Mattheson observes, is a knowledge which 'transcends all words' and 'is the highest perfection of music, and it can be attained only through considerable experience and great gifts.'

By refusing to use the Italian terms, the French apparently created some confusion among their own ranks. Couperin, for instance, explains,

> I find we confuse Measure or Time with what is called Cadence or Movement. Measure defines the number and quality of the beats; and Cadence is literally the intelligence and the soul which must be added to it.⁴³

We find this same concern expressed in Jean Rousseau's viole treatise of 1687.

> There are people who imagine that imparting the movement is to follow and keep time; but these are very different matters, for it is possible to keep time without entering into the movement, since time depends on the music, but the movement depends on genius and fine taste.

Sebastien de Brossard, in an early dictionary of music (1703), considered time from a different perspective with regard to the recitative. Writing of rubato in Largo tempo, he observes,

> In Italian recitatives we often do not make the beats very equal, because this is a kind of declamation where the Actor ought to follow the movement of the passion which inspires him or which he wants to express, rather than that of an equal and regulated measure.⁴⁴

With the hope to bring order to the general confusion regarding the designation of tempi there were a number of private inventors, caught up in the enthusiasm of the Industrial Revolution at the beginning of the nineteenth century, who worked toward creating a mechanical device for standardizing tempo. The winner of this race was the quack-inventor, acquaintance of Beethoven and emigrant to America, Johann Maelzel.⁴⁵ Maelzel's Metronome held promise for some, but for authentic musicians it only represented another rigid form of tyranny contradictory to true musical feeling. Beethoven, for example, who made the instrument known, wrote on a score following the indication, '100 according to Maelzel,'

---

41 Jean Rousseau, *Methode claire, certaine et facile pour apprendre a chanter la musique* (Paris, 1678).

42 Mattheson, *Der vollkommene Capellmeister*, II, vii, 18ff.

43 François Couperin, *L'Art de toucher* (Paris, 1717, reprinted Wiesbaden: Breitkopf & Härtel, 1933), 24.

44 Sebastien de Brossard, *Dictionaire de Musique* (Paris, 1703), 'Largo.'

45 He more or less stole the idea from Dietrich Winkel of Amsterdam.

But this must be held applicable to only the first measures, for feeling also has its tempo and this cannot entirely be expressed in this figure.[46]

Beethoven may have revised his thinking with more experience, for Franz Liszt claimed that when asked about the metronome, Beethoven replied, 'Better none.'[47] Here is a sampling of later views.

Berlioz,

I do not mean to say that it is necessary to imitate the mathematical regularity of the metronome, which would give the music thus executed an icy frigidity; I even doubt whether it would be possible to maintain this rigid uniformity for more than a few bars.[48]

Brahms, regarding his *Requiem*,

I think … that the metronome is of no value … The so-called 'elastic' tempo is moreover not a new invention.[49]

Verdi, a note in his Te *Deum*,

This entire piece ought to be performed in one tempo as indicated by the metronome. This notwithstanding, it will be appropriate to broaden or accelerate in certain spots for reasons of expression and nuance.[50]

Wagner, regarding *Tannhäuser*,

As to the 'tempi' of the whole work in general, I can only say that if conductor and singers are to depend for their time on the metronomical marks alone, the spirit of the work must stand indeed in sorry case.[51]

Bruno Walter,

The metronome marking is good only for the first few bars.[52]

---

[46] Quoted in Erich Leinsdorf, *The Composer's Advocate* (New Haven: Yale University Press, 1981, 165.
[47] Letter to Breitkopf and Härtel, Nov. 16, 1863.
[48] His Essay on Conducting.
[49] Ibid., 129.
[50] Ibid., 130.
[51] Wagner, *Prose Works*, III, 190.
[52] Walter, *On Music and Music-Making* (New York: Norton, 1957), 43.

Erich Leinsdorf,

> I do not consult the little clock.[53]

Well, the metronome *is* a horrible concept, a return to rigid formalism and the tyranny of rules. It is also unnecessary, for all the information on tempo is already provided by the composer—in the music itself. Thus, Franz Liszt wrote to a correspondent,

> A metronomical performance is certainly tiresome and nonsensical; time and rhythm must be adapted to and identified with the melody, the harmony, the accent and the poetry.[54]

And, when one considers the general limitation of our notational system, perhaps Mendelssohn said it best when he admits ignoring even the notation completely,

> I think the movement might be taken too slow, which I found to be the case at the first rehearsal, until I no longer paid any attention to the notes or the heading, but adhered to the sense alone.[55]

So where does this leave us today? Are we allowed to make alterations in tempo within a movement? Yes we are, for as Beethoven said, 'feeling has its own tempo.' One arrives at the tempo from the music itself and from nothing else. But we caution, this is an aspect of musicianship and you will be so judged by the listener.

For discovering tempo while studying scores I recommend, in places of doubt, singing. Singing somehow brings us into touch with the universal aspects of music and one should put some faith in your own inner, genetic, feeling in this regard. Certainly any form of classroom theoretical analysis will reveal nothing of tempo. Better to take the advice of Mattheson, study the score 'to find your own soul.'

Dynamics

The same freedom in performance allowed in tempo is also extended to dynamics, according to Praetorius.

> Besides, it adds much charm to harmony and melody, if the dynamic level in the vocal and instrumental parts is varied now and then.

---

[53] Leinsdorf, *The Composer's Advocate*, 130.
[54] Letter to Siegmund Lebert, Jan. 10, 1870.
[55] Letter to Nicolas Gade, March 3, 1843.

Praetorius returns to the subject of dynamics, in another place, mentioning that the Italians are beginning to use *forte*, *piano*, etc., to mark changes within a concerto. It is interesting that, once again, he suggests that the conductor is free to alter both dynamics and tempo.

> I rather like this practice. There are some who believe that this is not very appropriate, especially in churches. I feel, however, that such variety [in dynamics] and change [in tempo] are not only agreeable and proper, if applied with moderation and designed to express the feelings of the music, and affect the ear and the spirit of the listener much more and give the concerto a unique quality and grace. Often the composition itself, as well as the text and the meaning of the words, requires that one [change] at times—but not too frequently or excessively—beating now fast, now slowly, also that one lets the choir by turns sing quietly and softly, and loudly and briskly. To be sure, in churches there will be more need of restraint in such changes than at banquets.[56]

Finally, it is particularly interesting here, that Praetorius gives one Latin term, *lento gradu*, which he says was understood to mean that the voice was both softer and slower.

It is true there is enormous liberty in performance when it comes to dynamics because all the symbols are relative and without any precise definitions. Everyone has his own definition of *piano* and *forte*. My old friend, Mark Hindsley, a man trained in science before he became a conductor, once, after some cost and effort, developed a machine which measured dynamics and then lit up a series of colored light bulbs according to the relative dynamics. Everyone thought it was a fine idea, but no one knew how to use it. It measured relativity, but had no recognized base to begin from.

In spite of all these characteristics, dynamics remains the more important tool available to the musician for shaping melody and thus for helping give meaning to music. Marcel Tabeteau, Principal Oboe of the Philadelphia Orchestra, used to give his students a melody and then require them to number each note, 1 through 10, with ten being the most important melodic note in their view. This is very difficult, requiring one to constantly change one's mind about some insignificant looking note on the way to the climax, 'no, this is a 3, not a 4,' etc. But, conscious or unconscious, one has to do this with every phrase one plays. The first difficulty is that we are not trained to think like this in our youth. We sit behind an etude, notes utterly without meaning, without dynamics and we start to play. Our only goal is to get it right, in some technical definition. Years of practicing and playing, but with no music.

IMPROVISATION

On Improvisation in Harmoniemusik Literature

Today the composer hopes for as many performances as possible for his composition, indeed he even hopes that listeners yet unborn will hear his work. But the composer of the Baroque and Classical Period generally composed for a single performance by a specific body of performers and in most cases the composer expected to be present. The court composer, with his

---

[56] Ibid., 132 (112).

requirement to constantly produce music on demand, did not have the luxury of time to think of posterity. Earlier composers were also heir to a rich tradition of improvisation by all instrumentalists, a tradition as old as music itself. Indeed, it was only as recently as in the Renaissance that players began to read from written music on a regular basis.

For all the above reasons, we can understand why earlier court composers frequently wrote music in a simple form, anticipating that the player would 'finish' the composition by improvisation in performance. In slow movements, in particular, this was commonly expected. As Charles Burney observed,

> An adagio is, generally, little more than an outline left to the performers abilities to color. [If he does not, he will] soon excite languor and disgust in the hearers.[57]

When, in late Bach and Handel, we find the composer beginning to actually write everything out, the performers complained that the composer was taking away their role and furthermore making the music incomprehensible. Thus Johann Scheibe wrote of Bach that by his writing everything out he 'makes the melodic line utterly unclear.'[58]

It is less widely understood that this same tradition continued to some degree during the Classical Period. Indeed, we have eye-witness reports by Spohr and Berlioz that players were even continuing to freely improvise well into the nineteenth century.

In the following discussion of improvisation in Harmoniemusik, I will omit the entire category of single ornaments and instead concentrate on compositional circumstances which call for true improvisation.

First, it is clear that the type of melodic elaboration which was so commonly executed during the Baroque continued during the Classical Period. There are a number of cases where we have both the original form of the notation and what the player actually performed. Among such examples in Mozart's own handwriting, perhaps the most striking is found in a letter of 9 June 1784, to his father. Mozart's sister had apparently questioned if a passage in the *Concerto in D*, K. 451, should really be performed as written. 'Oh, no,' Mozart responded,

> in the Andante of the Concerto in D there is no question that in the solo in C something needs to be added. I shall send it to her as soon as possible.

In the solution he provided we can see how far removed his performance suggestion was from his original notation.

A similar example of melodic elaboration can be found in an early eight-wind version of the *Gran Partita*, K. 361/370a. In the example provided, which dates before January 1791, we can see how a clarinet player has written in the margin of his part the version he prefers in place of Mozart's.

---

57   Charles Burney, in 'Adagio,' in Rees' *Cyclopedia* (London, 1819).

58   Johann Adolf Scheibe, *Critische Musicus* (Hamburg, 1737), I, 12.

The next two conditions which call for improvisation in Harmoniemusik might be classified as 'short-hand,' places where the composer simply did not take the time to write out the music, leaving it to the player.

The first type of 'short-hand' notation has to do with the filling of wide leaps, something I believe the composer must have regarded as obvious. We find a typical illustration in the second movement of the Mozart *Piano Concerto in C*, K. 503, where, following a series of running thirty-second notes, Mozart simply outlines (for himself) how these fast notes will continue in performance. Surely no one today would contend that these widely leaping slow notes should be played as written. Similarly, Josef Triebensee in the first oboe part of his partita, *Variations on a Theme of Mozart*, simply outlines a two-octave leap to be filled by the player. This, by the way, is surely what Weber expected in those passages of great leaps in his solo works for clarinet, yet today we generally hear players squawking back and forth from the top to the bottom of the register of the instrument.

In concerti of the Classical Period one will sometimes see the solo part running along in sixteenth-notes, then suddenly one measure of two half-notes followed by more running sixteenth-notes. In this case, the composer is indicating a place to breathe, with the rest of the bar to be filled in with sixteenth-notes.

Another type of musical short-hand by early composers involved 'chord symbols.' It is important to remember that the figured bass symbols, so common to the Baroque and pre-Classical Periods, were not used in the upper voices and those composers did not yet have our modern device of representing chords by the use of Roman Numerals. So how could these composers notate a 'chord symbol'? The answer is by simply outlining the chord itself, usually in simple triadic fashion. During the Baroque this was done by 'Alberti bass' figures. A perfect example is founding the well-known Vivaldi *Piccolo Concerto in C*, in which the solo part alternates between genuine melodic material and dull, repetitive Alberti bass measures. In this work, written for his students, it is clear that Vivaldi, in writing a measure in Alberti bass, was saying to his student, 'Play what you will, but play in sixteenth notes and here is the chord.' This is nowhere more evident than in the initial entrance of the piccolo in the first movement. The solo part consists of ten measures of Alberti bass notation, 'music' of utterly no interest whatsoever, indeed one cannot call it music. But, perhaps the orchestra is doing something interesting? No, the orchestra has ten bars of a repeated C major chord! Clearly, *anything* the soloist plays here would be more interesting than what Vivaldi wrote!

We recall a similar kind of notation during the Classical Period in a wind instrument *Serenade* by Salieri. In the Minuet, the oboe has a beautiful melody throughout. But in the Trio we see only the outlining of triads. It seems clear that the oboist was expected to improvise, using the chord symbols provided by Salieri. Another obvious example of this kind of notation can be found in the first movement of the Mozart Clarinet *Quintet*. The first theme and its repetition are separated by a brief little passage for the clarinet, a fragment which sounds to us like what clarinet players play when warming up—and in a sense, this is what the soloist is doing in this the beginning of the first movement. In the development section, Mozart suddenly gets carried away and composes the entire development section not on the principal themes but on this little 'warm-up' figure. He provides each string instrument with an extended written-out improvisation of this figure. But when it is the soloist's turn, for the clarinet he merely indicates the chords, again by outlining the triads. It is quite clear to us that Mozart never anticipated that a clarinet soloist would actually play what he wrote, although that is exactly what every clarinetist does today!

The final circumstances calling for improvisation in Classical Period music are those places marked by a fermata symbol where a cadenza or an *Eingang* is required, a topic we have discussed above. Thus it may come as a surprise to clarinetists to learn that there are *no* cadenzas in the Mozart *Clarinet Concerto*, but there are three *Eingänge*.

In closing I should recognize that there is a growing tendency to encourage some improvisation on repeated material, such as in minuets, which I encourage. However the goal should not be just to wiggle some fingers or to add some turns and trills. Aside from a few sopranos during the Baroque who were showing off technique for the audience, most surviving examples of written out improvisation from that period show that the performer in his improvisation was attempting to increase the emotional meaning of the work. So encourage the student-improviser today to introduce his feelings as an expression of the feelings he feels from the composer. If we are going to improvise, let's add music, not technique.

PART IV
Score Discussions

Applied Performance Practice

Mozart, Gran Partita, K. 361

This is one of the great compositions by Mozart, and is his longest instrumental work. It was composed early in 1784 and before the premiere the word was out, one newspaper writing in advance that the concert would include a 'great wind piece of a very special kind composed by Herr Mozart.' And indeed a reviewer afterward wrote, 'I heard music for wind instruments today, too, my Herr Mozart, in four movements—glorious and sublime! … Oh, what an effect it made—glorious and grand, excellent and sublime.'

The fact that the work is scored for twelve wind instruments and string bass should pose no surprise for there is a long history of the twelve-member wind band. The *Les Grands Hautboisten* of Louis XIV consisted of twelve players. When this practice spread to Germany, beginning in 1690, those groups were also twelve players, one of whom called themselves, 'the Apostles.' The Handel *Fireworks music*, which we associate with the huge doublings of the first performance in England, appears in the autograph score as a work for twelve players, eleven winds and timpani. The Gossec *Te Deum*, the earliest work of the French Revolution repertoire was for twelve players on paper. And finally, one can find a number of late eighteenth and nineteenth century works composed for a twelve-member ensemble.

First movement, *Largo–Molto Allegro*

In the very first bar we see one of the important idioms of the Classical style, the stair-step cadence with all three of its parts: the strongest first note,[1] the need for double dotting and the last (fourth) note played half the written value. Because the third and fourth note thus become short, a sixteenth-note and an eighth-note, and have the potential to be a bit rough. I slur these two notes, which gives them an elegant quality.

Because the fourth note in the ensemble is now an eighth-note, notice that it is out of the way and does not conflict with the solo clarinet's entrance. It demonstrates that Mozart was aware of the Viennese custom of making a note followed by rests one-half of its written value. Nothing would be gained by blotting out the soloist's entrance. For the solo Mozart has written '*dolce,*' a term he used as we would write today 'solo part.' Notice also that he needed one more note to complete the diatonic line and so he added it as a grace note in bar two. There is absolutely nothing in the style of this period which would suggest a Baroque appoggiatura here or any other solution which makes this grace note become part of the first beat of bar two. It was also out of the style, and likewise it would have never occurred to Mozart, to cre-

---

[1] Since it was expected that a first movement would be *forte*, it was very common, to save time and ink, that composers did not bother to notate the initial *forte*.

ate a quintuplet to accommodate this needed extra note. The soloist simply works the extra note in smoothly or the players just wait—a very common practice in the late Baroque internal cadences.

There is a very minor performance problem in bars [12] and [13]. As Mozart would not have departed from tradition by creating a quintuplet in [1], here again a problem is created by the traditional notation. Arithmetically speaking, in [12], the first note of the third and fourth beat of the basset horns is not long enough to allow the listener to hear the harmonic resolution of the oboe part. The conductor needs to have the basset horn players play these notes slightly longer, until their ear hears the oboe resolve, etc.

In [14] the very short note Mozart has written before the fermata is to balance in the memory of the listener the remembered short note of the double-dotted figure in the first bar. It proves, in retrospect, that Mozart was thinking double-dot in bar one. The fermata over the half-note meant 'end of the Largo' for Mozart and it probably should not be elongated beyond two beats. The *Eingang* should be played by the solo clarinet player. I have suggested above the solution I prefer, but this *Eingang* could also be some figure which picks up speed, setting up the Molto Allegro. In any case the *Eingang* should not interfere with the Molto Allegro beginning *piano*—has anyone ever heard a performance which began *piano*?

The second bar of the Molto Allegro deserves some attention, due to poorly edited previous editions. There is a grace note in [2] of the clarinet part, not an appoggiatura. As a grace note it is played before the beat, which means before the bar line.[2] In effect, the clarinet on the third and fourth beat of the first bar should have a quarter-note tied to a dotted eighth-note followed by a sixteenth-note (the written out grace note). I have seen this very pattern, over both bars, written out by other composers, but the very awkward way it reads when I wrote it out in prose is exactly why the grace note version is so much easier to read.

The second quarter-note in the second bar of the Molto Allegro is followed by rests and is therefore played as an eighth-note. This conforms to the performance style: a strong first note followed by a second quarter-note which retreats. Equally long quarter-notes was not intended and would sound too aggressive and, moreover, would lead the listener to expect yet another note.

Almost all Mozart first movements are notated in common time, but were expected to be conducted alla breve. To conduct in four creates the same effect as hammering nails into a board. In alla breve the music takes flight. The proof of this can be seen when the *forte* finally comes, in [19], because this is a syncopation *only* if the music is alla breve. If the music is in four these notes are *on* the beat. This is followed in [39] by a typical Mozart practice in actually notating the first note of the stair-step cadence an octave higher.

In [49] it was a performance tradition to elongate the first note of a slurred figure, as here in the oboes.

I hesitate to mention something so obvious, but Mozart would have expected a crescendo and diminuendo in each bar of the clarinets in [59], and following.

---

2   Mozart makes this clear in the second half of the second trio in the first minuet. See bar [118] and following.

In [88], three bars before the repeat sign, on the second and fourth beats Mozart wrote the familiar pattern of appoggiatura, eighth-note, two sixteenth-notes which was an available means of ensuring an accent on the second and fourth beat. This cadence, in other words, should have a distinct up-beat 'kick,' giving a kind of syncopated feel.

The cadence, beginning in [136], is intended to make the listener think the recapitulation is at hand. Therefore performance tradition allows, and I would recommend, a slight ritard. in this cadence. Making the recapitulation *piano* is important for setting up the great surprise of the (only) *forte* appearance of the first theme in [152].

The fermata in [220] is a Grand Pause, in the sense that nothing happens. But it is *in tempo*, as it represents the first two alla breve beats of the macro meter in which each two bars is perceived as one bar. The fermata is therefore a great surprise, as a missing down-beat. The conductor must not make a cut-off gesture here, but rather simply holds the baton steady and then gives the next bar as a third beat, not as a down beat.

The next fermata is a real fermata in which time is suspended. The following music is not only very mysterious and beautiful, but is typical of the rather unappreciated joy Mozart found in doing weird things harmonically. Here we are at the end of the movement and we expect a B♭ tonality. But in the second bar, [224], we hear F♯ which briefly flirts with the tonality of B natural in the following bar!

The micro meter feeling continues through the 'dance' cadence which is discussed in the previous chapter.

Second Movement, *Menuetto*

It had been a very long time since anyone in Vienna had danced a minuet, maybe since the time of Louis XIV. The minuet had become strictly a stylized instrumental form, as had many of the other Baroque dance forms, such as the sarabande, which were no longer danced. At this time the Vienna composers were moving toward the faster style we associate with Beethoven in his scherzo third movements. One sees among Vienna composers such as Triebensee now a movement called 'Minuet allegretto.' Mozart, even as a child, demonstrated extraordinary skill in picking up by ear the idioms around him and therefore in this Partita he writes two minuets, this one in the old style and the next one in the new style. From a conducting perspective this one is in three, the next one is in four. Being in the older style, this first minuet should not be too fast, but rather on the stately and elegant side.

One needs to consult the autograph score to see the careful markings in the little development section after the first double bar. Mozart has carefully notated alternations of *sfz* and *piano* so bizarre as to make one wonder what he was thinking. Was he trying to make everyone out-of-step in their minds, or are these a rocky passage in this movement which so resembles a little stream with its little waves caused by the rowing of the boat?

Third Movement, *Adagio*

Long before band directors discovered the *Gran Partita*, this movement was known among Mozart specialists for its intense depth of emotion. One early scholar wrote that this movement was the 'crown' of the composition and another said, 'Yes, and the accents in bars 25 and 26 are the thorns in the crown!'

The second bar needs a crescendo and the third bar a decrescendo. This follows an old tradition of adding a sense of motion to a passage such as this to make it come alive as music; without this it seems to the listener that something is missing. I also do this for the fourth and fifth bar to give life, and to give support, to the solo lines.

I think there is little question that Mozart intended the leaps in the woodwinds to be filled, in ⑦, and especially in ⑪ and ⑫, etc. Any diatonic fillings adds great tension and strengthens the emotion and it becomes quite moving. But it should not be over done, should not be thought of as a cadenza, should include no ornaments or accidentals. The players should think only of adding to the emotion. The alternative of playing what is written would be quite absurd as it would be out of the style.

The final cadence with its ritard. has been discussed above. It is played the equivalent of a 'sigh,' making it possible for the listeners, and players, to release their emotions.

Fourth Movement, *Menuetto Allegretto*

This menuetto is the new style one, with four-bar macro meters. In the macro meters in this movement Mozart treats each fourth beat (bar) as a cadence. The conductor can feel exactly what Mozart felt by making the fourth beat simply bounce back counter-clockwise to the center of the body, not a fourth beat that goes up in the air from the third ictus. At the first double bar, going forward, this same gesture helps the baton get back in the center for giving a piano gesture for the next phrase. This conducting pattern can be used for both trios as well.

In the final bar at the end of the second trio, the string bass plays both notes the first time, but on the repeat before the *da capo* only the first note is played.

Fifth Movement, *Romance Adagio*

Here we come to the tendency of playing Mozart slow movements too slow, especially when marked adagio as here. The reader will recall from the previous discussions Mozart's own statement that he had never composed a really slow piece. The real problem here is beginning with a lack of motion. I recommend that the conductor think silently of the seventh and eighth bar, to hear a tempo in which the sixteenth-notes are graceful, melodic and not labored. When you feel that tempo, that is the one you want at the beginning. You want this movement to sing, not get bogged down.

The *piano* for the cadence in the seventh and eighth bar means a ritard. Going forward one might consider keeping a slightly slower tempo, otherwise the oboes in ⟨13⟩ and ⟨14⟩ sound a little wild. The purpose of the subsequent fermata and *Eingang* is to prepare the original tempo. The real significance of the cadential ritard. is seen in ⟨23⟩ and ⟨24⟩. A ritard. brings the tempo back naturally for the next section which is marked only Allegretto. If one does not make the ritard. then a faster tempo results at the Allegretto and the bassoons sound like a machine gun. At a slower Allegretto the bassoons are still heard as the solo part, still heard as a technical marvel.

The last time the cadential ritard. is heard, beginning in [110], the second bar of the cadence is not played, as indicated in the autograph score. Instead give a slight pause as you lift your arms high and give a delicate entrance for the beautiful and haunting coda. The final cadence we have discussed in the previous chapter.

Sixth Movement, *Theme and Variations*

This movement should be conducted in two beats per bar, not four. The only performance problem in this lovely set of variations is again the tempo of the adagio in the fifth variation. Most conductors look at those thirty-second-notes and begin to conduct very slowly, which results in melodic material which dies from lack of motion. To understand this movement the conductor needs to sing the oboe part, thinking like a singer, to find a proper tempo. Then, at first, those thirty-second-notes underneath will sound too fast, but if you ask them to add a little crescendo and decrescendo on each two groups they will sound musical.

If the tempo is too slow then it is [137] which really calls attention to itself as being unnatural. Do note those accompanying thirty-second-notes in [136] are marked *pianissimo*, a rare designation by Mozart and the reason should be apparent.

In the final variation the conductor will feel more in a position to shape things if he puts those down-beats into a pattern of four, for once again this is a macro meter. The final two bars is an inversion of the familiar stair-step cadence, therefore it is kept strong, with the final three quarters being the Masonic knock on the door.

Seventh Movement, *Finale, Molto Allegro*

The challenge in this fast-paced movement is to create variety within the rondo form, which, of course, is what one usually expects in a rondo form.

The first subordinate section is based on the three Masonic knocks. We should hear them clearly in the pick-ups to ⟨17⟩ and ⟨21⟩. This is important because after the repeat when the listener has now heard them four times, Mozart plays a little joke at ⟨25⟩. Here we hear the first knock, on the down-beat of ⟨25⟩, then the second knock on ⟨26⟩, then a bar delay before the third knock is heard on ⟨28⟩. In the next section the Masonic knocks are regular and obvious.

The next subordinate section, beginning at ⟨57⟩ is a little satire on opera *prima donnas*. A tenor begins, a forward and lusty solo in ⟨57⟩ and answered in ⟨59⟩ by the soprano. Now when they are really ready to compete with each other, Mozart shuts them down by thumbing his nose at them in ⟨63⟩ and ⟨64⟩.

During Mozart's lifetime the rare newspaper reviews outside of Vienna sometimes said 'Mr. Mozart's music is exotic.' It is a term which would never occur to us, but the section beginning at ⟨65⟩ is the kind of music they called 'exotic.' Each of the next two sections are miles apart stylistically and should be performed that way—a football fight song and the spooky bassoons.

I should like to beg the reader's forbearance while I give my interpretation of the curious ending of this movement, a patchwork of changing styles. It has always seemed clear to me, and I think many people would agree, that if Mozart could have had his choice he would have been most content to write opera and nothing else. He loved the stage and from time to time one hears music which seems like it is describing some stage characters. For me this ending is such an occasion, 'a soldier's Tale,' and since it is not difficult to find the titles of the various operas heard in Vienna in the Winter of 1783–1784 I am convinced someone will find an opera by somebody which has a brief scene just like this on the stage.

My thinking on this began with [104] and wondering what are these four bars? Not quite a vamp, but certainly marking time. Then it became quite clear to me that this is a little military cadence, complete with the famous 'roll-off' in the oboe-drums. It is a young Austrian soldier who is attracted to the bright uniforms and the glamour of the military and he wants to join. But then he remembers, soldiers get killed and 'I have a wife and children'—this thought comes as a headache, with his hand to his forehead in the form of the downward chromatic line in [108]–[109]. He snaps out of it, and resumes his marching. But the thought returns, now longer and more painful. You can almost hear him at the fermata crying 'Oh!' Beginning in [124] we have the battle and just like the 'battle music' in a number of Baroque instrumental compositions where what is represented is the confusion and the running of feet. So it is here, with even the climbing of a ladder. Bar [132] is 'Finale Music' and could come from the ending of a thousand operas. Bar [138] is where the final curtain begins to fall and we can be sure the crowd is cheering and yelling 'Bravo!' during the final five bars of cadence.

Mozart, *Partita in C minor*, K. 388

The Mystery Partita

Here is a Mozart composition which has kept Mozart scholars in total bewilderment for more than a century.[3] It is not just a quality work, it is one of the very best of all Mozart's compositions, a work of great depth of feeling, yet there is no record of any commission, no early performance nor any reference in Mozart's correspondence. Indeed one indication of just how

---

3   The autograph score has 'Serenada,' but it is in a different hand and clearly written over Mozart's original 'Parthia.' To me it also appears to have Mozart's name in his handwriting, with the date 1782 beneath. The date is a bit faded and Nissen has written in darker ink beneath it, '1782.'

special this composition was to Mozart himself is that fact that this was a very rare score that he never gave out, never gave it to his wind player friends nor gave it with so many other of his manuscripts to Johann Traeg to sell copies of. He kept it on his desk until he died. Later he arranged it for strings, but in doing so he directly transcribed it, changing nothing of significance. Ordinarily when Mozart rearranged a work, he rewrote.

It is clearly the first great work of the Vienna period, but why was it written for winds? Earlier scholars always assumed that any sort of chamber work for winds must have been for some light, outdoor entertainment. The year before, in 1781, Mozart had dashed off the traditional sounding *Partita* for six amateur players, the K. 375, but the K. 388 is a world away, more personal and more symphonic.

A 1781 Mozart's letter to his father mentions work on a '*nacht musique*,' which is otherwise unknown, and so early scholars assumed this K. 388 must be that piece. I was the first person to say in print that the quality of this work makes it impossible for it to be this little evening serenade, and the later publication by Tyson on the water marks of the paper Mozart used proved me correct. The paper was not available before 1782.

I believe it is possible to firmly date the composition of this work as April 1782, but to understand the very personal depth, especially in the first three movements, one must stand back and look at Mozart's state of mind for the previous year.

The year 1781 for Mozart begins in Munich, where the premiere of his opera *Idomeneo*, K. 366, was given. This had to have been a wonderful experience for Mozart, because aside from the public interest in him because of the opera, Munich was, and is, a wonderful city and in every way a greater cultural and cosmopolitan environment than Salzburg.

But in March 1781 the Archbishop Colloredo, Mozart's employer, read 'owner,' is in Vienna for the ceremonies celebrating the accession of Joseph II to the Austrian throne. To play his role among the aristocrats in Vienna, Colloredo wants to be surrounded by his own staff so he orders Mozart to leave Munich and come to Vienna. Because of the opera's success in Munich, and his widely known reputation as a child prodigy, Mozart's name was known among musicians in Vienna. But Colloredo treated Mozart as if he were a rare painting that he owned but never showed to anyone. He made Mozart join him in Vienna but then refused to make him available to aristocrats who wanted to meet him. Mozart had an offer from the Countess Thun to perform in her palace on an occasion when the Emperor would be present and for a very large fee. Colloredo would not let Mozart accept. Furthermore, Colloredo housed Mozart in a building together with his lowest servants. Colloredo's treatment was obvious and Mozart was understandably offended. In May Mozart asks to be relieved from his service under Colloredo and was refused. Then the following month Mozart asks Colloredo again to be set free, the Archbishop, deciding to teach him a lesson and let him starve to death, releases Mozart from his service and his dismissal is punctuated when the archbishop's chamberlain Count Arco, sends Mozart out the door with a kick in the pants. Mozart is angered and humiliated.

We must assume that during these months in Vienna that Mozart, in spite of his growing frustration and anger, must have been meeting and talking with influential musicians in town, who were no doubt assuring him that he had a bright future if only he came to Vienna to live and work. With his youthful confidence, and judging by the music he was hearing around him in Vienna, Mozart had no difficulty in deciding to locate there as a freelance performer and composer.

Almost immediately after his arrival in Vienna, Mozart was circulating among and making friends among the aristocrats. He writes his father on 23 January 1782 that he already has several interesting possibilities. One, he explains, was with the emperor's brother, Maximilian.

> Now of him I can say that he thinks the world of me. He shoves me forward on every occasion, and I might almost say with certainty that if at this moment he were Elector of Köln, I should be his Kapellmeister.

Maximilian soon did become the Elector at Bonn and almost immediately founded his own Harmoniemusik in imitation of the one his brother founded in Vienna in April 1782. Had Mozart become the Kapellmeister for this court, he would have had among the members of his orchestra the young Beethoven.

But for Mozart the more immediate opportunity seemed to lie with one of the great princes of Vienna, Prince Liechtenstein. Mozart, in this same letter, indicates some discussions had in fact taken place.

> Young Prince Liechtenstein, who would like to collect a wind-instrument band (though he does not yet want it to be known), for which I should write the music. This would not bring in very much, it is true, but it would be at least something certain, and I should not sign the contract unless it were to be for life.

Wind conductors today can only dream of the affect on our profession if Mozart would have been writing wind music the last ten years of his life! The element of secrecy involved here was because the emperor himself was thinking about founding a Harmoniemusik, made up of the principal players of his opera orchestra, and naturally no other aristocrat could afford to do this before the emperor did.

In fact, the emperor did organize his Harmoniemusik two months later, in April 1782, the same month we associate with the composition of the *Partita*, K. 388. Mozart must have been talking with these leading wind players, otherwise he would not have heard about the rumor of Liechtenstein forming a Harmoniemusik. But Mozart, as we know from this same letter, was known to the emperor and felt some opportunity existed there. Of his possible opportunities, he tells his father,

> The second (in my estimation, however, it is the first) is the Emperor himself. Who knows? I intend to talk to Herr von Strack about it and I am certain that he will do all he can, for he has proved to be a very good friend of mine; though indeed these court flunkeys are never to be trusted. The manner in which the Emperor has spoken to me has given me some hope.

We know the Emperor was well acquainted with Mozart's skill as a keyboard player, for the previous December he had arranged a competition between Mozart and Muzio Clementi to play in his presence. Mozart must have done well on this occasion for he writes his father on 12 January 1782,

> Clementi! plays well, so far as execution with the right hand goes. His greatest strength lies in his passages in thirds. Apart from this, he has not a kreutzer's worth of taste or feeling in short he is simply a *mechanicus*.

Four days later, Mozart writes his father with further details of this interesting competition.

> After we had stood on ceremony long enough, the Emperor declared that Clementi ought to begin. 'La Santa Chiesa Cattolica,' (the saint of the Catholic Church) he said, Clementi being a Roman. He improvised and then played a sonata. The Emperor then turned to me: 'Allons, fire away.' I improvised and played variations. The Grand Duchess produced some sonatas by Paisiello (wretchedly written out in his own hand), of which I had to play the Allegros and Clementi the Andantes and Rondos. We then selected a theme from them and developed it on two pianofortes. The funny thing was that although I had borrowed Countess Thun's pianoforte, I only played on it when I played alone; such was the Emperor's desire and, by the way, the other instrument was out of tune and three of the keys were stuck. 'That doesn't matter,' said the Emperor. Well, I put the best construction on it I could, that is, that the Emperor, already knowing my skill and my knowledge of music, was only desirous of showing especial courtesy to a foreigner. Besides, I have it from a very good source that he was extremely pleased with me. He was very gracious, said a great deal to me privately, and even mentioned my [prospective] marriage. Who knows? Perhaps what do you think?

One can imagine Mozart, having this kind of recognition from the emperor, must have had his hopes high that he would be taken into his permanent service, which would have assured his career in Vienna. By 10 April he writes his father that he really believed this was imminent.

> I have said nothing to you about the rumor you mention of my being certainly taken into the Emperor's service, because I myself know nothing about it. It is true that here too the whole town is ringing with it and that a number of people have already congratulated me. I am quite ready to believe that it has been discussed with the Emperor and that perhaps he is contemplating it. But up to this moment I have no definite information. At all events things are so far advanced that the Emperor is considering it, and that too without my having taken a single step. I have been a few times to see Herr von Strack (who is certainly a very good friend of mine) in order to let myself be seen and because I like his society, but I have not gone often, because I do not wish to become a nuisance to him, or to let him think that I have ulterior motives. As a man of honor he is bound to state that he has never heard me say a word which would give him reason to think that I should like to stay in Vienna, let alone enter the Emperor's service. We have only discussed music. Therefore it must have been quite spontaneously and entirely without self-interest that he has been speaking so favorably of me to the Emperor. If things have gone so far without any effort on my part, they can now proceed to their conclusion in the same way. For if one makes any move oneself, one immediately receives less pay, because, as it is, the Emperor is a niggard. If he wants me, he must pay me, for the honor alone of serving him is not enough. Indeed, if he were to offer me 1000 gulden and some Count 2000, I should decline the former proposal with thanks and go to the Count that is, of course, if it were a permanent arrangement.

After the angry confrontation with Archbishop Colloredo the previous year, and waiting around in hope that the emperor in Vienna would offer him a position, one can clearly see that Mozart is feeling stress. Defensively he says, 'well—I wouldn't take the offer anyway.' By April he was clearly anxious.

Adding to this stress was growing frustrations in his personal life. He takes a room in a rooming house run by Madame Cäcilie Weber, a relative of Carl Maria von Weber. Here he falls in love with her daughter, Aloysia Weber, but she rejects his advances. Next he turns his attention to her sister, Constanze, a lovely and, contrary to her musicological reputation, talented and educated young lady.

Upon his arrival in Vienna, Mozart was giving lessons to support himself and one of his students was Barbara von Auernhammer, a dilettante pianist of some ability. They played duets together, appeared in public together and to Mozart's naïve astonishment she fell in love with him.

> Well, I have told you how she plays, and also why she begged me to assist her. I am delighted to do people favours, provided they do not plague me incessantly. But she is not content if I spend a couple of hours with her every day. She wants me to sit there the whole day long and, what is more, she tries to be attractive. But, what is worse still, she is *serieusement* in love with me! I thought at first it was a joke, but now I know it to be a fact. When I perceived it, for she took liberties with me for example, she made me tender reproaches if I came somewhat later than usual or could not stay so long, and more nonsense of the same kind I was obliged, not to make a fool of the girl, to tell her the truth very politely. But that was no use: she became more loving than ever. In the end I was always very polite to her except when she started her nonsense and then I was very rude. Whereupon she took my hand and said: 'Dear Mozart, please don't be so cross. You may say what you like, I am really very fond of you!' Throughout the town people are saying that we are to be married, and they are very surprised at me, I mean, that I have chosen such a face. She told me that when anything of the kind was said to her, she always laughed at it; but I know from a certain person that she confirmed the rumour, adding that we would then travel together.

So, by April 1782, the letters of Mozart to his family are filled with his very complicated position. He has this history of relationship with young ladies, he is particularly concerned with this relationship with the Webers, he is in love with Constanze and he still had no means of support other than teaching and performing. It is no wonder the young man's *Partita in C Minor*, K. 388, is so emotional and personal in character, and for that matter, in a minor key.

I will give below the specific reasons why I date this work as April 1782, but in general it seems to me that Mozart is waiting around for the emperor to offer him something. The emperor in fact established his Harmoniemusik in this month and Mozart, with his friendships among the wind players and his negotiations with Prince Liechtenstein regarding a position leading his Harmoniemusik, must have thought that a similar position was going to be offered by the emperor. Preparing a high quality composition in advance for such an opportunity would have been a natural thing to do.[4] But the emperor never created such a position,

---

[4] After this month of April, Mozart was soon at work on his next opera, the *Entführung aus dem Serail* which had its first performance on 16 July. A letter of this July which mentions he is at work on a piece for winds is taken to be the revision of the six-part K. 375 for eight voices.

appointing his first oboe instead as the leader, and there was no occasion for Mozart to present this partita. Mozart's personal associations with this partita and his disappointment in this lost opportunity, together with all the feelings he had poured into this composition, may well explain why he laid it aside on his desk and could never bring himself to give it away. In particlar the apparent anger in the first movement may have seemed too personal to be appropriate to give to some other Harmoniemusik.

First Movement, *Allegro*

There is something about the way this movement begins which has always seemed odd to me. Certainly in terms of the definition of the sonata form as it was then understood, as a form based on tonal centers and not on themes, it meets its expectations. Rather it is the sense of the turmoil of anger, with starting and stopping, and its almost angry character at the beginning at ⑩ which is so startling. To me this is not a case of a composer who says this morning I will write the first movement and here is the theme. Rather it gives me the impression that there was a lot of emotional agitation before Mozart began. It is as if we are missing the first chapter. Nearly forty bars go by before the listener hears something which sounds like a traditional melody, and then it turns out to be the second tonal area.

It is in the dramatic closing section of the exposition section where we find the key to the agitation in Mozart's mind which lies behind this unusually personal movement. As we have said above, in the discussion of the ending of the Finale of K. 361, we suspect that if Mozart would have had the choice he would have loved to be a full-time opera composer. This is perhaps why we find from time to time in his music passages which seems to reflect the action of the stage more than just abstract instrumental music. The closing section of this movement we find a scene which must have been far too familiar in the life of a court musician, the rebukes by the angry court official and the humble responses of the court servant/musician. The emotions are so clear in this case that it seems apparent that Mozart had not yet freed his mind from the humiliation of his clash with the archbishop only a few months earlier, culminating with his loss of his court position as he was literally kicked in the seat and thrown out the door. In this closing section, then, we are observers of a very personal scene, one in which Mozart was the court servant having to take the abuse from a court official. It is this anger and frustration which must have still been with him which we believe was fully in Mozart's mind before he began to compose this very personal movement.

In terms of performance practice, like most Mozart first movements written in common time, this movement is clearly to be conducted in two and not in four.[5] The conductor should find the tempo in the lyrical melody which begins in ㊷.

---

5   Some earlier editions, in particular Kalmus, actually have a common time symbol at the beginning, but in the autograph score Mozart has clearly written the alla breve symbol. Kalmus also has a staccato dot over the first note in the clarinets in ⑤ which should be removed.

In the oboe solo in bars ⑥ – ⑨ Mozart wrote real ties. In modern calligraphy we would write a tie with the slur going from the first note of the tie to the note after; Mozart's version is not clear. In any case there is no intention that a breath accent should be made on these down-beats.

Bars ⑨ and ⑫ are clear opportunities for placement, that is ⑩ and ⑫ need not arrive in chronological time.

The ornament in ⑫ and following should be thought of only as accents at the *piano* level. In reality they can probably be little more than a mordant without sounding awkward. In ㉒ the conductor must be careful that the busy figuration does not prevent the listener from hearing the more important music in the bassoons.⁶ By the way, the NMA gives stroke accents to all these tongued eighth-notes, but in the autograph they are clearly only single dots. As discussed above, it is likely the dot means a form of accent here, but it would definitely be a lesser accent than the stroke accent.

In ㉖ – ㉗ Mozart in the autograph score does space the letters for 'calando' across both bars making it clear the calando is evenly spread over both bars.⁷

In ㉘, ㉚ and ㉜ the NMA is incorrect in its placement of the dynamic markings. There are all clearly *fp* meaning only an accent at the *piano* level and *not* half a measure *forte* and half a measure *piano*.⁸

According to the practice in Vienna at the time, Mozart expected ㊳ to be performed as a quarter-note and it certainly should be. He also assumed, of course, that the second clarinet part beginning in ㊷ be entirely slurred.

It is interesting to me that Mozart writes 'dolce,' which he used to mean 'the solo part,' only in ㊷, even though the oboe has been the *only* person playing in ㊵ and ㊶. When I look at this, I cannot help but believe this is another example of placement, meaning that Mozart considered the oboe free for two bars, perhaps in playing a longer half-note in ㊶, or maybe even a small improvisation, like an *Eingang*, and that the placing of 'dolce' in ㊷ then designates that here the music is back in tempo.

In ㉰ because the dynamic level is still clearly *piano*, and because Mozart rarely bothered to add slurs to such running wind lines, I would presume that Mozart intended the bassoons to be slurred in this passage.

---

⁶ In the new NMA edition they give the *f* on the first note of ㉒, but this is misleading. Mozart wrote 'For:' with the colon after the first beat. Then to clarify he repeated the 'for' under the third beat in this same bar, where it properly belongs. Since Mozart was always thinking in terms of the melodic line before he wrote anything else, it seems clear here that he first wrote 'for:' anticipating that the next section would be *forte*. Then as the music of the bar was being written he did not bother to cross out this first 'for' but rather added it *again* under the third beat.

⁷ In practice I have found in all such cases, including crescendi, that if the sound is evenly spread over more than a bar, the listener does not perceive it as having happened. Psychologically it is necessary to do most of the diminuendo or crescendo near the beginning for the listener [who has no score] to perceive it.

⁸ It is true that Mozart is not clear in ㉘, but the very same music in ㉚ and ㉜ are very clearly *fp*. His intention is beyond doubt.

In [66], the beginning of the closing section, if one has been able to maintain the previous *piano* level to this point, the horns with their *subito forte* should sound as a surprise, even startling, event. Again, as mentioned above, this movement has a certain angry quality lying behind it and one certainly feels in this passage which begins a virtual dialog between the angry court official and the obsequious court employee. Thus when the same cadence is repeated *subito piano*, in [75], it has almost the effect of the court employee repeating what he has been told, apologizing for his outburst. In [79] the angry reprimand followed in [82] by a whole-note *subito piano* and in [83] another whole-note *piano* with the *sf* only being an accent at the *piano* level. Again, as if the court employee has said 'Oh,—*sorry!*' followed by two more bars of reprimand.[9] Then in the autograph manuscript Mozart has circled these last four bars, a late decision to repeat this exchange and so emphasize it by its repetition of two bars of *piano* apology and two bars of angry reprimand. Following this, the cadence which begins at [90] can only be heard as the humble employee rapidly tip-toeing away and then when out of the range of the court official's hearing, in [93], the employee has the last laugh! The final two notes, with stroke accents, can only mean 'Take That!,' or probably something more obscene.

The development section is again very unusual, beginning not with thematic material but with the falling diatonic lines in the bassoon and second clarinet and the solo clarinet part seemingly lost in purpose. It is like a long 'sigh,' a long let down from the agitation of the end of the exposition section. The dot over the fourth beat in [98] of the clarinet solo is not a staccato note but an accent to prepare for the second and fourth beat accents in the following bars. Let me remind the reader that all these *sfp* signs are only accents at the *piano* level, nothing more than that. There should be no tie in the first clarinet between [101] and [102].[10] This whole passage from [99] through [106] has the quality of the feeling of a small headache, I think, with the marking time feeling one often feels under such a condition. What follows in [107] is neither a Grand Pause, nor four beats of rest. It is a classic example of the kind of pauses found in Baroque music, which we call Placement. The arrival of [108] is not determined by chronological time. It is determined by the feelings of the conductor or players, if no conductor. Furthermore, since it is a quotation of that angry outburst of [10] at the beginning, it is even more critical that the conductor *feel* when the precise moment comes for this outburst.

Now comes four *piano* bars of painful cries, in all voices, reminding one of those similar leaps in the Adagio of K. 361. Mozart now makes the cries *forte* and in imitation, against a background of agitation.[11] Then in [126] and [127] the music seems to break down in a hopeless sigh. Mozart did not write diminuendo in [126] and [127], but he surely assumed this would be evident, especially in the effect of the falling bass line, as otherwise a *subito piano* in [128] would call too much attention to itself. And here another Placement occasion. Bar [129] is empty, it is again neither a Grand Pause nor four chronological beats of rest. As what follows is twenty-three bars of recapitulation, the purpose of this silence in performance has to do with the

---

9   In the autograph score Mozart does not write *forte* in either [84] or in its repetition in [88], but because of the clearly notated *piano* in all voices in [90] one can only conclude in retrospect that these bars, [84]–[85] and [88]–[89] were intended to be *forte*.

10 The NMA fails to observe this.

11 All the 'little notes' [vorschlage] are grace notes played before the bar line and not Baroque type appoggiaturas.

preparation of the listeners to the *forte* music of the beginning. But it is an example of a 'false recapitulation,' something which Classical Period composers began to do after the public had come to know the sonata form and to expect the return of the original material. We have a little more development section left. Here are again some significant errors in the NMA. Bars [159], [161] and [163] are ***fp*** accents in the autograph score and not a half-bar of *forte* and a half-bar of *piano*. In [165]–[168] Mozart did *not* write accents over the unison eighth-notes as they are quite strong enough as they are.

The little cadence which transitions to the recapitulation is one of the most lovely moments in Mozart. The reader must be reminded that the written half-note in [170] was, according to this idiom in Vienna at this time, expected to be made a quarter-note by the players. This leaves the horns holding a *forte* for rather a long time before the lovely passage begins in [171]. Certainly one might ask the horns to diminuendo to their *piano* in [171]. An early nineteenth-century edition gives the horns a ***fp*** in [170], which would be appropriate only in the twentieth century use of ***fp*** meaning *forte* then an immediate drop to *piano*.

The recapitulation arrives with the appearance of a new melody, which should not surprise us as in the eighteenth century the sonata form was still based on key relationships and not on thematic material as become the case in the nineteenth century. But this six-bar melody, which is repeated adding the horn an octave lower, immediately catches the eye by its appearance. It is essentially a single melody with accompaniment which could be a guitar, with the second bassoon playing the role of a string bass, and with nearly half the instruments with tied whole-notes, the second oboe with nine tied bars of a single pitch. It is as if we are hearing a trio of street musicians playing a somewhat plaintive song. More likely it is a quotation from an opera being heard in Vienna. If some future person can identify this music, the words which accompany this melody will surely tell us something important about what Mozart was feeling at this moment.

This is followed by the melody which we would have expected from the exposition section[12] and a recapitulation of the entire angry dialog of the closing section, only here it is even more furious. Instead of the apologetic servant's *piano* whole-note followed by a *piano* whole note with a little accent which we heard in bars [82]–[83] and [86]–[87], now we hear only *one* bar of the *piano* whole-note apology which is interrupted by four bars of *forte*, four bars of syncopation sounding like an even more angry response. This is repeated, then the final cadence with the servant running away, his laughter and now his final two-word comment even stronger by virtue of octave extension although they are without the stroke accents.[13]

---

[12] Again in the NMA we find stroke accents in [190] and [192], where as the autograph score has simple dots in [190] and nothing at all in [192].

[13] NMA takes it upon themselves to add them anyway.

Second Movement, *Andante*

The second movement is one of the two movements which I believe point to the composition being written in April 1782. This movement begins with the lyrical tranquility of a traditional slow movement for chamber music of this period. But at the point the development section begins, something fundamental has changed. Suddenly it seems as if Mozart's thoughts are miles away. Three times he begins the first theme and leaves it hanging unfinished in space. The effect is haunting and sad. Even when he decides to begin the recapitulation he makes a mistake, creates a unique symbol changing a *da capo* to a *dal segno*—his mind still wasn't back in the present tense. What had taken over his mind?

On 23 March 1782, aside from the arrival in Vienna of the Pope, the father of the girl who was in love with him, Herr von Auernhammer, died. Mozart liked him, calling him a good and kind man. Then on 10 April Mozart heard that Johann Christian Bach had died in London, causing Mozart to write his father saying, 'What a loss for the Musical World!' On the first big tour to London, when Mozart was a child, Bach had treated him and his father with greater cordiality and offered more help than any other host in any other city they visited. Mozart had always retained a fond memory of Bach from that visit. Two days latter, on 12 April, in Vienna, the poet Metastasio died. It was his work which had inspired the libretto of Mozart's *Idomeneo* which premiered the previous year in Munich. These last two deaths of people who meant a lot to Mozart, coming two days apart, must have given Mozart pause. For one with a long history of illness since childhood, it is possible that he was for the first time thinking of his own mortality. I personally think it would not be too far a leap to suggest that the news of the second of these, the death of Metastasio, might well have corresponded with the day Mozart began to write the development section of this Andante.

Regarding performance practice, first the conductor must not allow a causal glance at all the ligatures to conclude that the tempo must be very slow. The ligatures are there only because the meter is $\frac{3}{8}$. In the Classical Period the Andante was considered the slowest of the fast tempi.

Nevertheless the extra set of ligatures does cause us to stop and try to hear what Mozart heard as things do look different. For example the *vorschlag* in the oboe in 23 is part of a standard idiom in which often we would realize the figure as thirty-second-, sixteenth- and thirty-second-notes, written in this style in order to achieve an accent on the first note.[14] If Mozart had wanted this common realization he should have written a sixteenth-note *vorschlag*, with a slash through it.[15] But that is not what he wrote, he wrote an eighth-note *vorschlag* with a slash, leaving open the possibility, in my opinion, that here he intended the *vorschlag* to be a grace note, which would render the figure more graceful in performance.

---

[14] NMA clouds the water a bit by writing the *vorschlag* as a sixteenth-note, with a thirty-second-note in parenthesis above the staff, which would indicate the editors belief in the standard idiom, even though that is not what Mozart wrote.

[15] In 30, for example, Mozart correctly writes a *vorschlag* as a sixteenth-note with a slash, which results in the realization of four thirty-second-notes with an accent on the first note.

I believe most early music specialists would agree that the ornament in ⟨29⟩ was intended to be a four-note turn, leaving two sixteenth-notes on the third beat. The question is, is the turn on the second beat or after the second beat. I prefer the more lyrical choice of placing it on the second beat. My experience, in either case, is that one should actually write the resolution out on paper for the student musician. A verbal explanation is too confusing—as the reader has just experienced.

The new music at ⟨32⟩ is in the character of a somewhat faster peasant dance[16] and the tempo should reflect this. It should be just enough faster to give verisimilitude to the kicking foot in the bassoon. It was in the style to make these kinds of tempi modifications so long as it was done smoothly, which in this case means getting back to the original tempo for the more tranquil closing section. Mozart goes to some length to do this in ⟨38⟩ by not only marking it ritard.[17] but by writing clear and easy beats with which to achieve a ritard. The final two eighth-notes of the exposition section, bars ⟨45⟩–⟨46⟩, are marked with a stroke accent in the autograph score, not as staccato as given in the Kalmus edition.

The haunting and melancholic phrases of the development must be set off with Placement. The two eighth-note rests were not intended to be observed in chronological time as part of the previous tempo. They are just like such rests as might follow a fermata. They have no time definition whatsoever until the music resumes. In other words, the conductor lets these phrases hang in the air until his feeling tells him to begin again. The one crescendo, in ⟨57⟩, is only there so that the notes after the octave leap up will not stick out, a solution which had been known since the seventeenth century in choral music in particular.[18]

The final cadence recalls the emotional impact of the development section. Mozart therefore now eliminates the strong accents[19] on the eighth-notes and now allows these two eighth-notes to gracefully ritard., which allows for the release of the emotions in the listener.

Third Movement, *Minuetto in Canone*

For anyone who is familiar with music of the Classical Period this Minuet catches the attention in even a momentary glance.[20] It stands as an anomaly among thousands of minuets which as a genre tend to be in a pleasant dance style with mild emotional content. It is beyond unconventional, it is fantastic to see a minuet begin in a contrapuntal style associated with ancient Church Scholasticism.

---

[16] The NMA makes all articulations in this passage as slash accents. Mozart does appear to have done this in ⟨33⟩ in the oboes, which does add to the peasant quality. However, Mozart wrote only staccato dots in the bassoons and in both oboe parts in ⟨37⟩. If by their realization the NMA editors meant to confirm that the single 'staccato' dot could mean 'accent,' we would agree.

[17] One of the standard definitions for *p* was slow.

[18] Instrumental conductors are familiar with this problem relative to the 'pyramid' solution.

[19] This is very clear in the autograph score. The modern score published by NMA is simply not correct.

[20] The ending of the second movement and the beginning of the Menuetto are on the same page, but there is clearly a change of ink before the Menuetto was set on paper, suggesting at least some interval of time between the composition of these movements.

But the purpose of music is not to communicate counterpoint, the purpose of music is to communicate feelings. And I, for one, have always heard the initial Minuet as being angry. One thinks of the Minuet of the *G Minor Symphony*, which also has similar striking hemiolas, but it does not sound angry.

It is the very character and presence of this movement which point to April 1782. On 10 April he writes his father,

> I have been intending to ask you, when you return the rondo, to enclose with it Handel's six fugues and Eberlin's toccatas and fugues. I go every Sunday at twelve o'clock to Baron van Swieten,[21] where nothing is played but Handel and Bach. I am collecting at the moment the fugues of Bach not only of Sebastian, but also of Emanuel and Friedemann. I am also collecting Handel's and should like to have the six I mentioned.

And ten days later, he writes his sister,

> Baron van Swieten, to whom I go every Sunday, gave me all the works of Handel and Sebastian Bach to take home with me (after I had played them to him). When Constanze heard the fugues, she absolutely fell in love with them. Now she will listen to nothing but fugues, and particularly (in this kind of composition) the works of Handel and Bach. Well, as she had often heard me play fugues out of my head, she asked me if I had ever written any down, and when I said I had not, she scolded me roundly for not recording some of my compositions in this most artistic and beautiful of all musical forms, and never ceased to entreat me until I wrote down a fugue for her.

If anyone besides me hears some anger in the contrapuntal music of this Minuet, my guess is that Mozart was just tired of hearing all the talk about the admiration of those other masters of the fugue. In any case, there is no other period of Mozart's life when there is such a concentration on this style and for this reason I believe this movement and this *Partita* must be associated with April 1782.

There is another factor here which I feel I must mention. Mozart, with his extraordinary ability in composition, from time to time could not help himself from showing off. I think, for example, of the first movement of the *Clarinet Quintet* where between statements of the principal theme Mozart writes a little bridge which is nothing more than an imitation of the 'noodling' clarinet players do to warm up once their instrument is put together. At the beginning of the development section Mozart states the principal theme, and then the 'noodling' little bridge, and then he gets carried away and develops the entire development section on this figure, as if to show that he can make a perfectly good development section out of nothing.

So it is my belief that after hearing all this talk on Sundays about the fugue technique, and while he had no reason at the moment to write a strict fugue, he was just showing off by writing an extraordinary example of counterpoint in the last place in the world anyone would expect it, in a minuet!

---

[21] Baron van Swieten was a busy and influential man around town in Vienna and was one of the people Constanze asked to finish the *Requiem* after Mozart's death. Baron van Swieten tried but only succeeded in covering some of the autograph score with pencil as he attempted to fill in missing horn and woodwind parts before he gave up and returned the score.

The Trio of this minuet is quite a different story. The listener expected in the Trio to hear contrast with the Minuet, usually in everything except form. Mozart's contrast here is more psychological, instead of the rigidity of counterpoint here one feels the music takes flight, sounding *very* free. Could we have here a little drama with a residual echo of the rigid life under Archbishop Colloredo versus his present freedom?

Or maybe there was another factor. We don't hear much about it this country, but the success of the American Revolution had an enormous influence on the people of Europe. For five years as the battle raged on, no one in Europe thought the American farmers could defeat the mighty British Empire. But when they did, suddenly the idea of ordinary people throwing off the chains of the monarchy which existed in every country started everyone thinking and was the topic of wide conversation. The contribution to the French Revolution is an obvious example. The actual end of the American Revolution came with the surrender of Cornwallis at Yorktown on 19 October 1781. News traveled slowly in the eighteenth century and judging by the four months it took before Mozart heard of the death of Johann Christian Bach, then it might have been only a few weeks before April 1782, when this news reached Mozart. Perhaps the widespread celebration felt in Europe on the idea of being free contributed to the outpouring sense of freedom one senses in this Trio. This is no Classical four-bar structured melody; something is bursting across the bar lines.

We should also point out that the Trio is composed for only half the ensemble, the oboes and bassoons. Most of the later Harmoniemusik minuets keep the same instrumentation in the trio, but it was common in the Baroque wind band minuets to have a smaller instrumentation in the trio, sometimes only two bassoons alone. Since this Trio is for oboes and bassoons it really is like a Baroque wind band, the *Hautboisten*, because those were the instruments they used, as did the typical military band of the American Revolution. Perhaps Mozart was aware of this earlier tradition, or maybe in his travels he had actually heard some older players performing *Hautboisten* repertoire.

The beginning of the Menuetto has no dynamic marking, but this was a common practice in Vienna if it were assumed the movement began *forte*. I have found in conducting this movement that because of the strong tone of the modern French oboe, together with the hemiola structure, the beginning always seems to be very aggressive, even angry. I have found over the years that asking the players to just play *mezzo forte* is quite enough contrast with the *mezzo voce* of the Trio.

In any case, after the double bar, the second part of the Menuetto is *piano* for eight bars. The *subito forte* in [25] has the stroke accents only in the second bassoon, although the NMA adds them in all voices. Mozart again marks the oboes *forte* in [29] and the bassoons in [30], but this is probably for the purpose of indicating the return of the initial music.

The final measure of the Menuetto is again a written half-note, which in the Viennese tradition was expected to be performed only as a quarter-note. The second bassoon plays all three quarter-notes the first time and only one quarter-note on the repeat (which confirms the Viennese principal, as quarter-notes are what the other players will also play).

While the final cadences of the Menuetto have no articulation marks, the final cadences of the Trio are with the stroke accents. Why should this lyrical *mezza voce* Trio for only four instruments end so heavily marked? Perhaps if this Trio is expressing the momentary freedom, as discussed above, maybe Mozart returns to the reality of the court musician and has the four stroke accents in the second bassoon represent the archbishop's chamberlain Count Arco snarling, 'Get back in line!' Or maybe it is just a comment intended for those friends who were admiring Handel every Sunday, after writing here a canon with the second voice in mirror image of the first one, Mozart was saying, 'How's That!,' or some comment to refer to the fact that he was doing something more difficult than usually found in traditional fugues.

Someone, probably Johann André, who owned this autograph score after Mozart's death had the bindings stitched to hold it together. At that time they inserted a sketch of two bars by Mozart for Harmoniemusik. It is in C minor and may well have been the original beginning of the final movement. But it abruptly stops after two bars, maybe because it seems a little too grand. In any case it is a loose sheet of paper and not part of the folios which make up the rest of this composition.

Fourth Movement, *Allegro*

The final movement, like all the other movements of this extraordinary partita, is unusual and special. It has a lighter mood, even though it is in a minor key. Instead of the typical Rondo, here we have a Theme and Variations with great variety in character and a great display of fine wind playing. It has always seemed to me that this work is a tribute to the Emperor's Harmoniemusik, maybe because of the 'oboe contest' beginning in [144]. There were a lot of fine oboists in Vienna at this time and the two who were members of the Emperor's Harmoniemusik, Georg Triebensee and Johann Wendt, were probably the best. This variation was for them to show off and the modern players should employ good body motion when it is their turn to show off. Similarly, the bassoons were given far more exposure in this movement than one would find in most partitas.

In any case it must be judged unusual in how it begins, the movement not only begins *piano,* but once more with only half the ensemble, the little Baroque *Hautboisten* band of the previous movement, a double-reed band of oboes and bassoons.[22]

The First Variation is a million miles away stylistically, Everyone plays now, and *forte*, and the style is an outdoor flamboyant country dance. Again, in the final bar of this variation, everyone plays an eighth-note, rather than the notated quarter-note and the second bassoon plays all his notes the first time and only the first eighth-note on the repeat.

---

[22] The NMA creates stroke accents for all the articulations in this Theme, whereas they appear in the autograph score to me as simple dots over the notes and in most cases there is nothing at all. Certainly the stroke accents seem too strong for this little four-man band playing piano.

The Second Variation, at ㉝, is again *piano* and features the first oboe.[23] I would recommend this variation as a marker for the conductor to find the Allegretto tempo[24] for the beginning of this movement. If the tempo is very fast the oboe part quickly begins to sound awkward and rushed instead of simple and lyrical; if the tempo is too slow it begins to sound a bit seasick.

The Third Variation is an example of the kind of music eighteenth-century critics called 'exotic' in the music of Mozart. It certainly has a sence of mystery and Mozart has carefully made the instruments which play the beats only *pp*. The final note in both cadences should be played as an eighth-note, not a quarter-note, as was the Viennese style at this time.

Variation Four is another country dance with all the accents having an outdoor rough quality, as for example in the stroke accents on the upbeat of the first beats. During the running bassoon line the placement of a trill on the second beats of the oboe is to create an accent on the (wrong) second beat. I doubt very much that Mozart expected the bassoons to tongue every note during the solo. If I were a bassoonist I would slur the first two notes in ㊵, then slur all eight notes in ㊹, as they really represent a chord here. Then slur the first two notes of the scale passage in ㊺, slur all eight in ㊻, etc.

Variation Five gives the clarinet a solo. The clarinet has an accent *fp* in [106] and [108], whereas everyone else has an accent *mfp*. No one today knows exactly what quality of accent was meant by the traditional *fp*, but whatever it was, we can presume *mfp* was half that value. In [111] in the clarinet Mozart expected a quarter-note followed by two eighth-notes, the first of which was accented.

At the double bar, [112], I believe eighteenth-century players would have, as a matter of routine, made a crescendo into the *sf* accent and for the next six bars would have added crescendi and diminuendi supporting the directions of the melodic line.

Variation Six, after a reprise of the music for clarinet and horns, is the famous oboe contest, each oboe playing the same melody in a contest of musicianship. Since the parts are identical on paper, this stands as clear evidence that players at this time did much more than play what is on paper. Undoubtedly they added crescendi, diminuendi, accents and perhaps a bit a improvisation.[25]

Variation Seven, beginning in [176], is another *pianissimo* mysterious, exotic passage with the kind of harmonic wandering around which Mozart loved to do, and which he may have regarded as just showing off.[26] Here especially we wish we could ask him the distinctions between *mfp*, *sfp* and *fp*. He has so carefully placed them and we can only guess at their meanings.

---

23 NMA writes 'Solo' at the beginning, but this is not in the autograph score.

24 The NMA editors have elected to call the tempo abbreviation in Mozart's hand, 'Allegro,' but after years of looking at manuscripts from this period, I read it as the abbreviation for 'Allegretto.'

25 I think, for example, [149] is a bar where the figuration could be altered without affecting the nature of the melody. In these solos NMA gives stroke accents for what in the autograph score are merely dots above the notes. In [145] in the bassoon the second beat is the most common, yet rare, form of the Baroque style appoggiatura used in the Classical Period. It is played as four sixteenth-notes, slurred two and tongued two and with the first note accented.

26 A similar, but shorter, passage can be found beginning in [211] of the first movement of the *Partita*, K. 375.

The quarter-notes in the cadence beginning at [208] should all be played as if they were written eighth-notes. In the sixth of these, [214], Mozart surprises the listener with a written-out fermata. I have always felt that bars [212]–[215] should also be played with a crescendo.

It would have been expected that the first oboe played an *Eingang* which leads into the coda in the major key. It need not be long and I would prefer one which ends *mi fa sol*, the *sol* being the written G.

In the first edition of his famous catalog, Köchel wrote that the final page of this score was lost and that a different person had composed the final page. The editors of the new NMA agree and take the position that whoever wrote this final page did so on the basis of an extant, but unidentified, set of parts.

I will not feel comfortable with this conclusion until I have an opportunity to see the actual autograph score in Berlin. I see a few details, such as the symbol for the quarter-note rest, and the braces which set apart the two scores on this page, which look like Mozart to me. I have a digital copy made for me by Berlin and I have seen an older microfiche reproduction, but some fundamental questions I have can only be answered by seeing the original in person. For example, the last six bars of the previous page demonstrate that Mozart's ink was rapidly fading. I had wondered if the following, and final, page was originally very faint and had been inked over by someone like Nissen. The note-heads in particular are a very dark black ink. But if there is any inking over of earlier notation here it will not be seen except in the original manuscript.

It may be argued that this is not an important issue since presumably the music of this page is the same as that found in the later string version by Mozart; this is the position taken by the NMA.

There is one small problem here, and it may be Mozart's error. The final chord of the wind version has no third, although there is one in the string version. The NMA have taken it upon themselves to rewrite the final two bars in order to produce a complete chord at the end, although in so doing they write a C♯ for the horn which is not an easy note to create on the natural horn in E♭.

Years ago, when I began pointing this out, one conductor told me that he believed Mozart wanted to end the work with a Medieval flavor. If Mozart had that in mind then it is a thought too impenetrable for me, but, *C'est la vie!*

About the Author

Dr. David Whitwell is a graduate ('with distinction') of the University of Michigan and the Catholic University of America, Washington DC (PhD, Musicology, Distinguished Alumni Award, 2000) and has studied conducting with Eugene Ormandy and at the Akademie für Musik, Vienna. Prior to coming to Northridge, Dr. Whitwell participated in concerts throughout the United States and Asia as Associate First Horn in the USAF Band and Orchestra in Washington DC, and in recitals throughout South America in cooperation with the United States State Department.

At the California State University, Northridge, which is in Los Angeles, Dr. Whitwell developed the CSUN Wind Ensemble into an ensemble of international reputation, with international tours to Europe in 1981 and 1989 and to Japan in 1984. The CSUN Wind Ensemble has made professional studio recordings for BBC (London), the Köln Westdeutscher Rundfunk (Germany), NOS National Radio (The Netherlands), Zürich Radio (Switzerland), the Television Broadcasting System (Japan) as well as for the United States State Department for broadcast on its 'Voice of America' program. The CSUN Wind Ensemble's recording with the Mirecourt Trio in 1982 was named the 'Record of the Year' by The Village Voice. Composers who have guest conducted Whitwell's ensembles include Aaron Copland, Ernest Krenek, Alan Hovhaness, Morton Gould, Karel Husa, Frank Erickson and Vaclav Nelhybel.

Dr. Whitwell has been a guest professor in 100 different universities and conservatories throughout the United States and in 23 foreign countries (most recently in China, in an elite school housed in the Forbidden City). Guest conducting experiences have included the Philadelphia Orchestra, Seattle Symphony Orchestra, the Czech Radio Orchestras of Brno and Bratislava, The National Youth Orchestra of Israel, as well as resident wind ensembles in Russia, Israel, Austria, Switzerland, Germany, England, Wales, The Netherlands, Portugal, Peru, Korea, Japan, Taiwan, Canada and the United States.

He is a past president of the College Band Directors National Association, a member of the Prasidium of the International Society for the Promotion of Band Music, and was a member of the founding board of directors of the World Association for Symphonic Bands and Ensembles (WASBE). In 1964 he was made an honorary life member of Kappa Kappa Psi, a national professional music fraternity. In September, 2001, he was a delegate to the UNESCO Conference on Global Music in Tokyo. He has been knighted by sovereign organizations in France, Portugal and Scotland and has been awarded the gold medal of Kerkrade, The Netherlands, and the silver medal of Wangen, Germany, the highest honor given wind conductors in the United States, the medal of the Academy of Wind and Percussion Arts (National Band Association) and the highest honor given wind conductors in Austria, the gold medal of the Austrian Band Association. He is a member of the Hall of Fame of the California Music Educators Association.

Dr. Whitwell's publications include more than 127 articles on wind literature including publications in Music and Letters (London), the London Musical Times, the Mozart-Jahrbuch (Salzburg), and 39 books, among which is his 13-volume *History and Literature of the Wind Band and Wind Ensemble* and an 8-volume series on *Aesthetics in Music*. In addition to numerous modern editions of early wind band music his original compositions include 5 symphonies.

David Whitwell was named as one of six men who have determined the course of American bands during the second half of the 20th century, in the definitive history, *The Twentieth Century American Wind Band* (Meredith Music).

A doctoral dissertation by German Gonzales (2007, Arizona State University) is dedicated to the life and conducting career of David Whitwell through the year 1977. David Whitwell is one of nine men described by Paula A. Crider in *The Conductor's Legacy* (Chicago: GIA, 2010) as 'the legendary conductors' of the 20th century.

> 'I can't imagine the 2nd half of the 20th century—without David Whitwell and what he has given to all of the rest of us.' Frederick Fennell (1993)

About the Editor

CRAIG DABELSTEIN began studying the piano at age seven and took up the saxophone at age twelve. Mr Dabelstein has Bachelor of Arts (Music) and Bachelor of Music degrees from the Queensland Conservatorium of Music, where he majored in the performance of classical saxophone repertoire. He also has a Graduate Diploma of Learning and Teaching and a Graduate Certificate in Editing and Publishing from the University of Southern Queensland.

He has held the principal alto and tenor saxophone chairs in the Australian Wind Orchestra and has been an augmenting member of the Queensland Philharmonic Orchestra, the Queensland Symphony Orchestra, and the Queensland Pops Orchestra. For many years he was also a member of the Queensland Saxophone Quartet.

He has been a casual conductor of the Young Conservatorium Symphonic Winds, and has previously been a saxophone teacher at the Queensland Conservatorium of Music. He is a regular conductor of the Queensland Wind Orchestra, having served as their artistic director and chief conductor from 2004 to 2009.

Craig Dabelstein is a research associate for the *Teaching Music Through Performance in Band* series of books, contributing analyses to volumes 7, 8, 1 (rev. edn), and the *Solos with Wind Band Accompaniment* volume. He served as the copyeditor and layout designer of the *Australian Clarinet and Saxophone Magazine* from 2007 to 2009 and he has written many CD and book reviews for *Music Forum* magazine. He is the editor of the second editions of the books by Dr. David Whitwell including *A Concise History of the Wind Band*, *Foundations of Music Education*, *Music Education of the Future*, *The Sousa Oral History Project*, *Wagner on Bands*, *Berlioz on Bands*, *The Art of Musical Conducting*, and the *Aesthetics of Music* series (8 volumes) and *The History and Literature of the Wind Band and Wind Ensemble* series (13 volumes). From 1994 to 2012 he was a staff member at Brisbane Girls Grammar School. He now teaches woodwinds and conducts bands at St. Joseph's College, Gregory Terrace, Brisbane, Australia.

www.ingramcontent.com/pod-product-compliance
Lightning Source LLC
Chambersburg PA
CBHW080733300426
44114CB00019B/2574